Off the Beaten Path

Edited by

Joseph Barbato and Lisa Weinerman Horak

of The Nature Conservancy

Introduction by Barbara Kingsolver

North Point Press
A division of Farrar, Straus and Giroux
New York

Off the Beaten Path

Stories of Place

North Point Press
A division of Farrar, Straus and Giroux
19 Union Square West, New York 10003

Copyright © 1998 by The Nature Conservancy
All rights reserved
Distributed in Canada by Douglas & McIntyre Ltd.
Printed in the United States of America
Library of Congress catalog card number: 98-066419
Designed by Jonathan D. Lippincott
First North Point Press edition, 1998
First paperback edition, 1999

The Nature Conservancy is grateful to the authors for their generous donation of original work. These short stories are works of the imagination. The views expressed in them are the authors' own and do not necessarily represent the opinions of the organization.

*For writers and readers everywhere
who know the wonder of wild places*

CONTENTS

Off the Beaten Path

PREFACE

On a recent trip to the Rio Bravo conservation area in the jungles of Belize, our group came across a set of fresh jaguar tracks. It was an exciting moment—evidence that The Nature Conservancy and its local partner, the Programme for Belize, are successfully preserving the biological diversity of this lush region, including its top predator.

But something else happened when I glimpsed those tracks. I recalled that the elusive jaguar was sacred to the ancient Maya that lived here and one of the nine lords of their underworld. I suddenly felt caught up in the jaguar's lore of power, mystery, and death and in the drama of the animal's stealthy presence. Perhaps it was instinctive.

The screams of howler monkeys and the screeches of parrots provided accompaniment to vivid story lines racing through my brain. Suddenly, I was back two thousand years ago among the Maya. In my mind's eye, I could see the brightly clothed Maya living their workaday lives: building towering temples to bury dead rulers and priests; chiseling in stone the celestial order of the sun, moon, and stars; and holding elaborate ceremonies to please the gods, including, of course, the revered jaguar.

I want to share that experience because it illustrates how connected we are to the power of nature, and how that power can trigger the creative process. For this book, we have asked many of the nation's finest writers to do something unusual—to produce an original work of short fiction inspired by nature. We asked them not for a story *about* nature, nor for a nonfiction account of a place, as in our earlier book *Heart of the Land: Essays on Last Great Places*. Rather, we asked the authors to visit a place where The Nature Conservancy works, or to let inspiration flow from a place ingrained in their souls, and to let their imaginations run wild.

Of course, the natural world has always inspired authors. From the early American novelist James Fenimore Cooper, who celebrated "the holy calm of Nature," to the contemporary writer Annie Proulx, who has a story in this book (and who has said that "everything that happens to characters comes welling out of place"), our nation's authors have been moved by nature and often incorporated it into their work. Indeed, at a Conservancy panel session on nature writing in Charlottesville, Virginia, not long ago, the Pulitzer Prize–winning poet Henry Taylor went so far as to remark, "Isn't all writing nature writing?"

Taylor's question underscores the intimate connection between people and nature. Since we are all, to one degree or another, *of* the lands and waters, it is difficult to imagine any writing that cannot be traced to nature and the power of place.

In setting out on this project, we were inspired by Barry Lopez's observation that fiction allows him to get closer to the truth of the land than nonfiction. We wondered what would happen if we arranged for fiction writers to visit Conservancy sites of their choice and to write a short story inspired by the experience. We were delighted to find many of our foremost writers intrigued by the challenge.

As with *Heart of the Land*, we placed no constraints on what the authors wrote. Quite simply, we wanted to see where their imaginations took them, what sort of delicious mix of fiction would come out of the very places we work daily to conserve. And as with *Heart of the Land*, what we have is a wonderful literary jambalaya, stories of all varieties, from the steamy forests of the Dominican Republic to the achingly cold wilds of Alaska. Diversity is, after all, what the Conservancy is all about—not just biological diversity but working with diverse partners and using multiple creative methods to conserve our natural resources.

We are deeply grateful to our contributors. Our hope is that their stories touch the reader and awaken the deep connection to nature inherent in us all.

John C. Sawhill
President and Chief Executive Officer
The Nature Conservancy

INTRODUCTION:
KNOWING OUR PLACE

by Barbara Kingsolver

I have a place where I write.

I have two, in fact. In summer it's a log cabin in a deep, wooded hollow at the end of Walker Mountain. Our stoic little log house leans noticeably uphill, just like half the tobacco barns do in this rural part of southern Appalachia, where even gravity seems to have fled for better work in the city. The cabin was built of chestnut logs in the late 1930s, when the American chestnut blight was running roughshod through every forest from Maine to Alabama, felling mammoth trees more extravagantly than the crosscut saw. Those of us who'll never get to see the spreading crown of an American chestnut might view the blight as a tragedy, but the pragmatic homesteaders in this hollow saw a godsend. They harnessed their mule and dragged the fallen soldiers down off the mountain to build their home.

Now it's mine. Between May and August, my family and I happily settle our lives between its knobby, listing walls. We pace the floorboards of its porch while rain pummels the tin roof and slides off the steeply pitched eave. I love this rain; my soul hankers for it. Through a curtain of it I watch the tulip poplars grow. When it stops, I listen to the woodblock concerto of dripping leaves and the first indignant Carolina wrens reclaiming their damp territories. Then come the wood thrushes, heartbreakers, with their minor-keyed harmonies as resonant as poetry. A narrow beam of sun files between the steep mountains and butterflies traverse this column of light, top to bottom to top again, like fish in a tall aquarium. My daughters hazard the damp grass to go hunt box turtles and crayfish, or climb into the barn loft to inhale the scent of decades-old tobacco. That particular dusty sweetness, among all other odors there are, invokes the most reliable nostalgia for my own childhood; I'm slightly envious and have half a mind to run after the girls with my own stick for poking into crawdad holes. But mostly I am glad to watch them claim my own best secrets for themselves.

On a given day I might walk the half mile down our hollow to the mailbox, hail our neighbors, and exchange a farmer's evaluation of the weather (*terrible*: it truly is always either too wet or too dry in these marginal tobacco bottoms). I'll hear news of a house mysteriously put up for sale, a dog on the loose, or a memorable yard sale. My neighbors use the diphthong-rich vowels of the hill accent that was my own first language. My great-grandfather grew up in the next valley over from this one. Now I am known as the gal married to that young fella that fixed up the old Smyth cabin. We are suspected of being hard up (the cabin is quite small and rustic for a family of four) or a little deranged; neither alternative prevents our being sociably and heartily welcomed. I am nowhere more at home than here, among spare economies and extravagant yard sales glinting with jewel-toned canning jars.

But mostly I keep to the hollow. Hard up or deranged I may be, but I do know my place, and often go for days with no worldly exchanges beyond my walk to the mailbox. I'd just as soon listen for the communiqués of pileated woodpeckers, who stay hidden deep in the woods but hammer elaborately back and forth on their hollow trees like the talking drummers of Africa. Sometimes I stand on the porch and just stare, transfixed, at a mountainside that offers up more shades of green than a dictionary has words. Or I will step out with a hand trowel to tend the few relics of Mrs. Smyth's garden that have survived her—a June apple; a straggling, etiolated choir of August lilies nearly shaded out by the encroaching woods; and one heroic wisteria that has climbed hundreds of feet into the trees. I try to imagine the life of this woman who grew corn on a steeper slope than most people would be willing to climb on foot, and still needed to plant her August lilies.

I take walks in the woods, I hang out our laundry, I read stories and sing to my children, but mostly what I do with my days is write. I work in a rocking chair on the porch, or at a small blue desk facing the window. I usually write by hand, on paper, which—I somehow can't ever forget—is made from the macerated hearts of fallen trees.

The rest of the year I work at a computer on a broad oak desk by a different window, where the view is very different but also remarkable. In this house, which my predecessors constructed not from trees (which are scarce here) but of sunbaked mud (which is not), we nestle into what's called in the Southwest a *bosque*—that is, a narrow, riparian woodland stitched like a green ribbon through the pink-and-tan quilt of Arizona desert. The dominant trees are mesquite and cottonwood, with their contrasting personalities: the former swarthy and confident, the latter tall and apprehensive, trembling at the first rumor of wind. Along with Mexican elder, button willow, and bamboo, they grow densely along a creek, creating a shady green that is stretched long and thin. Picture the rich Nile valley crossing the Saharan sands, and you understand the fecundity. Picture the air hose connecting a diver's lips to the oxygen tank, and you begin to grasp the urgency. A riparian woodland, if it remains unbroken, provides a corridor through which a horde of fierce or delicate creatures may prowl, flutter, swim, or hop from the mountains down through the desert and back again. Many who follow that path—willow flycatchers, Apache trout—can live nowhere else on earth. An ill-placed dam, well, ranch, or subdivision could permanently end the existence of their kind.

I tread lightly here with my heart in my throat, like a kid who's stumbled onto the great forbidden presence (maybe sex, maybe an orchestra rehearsal) of a more mature world. If I breathe, they'll know I'm here. From the window of my study I bear witness to a small, tunnelish clearing in the woods, shaded by overarching mesquite boughs and carpeted with wildflowers. Looming over this intimate foreground are mountains whose purple crowns rise nine thousand feet above the Tucson basin. In midwinter, they often wear snow on their heads. In fall and early spring, blue-gray storms draw up into their canyons, throwing parts of the strange topography into high relief. Nearer at hand, deer and jackrabbits and javelina halt briefly to browse my clearing, then amble on up the corridor of forest. On insomniac nights I huddle in the small glow of my desk lamp, sometimes pausing the quiet click of my keys to listen for great horned owls out there in the dark, or the ghostly, spine-chilling rasp of a barn owl on the hunt. By day, vermilion flycatchers and western tanagers flash their reds and yellows in the tops of my tall windows, snagging my attention whenever they dance into the part of my eyesight where color vision begins. A roadrunner drops from a tree to the windowsill, dashes its full length, drops to the ground, and moves on, every single day, running this course as smoothly as a toy train on a track. White-winged doves feed and fledge their broods just inches from my window, oblivious to my labors, preoccupied with their own.

One day not long ago I had to pull myself out of my writerly trance, having become aware of a presence over my left shoulder. I turned my head slowly to meet the gaze of an adolescent bobcat at my window. Whether he meant to be the first to read the story on my computer screen, or was lured in by his own reflection in the quirky afternoon light, I can't say. I can tell you, though, that I held my breath and looked straight into bronze-colored bobcat eyes for longer than I knew I could hold my breath. After two moments (his and mine) that were surely not equal—for a predator routinely passes hours without an eye blink, while a human can grow restless inside ten seconds—we broke eye contact. He turned and minced away, languidly, tail end flicking, for all the world a *cat*. I presume he returned to the routine conjectures and risks and remembered scents that make up his bobcat life, and I returned to mine, mostly. But some part of my brain drifted after him for the rest of the day, stalking the taste of dove, examining a predator's patience from the inside.

It's a grand distraction, this window of mine. "Beauty and grace are performed," says Annie Dillard, "whether or not we will or sense them. The least we can do is try to be there." I agree, and tend to work where the light is good. This window is the world opening onto me. I find I don't look out, so much as it pours in.

What I mean to say is I have come to depend on these places where I write. I've grown accustomed to looking up from the page and letting my eyes relax on a landscape upon which no human artifact intrudes. No steel, pavement, or streetlights, no architecture lovely or otherwise, no works of public art or private enterprise—no hominid agenda. I consider myself lucky beyond words to go to work every morning with something like a wilderness at my elbow. In the way of so-called worldly things, I can't seem to muster a desire for kitchen gadgets or cable TV or to drive anything flashier than a dirt-colored sedan that is older than the combined ages of my children. My tastes are much more extreme: I want wood-thrush poetry. I want mountains.

It would not be quite right to say I *have* these things. The places where I write aren't actually mine. In some file drawer we do have mortgages and deeds, pieces of paper (made of dead trees, mostly pine, I should think), which satisfy me in the same way that the wren yammering his territorial song from my rain gutter has satisfied himself that all is right in *his* world. I have my ostensible claim, but the truth is these places own me: they hold my history, my passions, and my capacity for honest work. I find I do my best thinking when I am looking out over a clean plank of planet Earth. Apparently I need this starting point—the world as it appeared before people bent it to their myriad plans—in order to begin dreaming up my own myriad, imaginary hominid agendas.

And that is exactly what I do. I create imagined lives. I write about people, mostly, and the things they contrive to do for, against, or with each other. I write about things like liberty, equality, and world peace, on an extremely domestic scale. I don't necessarily write about wilderness, in general, or these two places I happen to love, in particular. This past summer on the cabin porch, while surrounded by summertime yard sales and tobacco auctions, I wrote about *Africa*, for heaven's sake. I wrote long and hard and well until I ended each day panting and exhilarated, like a marathon runner. I wrote about a faraway place I once knew well, long ago, and that I have visited more recently on research trips, and whose history and particulars I have read about in books until I dreamed in the language of elephants. I didn't need to *be* in Africa as I wrote that book; I only needed to be where I could think straight, remember, and properly invent. I needed the blessed emptiness of mind that comes from birdsong and dripping trees. I needed to sleep at night in a square box made of chestnut trees who died of natural causes.

It is widely rumored, and also true, that I wrote my first novel in a closet. Before I get all rapturous and carried away here, I had better admit to that. The house was tiny, I was up late at night while people were sleeping, there just wasn't any other place. The circumstances were extreme. And if I have to—if the furies should take my freedom or my sight—I'll go back to writing in the dark. Fish gotta swim, birds gotta fly, writers will go to stupefying lengths to get the infernal roar of words out of their skulls and onto paper. Probably I've already tempted fate by announcing that I need to look upon wilderness in order to write. (I can hear those furies sharpening their knives now, clucking, *Which shall it be, dearie? Penury or cataracts?*) Let me back up and say that I am breathless with gratitude for the collisions of choice and luck that let me work under the full-on gaze of mountains and animate beauty. It's a privilege to live any part of one's life in proximity to nature. It is a privilege, apparently, even to know nature is out there at all. In the summer of 1996, human life on earth made a subtle, uncelebrated passage from mostly rural to mostly urban. More than half of all humans now live in cities. The natural habitat of our species, then, officially, is steel, pavement, streetlights, architecture, and enterprise—the hominid agenda.

With all due respect for the wondrous ways people amuse themselves and one another on paved surfaces, I find this exodus from the land makes me unspeakably sad. I think of the children who will never know, intuitively, that a flower is a plant's way of making love, or what *silence* sounds like, or that trees breathe out what we breathe in. I think of the astonished neighbor children who huddled around my husband in his tiny back-yard garden, in the city where he lived years ago, clapping their hands to their mouths in pure dismay as he pulled *carrots* from the *ground*. (Ever the thoughtful teacher, he explained about fruits and roots and asked, "What other foods do you think might grow in the ground?" They knit their brows, conferred, offered brightly: "Spaghetti?") I wonder what it will mean for us to forget that food, like rain, is not a product but a process. I wonder how we will imagine the infinite when we have never seen how the stars fill a dark night sky. I wonder how I can explain why a wood-thrush song makes my chest hurt, to a populace for whom "wood" is a construction material and "thrush" is a tongue disease.

Oh, how can I say this: people need wild places. Whether or not they think they do, they *do*. They need to experience a landscape that is timeless, whose agenda moves at the pace of speciation and ice ages. To be surrounded by a singing, mating, howling commotion of other species, all of whom love their lives as much as you do, and none of whom could possibly care less about your economic status or your running-day calendar. Wilderness puts us in our place. It reminds us that our plans are small and somewhat absurd. It reminds us why, in those cases in which our plans might influence many future generations, we ought to choose carefully. Looking out on a clean plank of planet Earth, we can get shaken right down to the bone by the bronze-eyed possibility of lives that are not our own.

One of the remarkable stories in this book is about, believe it or not, a plane crash. That event is described in such fascinating detail that I'll now be content if I never experience it myself, but even so, the plane crash is not really the point. The point is that a woman whose soul is burdened ferociously with her husband's long-ago love affair must suddenly put that concern aside and figure out how to keep from freezing to death, or being damaged by a bear. She discovers new ways of thinking about time and survival, and an unexpected answer to a question she'd thought unanswerable. She finds these things in the Tengmiirvik wilderness of Alaska.

In another story, an aging Wasco man coping with regrets for a misspent life is passing through the Columbia River Gorge when he allows a doubtfully prestigious totem—a pair of mongrel dogs at the edge of a parking lot—to lead him into a place that restores his spirit and his hope.

In a different story, a man deeply pained by the clear-cutting of old-growth forest in Montana's Yaak Valley chooses to cut logs himself, more and more slowly, appreciating the life of each fallen tree, as a soulful form of protest. In still another story, two boys come face-to-face with nature after their truculent father shoves them out the door of a vacation cottage with a pocketknife and the absurd command to go out and kill something edible. The young narrator arrives at certain realizations about squirrels and rabbits, his parents, and survival, and he winds up chasing a be-mused cow around a pasture with a huge stick. The scene is funny, bitter, and unforgettable. This book is filled with the likes of such.

The stories are not, mostly, about wilderness. They are all about different things, and even if they were all about the same thing, I would not presume to say what that is. I believe that every act of literature is performed by two people together—the writer and the reader—and that, like sex and voting, it's a private and individual matter. Whatever works for you here, reader, is right and good, so don't let anybody tell you what you're supposed to feel in the af-terglow. I believe this so strongly, in fact, that when I speak to college students who have recently read one of my books and are about to take an exam on it, and are therefore moved to ask me what is meant by this symbol or that recurrent theme, I always ask, "Well, what do *you* think it means?" And then I say, "You are right." Of course the students think I'm being coy and evasive and don't want to help them make a good grade on the test. What they don't realize is that I might not score all that well on the test myself. I'm pretty sure Franz Kafka would have failed an exam I once had to take on "The Metamorphosis," in which most of the correct answers involved the terms "Christ figure" and "Freudian view." Which is not to say Franz Kafka wasn't thinking about religion or the human psyche when he wrote "The Metamorphosis." I just think he was also, possibly, thinking about cockroaches and laughing his head off. I believe he'd agree with me that there is no absolutely right or wrong way to read a story, except maybe with the book upside down. We authors do generally have something we want to teach you about the world, and, yes, we do put every one of those symbols and metaphors in there for a reason. But which part of that lesson you learn and how, precisely, it will matter to you depends on what you've lived, what you need, and whether you tend to listen with your ears or with your heart. The stories in this collection are about what human life seems to be about: people, and all the fascinating things we contrive to do for, against, and with each other.

And just like in real life, all these things happen in some *place*. But unlike real life, these stories all happen in places that are astonishingly wild and beautiful. It's not a coincidence.

This book was conceived and assembled by The Nature Conservancy, an organization that is in the business of trying to hold on to astonishingly wild and beautiful places. It attempts to protect them from the prevailing human tendency to pave such places over, build subdivisions on them, and name them things like "The Willows," or "Peregrine's Roost," or "Elk Meadows," after whatever it was that got killed there. Apparently it's hard for us to doubt, even for a minute, that this program of plunking down our edifices at regular intervals over the entire landmass of planet Earth is basically a good idea. To attempt to slow or change the program is even harder. The Nature Conservancy brings effort and ingenuity to the task, and this book is a fine example of both. In the hope of raising awareness, raising Cain, and raising money with which to spare more wild lands from the blade, the editors conceived this book. They called a dozen or so fiction writers and issued an invitation: visit one of the wild places the Conservancy is working to protect (you get to choose which one), then go home and write a story.

The story need not be about anything that happened during your visit, particularly. It need not even be about the place you visited. Just see where the inspiration takes you. Write a short story. The collection will be published as a book.

Let me tell you, this is not something we fiction writers hear very often from editors and publishers. We hear things like, "That deadline was two weeks ago, you know," and "Are you aware that it is now July?" not, "Hey, just see where the inspiration takes you." Most of us jumped at the chance.

It happened that when I received the call I was just about to leave for the Calakmul Biosphere Reserve in the lower Yucatán peninsula—a vast rain forest that The Nature Conservancy is working to protect, in cooperation with several Mexican conservation groups. I was going for other reasons, but I could certainly try to get inspired and write something for The Nature Conservancy's book while I was at it. I cautioned the editors, though, that I might not be able to produce a short story. As a person who has been asked nine million times, "Where do you get your ideas?" and who still has no answer to that question (except to declare solemnly like my friend Dave Barry: "Mail order"), at least I know where they *don't* come from. I can't, reliably, go to any particular place on this earth and come back with a story. I do set my stories in places I've lived or visited, but it's not like running down to the market to pick up a quart of milk. Once I watched a glorious sunset from the pier at the Berkeley Marina and exactly one year later wrote a story in which a character set her life askew by kissing a stranger in that very setting. Seven or eight years after I attended a picturesque celebration called the Covered Bridges Festival in southern Indiana, I reread what I'd written in my journal about it and drafted a short story (bearing no relation to anything that happened to me that day) called "Covered Bridges." Some three decades after I lived in a village on the Wamba River in central Africa, I began writing a novel set in that place. If current trends bear out, I may well write a story set in the Calakmul forest someday. But when the editors of this book said, "See where the inspiration takes you," I don't think they meant, "in the next fifty years." For me, the genesis of fiction is tenuous and labyrinthine and inscrutable and deeply inefficient, somewhat like the U.S. government agency that issues tax refunds. I can only begin to write a story after I know what the story will be *about*. It has to be something I know to be true. Then I think about how I know it's true, by remembering events in my life that taught this truth to me. Next I consider what sort of people could act out such a drama more instructively or comically or sweetly than anything that ever happened to me in real life, which is not to say my life is not comic or sweet, but it has never to my knowledge proceeded neatly from setup to development to revelation and climax and denouement, which a short story has got to do, in all fairness to the reader. So then, after I get a glimpse of the plot, I decide how character and setting will work to complement the theme. Like I said, you will get your government refund check and probably spend it, too, long before I get my story going.

What worried me, when I anticipated going to the rain forest and coming home with a short story in my cerebral suitcase, was that while I seem capable of writing *essays* about any darn thing under the sun—hermit crabs, go-go boots, and the Dewey decimal system included—when I write fiction it is always about people. I hoped to visit and maybe even learn something about the people who live in or near the Calakmul forest, and in fact I did. But in two weeks I did not scratch the surface of their language or their lives. I walked with Mayan women through their gardens, stepping carefully over the cilantro and the *nescafé*, and so I know what grows there. But I don't know the different scents of the kindling woods they use for cooking, what spices they use for the blessing, or the poetry with which they cajole their children to eat. I know nothing of the details of life in the Calakmul forest, and fiction is nothing but a collection of details piled carefully upon one another until they resemble a universe. If you leave out the details, you have a black hole. If you *make up* the details, you have either science fiction or bad fiction, neither of which I aspire to as a specialty. Aware of my limitations, I promised the editors of this book that, if I couldn't write a short story out of my visit to the Yucatán, I would write a foreword for the book instead. And so, here I am.

Deep in my wicked heart I suspect all other people of harboring my own deficiencies but just hiding them better, so I wondered how all these other fiction writers were going to manage an assignment that I found utterly impossible. Could they just take a hike through the Alaskan wilderness or the Point Reyes National Seashore or what have you, then beat it back home and crank out a story? Why, yes, it turns out, they could. You are holding the proof, a fine piece of work. You could read this book for the descriptions of setting alone, but you won't, because there is so much else, so many different angles on the human condition to run away with your imagination. Suffice it to say these writers did much more than take notes on the vegetation. They took pilgrimages, evidently, to places where they could think straight, remember, and properly invent. I am enthralled with what they brought back. I think you will be, too.

As I turned the pages of this manuscript and slowly got myself lost in one quiet world after another, I began to see how they managed it. The stories sort themselves roughly into two types. Some are told from the point of view of a visitor to a strange land who is somehow moved by the strangeness or by the land; these were written by authors who visited a place that was new to them. The other stories tell of characters deeply embedded in the culture and sense of a place, who often are moved by some outside force that is set upon the land; these came from the writers who, as Lee Smith says in her author's note, "seized the opportunity to look in my own back yard." Both kinds of stories met the assignment perfectly. Now, why didn't I think of that? There are, after all, only two plots in the English language: they begin "I set out on a trip . . ." or "A stranger has come to town. . . ."

Which brings us back to the matter of place. Whether we are leaving it or dealing with an outsider coming into it, it's *here* that matters. Whether we understand where we are, or don't—that is the question. To be *here*, or not to be. Storytelling is as old as our need to remember where the water is, where the best food grows, where we find our courage for the hunt. It's as persistent as our desire to teach our children how to live in this place that we have known longer than they have. Story is our grand explanation for ourselves, and it grows from place, as surely as carrots grow in dirt.

I've already warned that no one ought to tell you what a story means, and now I'm presuming to tell you what one *is*. I tell you this because I think it's true, and can't believe otherwise. A world is looking over my shoulder as I write these words: my censors are bobcats and mountains. I have a place from which I tell my stories. So do you, I expect. We sing the song of our home because we are animals, and an animal is no better or wiser or safer than its habitat and its food chain. Among the greatest of all gifts is to know our place. I write about people, but I believe I am a writer because I grew up among trees. These stories explore that mystery: the intimate relation of human passion and human place.

An earlier book produced by The Nature Conservancy, called *Heart of the Land,* is very much like this one, except that it's a collection of essays rather than short fiction. The contributors were given the same task of visiting one of the Conservancy's preserves and writing of that place whatever we wished. That collection is as compelling as this one, although the essays probably hold more to a common theme than these stories do. Barry Lopez had the task of suggesting what that theme might be, in the foreword, and he did it beautifully. He concluded from reading the essays that if our endeavor—the protection of natures other than our own—is to succeed "it will require that we reimagine our lives . . . It will require of many of us a humanity we've not yet mustered, and a grace we were not aware we desired until we had tasted it."

This book is a worthy sequel to that one, because fiction is all about the reimagined life. It's a chance to show what we could be, what we might have been, what character is and what it owes to circumstance. I learned in the eleventh grade that the three great themes in literature are Man against Man, Man against Himself, and Man against Nature. I've surmised since then that literature has room for more than just those three poor beleaguered Men and that, in fact, it doesn't always have to be *against*. Especially not Nature. Implicit within these covers is the acknowledgment that all the characters on a scene need not be human at all—here the white pelican is a character; the bear is a character; the cow ducking and lumbering from the wielded stick is a character; the dense, ancient logs in an old-growth forest are characters; the land itself is a character.

Here is a book made of the macerated hearts of trees, who died for the sake of these imagined lives. Remember that you are holding consecrated air and time and sunlight. Listen with your heart to the people on these pages who move through the land and are moved by it, in a hundred different ways. Like me, and like you, they have particular and beautiful places where they live, or work, or go, in order to come away changed. They have tasted grace and learned that they desire it; in one way or another, they need wild places. Please learn from them what you will.

THE CHAUFFEUR

by *Howard Norman*

My only client was Mrs. Moro. With what she paid me, I didn't need to drive anyone else. She lived at 1960 Jones Street, on Russian Hill, here in San Francisco. I live at 488 Columbus, Apt. 6-B, a few blocks up from North Beach. Every Tuesday, I picked her up at 6 a.m. In the almost two years she employed me, she was never ill or out of town.

The tableau soon became familiar. Mrs. Moro would be sitting on the dark red, wooden bench on the left side of her porch. I must say she looked childlike against the two-story brown house, with its tall door and slate shingles. It never varied, she'd be wearing cotton blue pants, a blouse, a sweater, and a black all-weather parka on top. This was her year-round attire. She'd either be sipping tea from a thermos, or holding the closed thermos on her lap. The few times she was asleep I didn't tap the horn. I simply kept the car idling until she opened her eyes, stood, smoothed both sleeves of the parka with her hands, took up her walking stick, and navigated down two levels of cobbled stairs to the curb. Naturally, I'd hold open the door. She was about five feet tall; she didn't have to bend much to get in. Then, I'd drive her across the Golden Gate Bridge, up Highway 1 past Mill Valley, out to Sir Francis Drake Highway, on through Inverness, and up to Point Reyes National Seashore, where she'd walk and bird-watch, rain or no rain.

Mrs. Moro was my patron, my driving companion, and, truth be told, one of the few people I had any sort of regular conversation with. And that was fine. Friendlier chauffeurs got extra work, word-of-mouth. I had Mrs. Moro, stuck with her, she stuck with me, and she paid me better than I could've ever imagined. Two people in a car for so many hours rely in equal measure on each other for things said and things unsaid.

Not that I hadn't had previous clients. I'd worked for Airport Limousine for five years before Mrs. Moro hired me. I was on call with a beeper. Mostly, I drove businessmen, airport to hotel, hotel to restaurant, to a nightclub. Waiting for a client on summer nights, I'd lean against my Lincoln Town Car, just looking at whatever street activity. Or sit in the car, reading one of my Joseph Conrad novels. Or Graham Greene. I did my book shopping at Clean Well-Lighted Place for Books. I had a small portable library in the front seat. It included some Italian authors, too; there was Elsa Morante, Dino Buzzati, Tommaso Landolfi, Natalia Ginzburg, my favorite. Whereas many of the chauffeurs I met at hotels, bar mitzvahs, concerts, weddings, and so on preferred music tapes to reading. I didn't have a single music tape. When my clients wanted music, I found something on the FM.

In this employment, I wasn't happy or unhappy, and it paid my rent. On occasion, I drove a stretch limousine, TV, wet bar, stereo system in the back, but I preferred the Town Car. In terms of human behaviors, life seemed less complicated with the Town Car. With the limousine, not often, but once in a while, there was love-making in the backseat, and then the awkward moment with the clients' mussed-up shirt or blouse, their extravagantly oversized tips out of embarrassment. Usually these were people who'd started out the evening all neatly tucked and tied, but ended up like a boozy scene in a film noir, or aspired to. From the get-go with my boss David Tallen, I refused prom nights or rich kids just out for a lark—you could tell by what my boss called their "on-phone demeanor." In a Town Car, there's no privacy from the driver, no privacy window, whereas in the limousine, there was, so in Town Cars the clients predictably acted in a more civilized manner. Only once did I ever say "Get another driver," and that guy was an out-and-out jerk, bully-the-chauffeur, obviously a show-off-for-his-girlfriend celebrity type, I think a weather channel host. I wasn't much bothered by it, really. I take things personally only from people I know personally. In that instance, I didn't even adjust the rearview in order to see his face after I'd dumped him back at his hotel. In fact, his girlfriend stayed in the car and I dropped her off at a party. Shame and embarrassment, just wanting to get away from the chauffeur, quite often resulted in hurried, oversized tips. I'm just describing human nature in such situations. Let's see, oh yes, and one time I had Dustin Hoffman and his wife in the car. They were very polite and friendly and kept driver-client exchanges very cut-and-dry, which a driver appreciates. They went out for dinner, then to someone's apartment, then back to their hotel at 3 a.m. Generous tip that time, too. I worked for a pair of Buddhist monk dignitaries, the cellist Janos Starker, and, a year before he died, the famous deejay Wolfman Jack, and they are the extent of my name-dropping. Whereas some chauffeurs go on and on, like they became personal confidants in a few hours. "Yeah, Harold Robbins—the author? His wife always requests me." And like that.

Mrs. Moro, born in Tokyo, a bird-watcher and nice person, was anonymous, as far as I knew, to the world at large. She struck me as a very private soul, so I appreciated our conversations, some of which were only a few minutes long. On our fifth or sixth drive together, she said, "Tuttle Albers"—she always used my complete name—"Tuttle Albers, I have a present for you. A little gift. It's a book." She set a book called *Rashomon*, by the Japanese writer Akutagawa Ryūnosuke, on the front seat next to me, then pronounced his name on my behalf. "Give it a try maybe." I read it while she was walking at Point Reyes, a murder story told from different points of view. When we started back to San Francisco, I said, "I read the book," and she said, "I'm pleased you read it so quickly. I know you did so because it was a gift, but I'm pleased just the same," and wanted to hear my opinion. In her questions, she was a bit like a schoolteacher, but I could tell she was enjoying herself. As usual, she fell asleep just as we got to the Golden Gate Bridge. I always had to wake her up when we got to her house.

· · ·

To put it simply, working for Mrs. Moro got me out into nature. I mean that in two old-fashioned ways.

First, at Point Reyes, there was never an absence of hawks, and there were the smaller flitting kinds of birds, the usual crows. All sorts of ducks, Mrs. Moro told me, "abounded"—she used that word—in the lowland estuaries. There are maybe ten hiking trails at the National Seashore, names like Five Brooks, Chimney Rock, Mount Vision, Muddy Hollow. Some of the trails meander back before reaching the sea, but Mrs. Moro walked the same trail every time, the Estero Trail, which went all the way to Sunset Beach. "I take a quick nap leaning against a fallen tree," she once told me. "I believe it was struck by lightning."

Parked next to the Estero trailhead entrance gate, I'd do pretty much what I did when I used to wait for clients in the city. I'd sit in the car, or, weather permitting, lie on the ground and read. Or listen to KPXP Country. I had my Joseph Conrads, my Italians, and, as the weeks went by, the Japanese novels generously given to me by Mrs. Moro: Tanizaki, Kawabata, more Akutagawa, and a number of others. "No reason to expect you'd ever read in Japanese," she said. "Still, I feel sorry for you, that you cannot." In short, Mrs. Moro had provided me with my entire Japanese library. Remarkable as it first seemed, that a woman her age could make the three-hour trek to the ocean and back, after a few trips her stamina didn't at all surprise me. And she had her nap on the way to Point Reyes, at the beach, on the way home. Some days, after I watched her disappear over the hill, I'd drive into Point Reyes for lunch, even catch a noon matinee at the art house in Mill Valley, but I'd always get back in plenty of time. I made sure to tell Mrs. Moro my exact plans and wrote out telephone numbers, the car phone, the police, the movie theater, even the general store in Point Reyes Station. She kept these numbers in a small notebook. A separate notebook from her bird lists. "Birds are my greatest pleasure," she once said.

Turn left off Sir Francis Drake Road, go down a quarter mile of blacktop, continue along the hard-packed dirt road for another mile and a half, and you get to the parking area at the Estero trailhead. It's situated between dry grassy hills. In summer, there are dust devils, even an occasional brush fire; the National Seashore has its own volunteer fire department, men and women from Inverness, Point Reyes Station, and other nearby towns. Volunteers had VFD decals on windshields, lower left-hand corner. To either side of the trailhead, cattle grazed up close behind fences. I'd hear cattle lowing all day. And as I mentioned, hawks were always in abundance. Hawks were a constant. They'd be circling overhead, buffeted by the wind, they'd drift and rise on the thermals and swoop down into the crag gullies, and hawks were always patrolling the fields as far as the eye could see. I'd watch them but not study them, really, although I knew that Mrs. Moro studied them and even wanted hawks to be a common thing between us, because she gave me a field guide. "Hawks may be the easiest to tell apart. They're observable for long periods," she said. "However, the true test is shorebirds. To distinguish one sandpiper from the other has, for the twenty years I've walked the same path, been my nemesis. I have almost given up."

"Why do you keep walking to the same beach?" I said.

"Oh, that is simple. I hope to see white pelicans. I hope to see them. But why should they be in any hurry to let me see them?"

"Maybe if you'd come up here more than one day a week," I said. "I'll bring you up here for free, an extra time per week, if you want."

"That holds out the possibility of my not seeing white pelicans twice a week, instead of once. I don't think that would be a good thing."

Second, there was human nature. Because during Mrs. Moro's walks to the sea, I would visit Grey Zamarkis, who was a resident research zoologist at the Tule Elk Reserve, out on foggy Tomales Bay, at the northern edge of the Inverness Ridge.

I looked this up in my appointment book, which I kept in my glove compartment: I met Grey the twenty-third time I brought Mrs. Moro to the National Seashore. I'd waited until Mrs. Moro drifted over the hill—the day was hazy and she looked a little like a mirage—and then I drove into Inverness to gas up the Town Car. I was standing next to the gas pump in front of the Inverness General Store when I saw this woman—I'm speaking of Grey, of course—putting air into the tires of her Land Rover. Not a candlelight dinner in sight, as the country-western song defined a romantic moment in a non-romantic setting. Not to leap ahead too far, but we ended up having country-western music in common; we made love to it and argued about it. For instance, one time I claimed that, although I enjoyed it, C and W basically promoted a drastically simple take on people. To support this, I cited a popular joke: What do you get when you play a country-western song backward? Well, you get your wife back, your kids back, your car back. "No, sir, uh-uh, nope," Grey said, shaking her head back and forth. "They may be drastic little soap operas, but they tell some basic truths about love and life. Just like great novels do. In less time, of course." Anyway, for the approximately six months Grey and I were together, we kept the radio on KPXP, and never changed stations, not in her Land Rover, the Town Car, or in her one-room "fisherman's hovel," as she called her rented clapboard structure at the end of a dock stretched out into Tomales Bay. Next to the Golden Hinde Boatel on Sir Francis Drake Highway. The dock slats were so unevenly rotted it was like walking on a long wooden xylophone; it made that many different hollow tones. Grey's rent was fifty dollars a month. She lived a twenty-five-minute drive from the herd of elk.

I met Grey on August 17, and later, as I mentioned, I entered our meeting in my work diary. I already had strong feelings for her, yet all I wrote was "Grey Zamarkis."

Standing at the gas pump, I'd noticed Grey's bumper sticker: I BRAKE FOR SASQUATCH. Now, normally, I'd have been repelled. Because driving as much as I did, I'd evolved an ever-narrowing tolerance for bumper sticker philosophies. I made it my obligation to disagree with each and every one of them, on principle. The principle being that any joke, platitude, Bible quote, political harangue, or ethical judgment that ends up on a bumper sticker asks you to be like-minded. But somehow, Grey's sticker didn't put me off. I felt generous toward it, willing to be persuaded that it declared that she was open to surprises in the natural world: should Sasquatch step out onto the road, she'd give it the right-of-way. I immediately thought of Grey as someone who'd defer to the mysterious. It's quite likely that all of this quick interpretation was based on the fact that Grey, at first glance and from that time forward, was so striking. The word "smitten" accurately applies to me, and I remember everything about that morning, including that her red hair was shaped into a tight configuration of braids, but was frizzed out anyway. When she stood up, I saw that she was taller than me by at least an inch; I am five foot eight. Though she was not a park ranger, a Smokey the Bear–type hat hung by a woven cord down her back. When she leaned over again to test the air pressure, the hat fell to one side. She got annoyed and flipped it back, and then must've felt me staring, because she turned and glared at me. She had a sprinkle of freckles along her nose. Since I thought she looked pretty elegant while just putting air in her tires, naturally I needed to watch her walk to the cash register, chat up the clerk, buy a pack of Neccos, go in and out of the ladies. And then I was both stupefied and pleased when she walked directly up to me and said, "Hate your car."

"Well, I'm a chauffeur."

She had a nice laugh. We had coffee while standing up in the store. Coffee and bagels to go. Conversation. Betraying no excitement. And two hours later, this was about 11:30 a.m., we were standing up in her open-top Land Rover, looking at a dozen or so tule elk. "I'm the only researcher in residence right now," Grey said. She handed me her binoculars and I looked through them at the elk. I could see that their noses were wet. I could see them scuffing up ground cover. I could see them nodding, shivering up along their thick necks, gazing in our direction, sniffing the air, nervously shuffling. "We're in the elk's house—the Indians who used to live around here said—and some days, it feels like heaven to me," Grey said. "But I'll tell you what, elk can be nasty. They've gone for my vehicle. The reserve gets socked in by fog, midsummer or not. And the forest—all these trees—can get like one enormous ventriloquist."

"How do you mean that?"

"Well, depending on the fog, how thick, how not thick, it's like an elk throws its voice. You hear one bellowing or coughing—it's more a chuffing bark—coming, say, from over to your left. But then suddenly the animal crashes right past you not ten yards away on your right."

"Could it be there's really two elk?"

"You don't get what I mean. Because you haven't experienced it yet. No offense."

"That's okay. We just met. I'm out here in my chauffeur's suit. These shoes. And these are the first elk I've ever seen, except for on Marty Stouffer's *Wild America* program."

"I hate that show."

"So do I—now."

"Yippee, our first thing in common."

Grey and I first started sleeping together two visits later. She had just turned twenty-eight that July 11, and my thirtieth birthday had been on March 14. She'd been married at nineteen in Fresno, moved to Castroville, and gotten divorced at twenty-three. "He— that being Eddie—wanted me to be an artichoke wife," Grey told me, our first noontime in bed. "His family business was artichokes. All the women he was raised around and by became artichoke wives. They took care of the house, kids, did the books, et cetera. And I was that for four years of my life, Tuttle, right out of high school. Except that I had no children. I was derided for taking night courses at the community college. In biology. They were tough courses. And I mean derided. Sitting with family or friends, in a bar? My own husband, Eddie—he'd say, 'And what does our local intellectual say about that?' Whatever the topic. I think he was jealous because he read comic books and the occasional farm report, and there was TV. I'd married him, though; nobody put a gun to my head. Going from artichoke wife to zoology major was twice around the planet Earth, considering where I started out."

Grey was working on what she called her "late doctorate" in zoology, at the University of California, Davis campus. She knew a dictionary's worth of zoological terms, and had a nonplussed way of simplifying for me all the important theories in her field. She expected me to be interested, but didn't ask me to read any of the Ph.D. thesis she was writing. She was up-front about her need to budget her study time. I admired her constancy. Whenever I drove up to spend a weekend, I admired that she took her time in bed, too. And admired when she'd then get up, go to her desk, open her notebooks, and work until 3 a.m. If I was there on a weekday night, she'd get maybe two, three hours of sleep, off goes the alarm, she'd drink half a pot of coffee, and leave for the Tule Elk Reserve.

The working title of her thesis was "Predator-Prey Relationship Between Saber-toothed Cats and Tule Elk." At Davis, she'd studied with one of the world's foremost experts on sabertooth—the large, extinct cat that used to roam California—behavior. His name was Dr. Peter Volk. He was British, and had supervised excavations at the La Brea Tar Pits. Grey said he was demanding. He gave every single one of his graduate students *The Autobiography of Charles Darwin* for inspiration. He'd made sure that Grey steeped herself in all the paleontological writings about sabertooths, and she had to cross-reference that with predator-prey studies about other large cats of the world. "Partake of hours and hours of imaginative thinking and daydreaming," Volk said, "and spend as much time with tule elk as possible." One of Volk's theories—the one that excited Grey the most, actually—was that present-day elk might have a genetic memory of being hunted, say a thousand years ago, by saber-toothed tigers. She once let me read her notebook: "Passing the exams will be child's play, for you, Grey," he'd told her during an office appointment. "But if you want to make real discoveries, stretch your brain, get obsessed by far-reaching possibilities."

"At first," Grey said, "with all his talk about a poetic approach,

I felt lost, and thought that Dr. Volk was patronizing me. That he didn't really think I had the scientific smarts. I mustered up the courage to confront him on this, and he said, 'I don't take just anybody into this program, Miss Zamarkis,' and that ended that discussion."

I admit I didn't grasp all of the ambitions of Grey's fieldwork, and very little of her thesis topic, but she made it sound exciting; I cared because she cared so much, and I told her that. She was dedicated. "I told Dr. Volk I was working long hours because I wanted to make up for lost time," Grey said. "He downplayed that. He said that, with a living animal—the elk, he meant, and then add this sabertooth deal to boot—you have to take your sweet time."

The first week in September I'd driven up on a Saturday afternoon to be with Grey. I got to her place at 4:15, and we were in bed by 4:30. That evening, we had dinner at The Station, in Point Reyes Station, a lively joint that specialized in Mexican. Grey was in a chatty mood. She'd gotten dressed up in a pleated, black Western skirt, a belt with a steer-horn buckle, a white cotton sweater, no bra, and a necklace of black pears. And cowboy boots. She had her hair up in one braid, and otherwise it tumbled down, frizzy as it was. "Tuttle," she said, the moment we sat down, "I'm going to play the jukebox. I actually went to the bank yesterday to get quarters, hoping we'd be here tonight."

"We can go three doors down to Max's afterward to dance, if you'd like."

"I'd just as soon go home."

"That's fine, too."

"Or there's a movie, *The Lacemaker,* with that beautiful Isabelle Huppert. Down in Mill Valley. My mother, I mentioned it to her on the telephone last night. She said she saw it when it first came out, *The Lacemaker,* and that it had the saddest ending of any movie she'd ever seen. The camera just holds on a brokenhearted Isabelle Huppert's face for at least three minutes. I said, Mom, you always thought that was me in the school playground, you know, sitting off by myself alone, and that's how I'd end up, too. But that was a movie star sitting alone, jilted and forlorn, at the end of a movie, not your own daughter, Mom."

"You just gave the ending away."

"It doesn't matter, does it? I mean, you only really experience the end by going through the whole story start to finish. A story's not ruined just by knowing the ending ahead of time. Only a limited person would think that. And that's not you, Tuttle. You're not in the least bit limited."

"Well, to a movie or back to your place. Either one's fine. I know you like to work up your notes on Saturday nights. Miss Lonelyhearts, huh?"

"I enjoy being alone sometimes, but not tonight. Tonight I'm sticking with you. And I'm extra happy. Want to know why? Because I felt like a sabertooth yesterday, all afternoon yesterday. Usually, I try to imagine—like Dr. Volk suggested—imagine myself as a tule elk, a female. Nibbling grass in the fog. Picking my way down to a rocky beach. You know, get inside an elk's head. But two nights ago, coffee, coffee, coffee, and the term 'predator-prey' came into my brain, and I thought, *hmmmmm*, that I'd been one-sided in my concentration all of these months. So, yesterday, I was out at the range at 4 a.m., and I had a pretty normal morning. But in the afternoon—pow! I really got into being a sabertooth. It made a big difference, emotionally at least. Now, if I could only somehow get that experience down on paper."

The waiter brought our salads first, then enchiladas and Dos Equis beers. Grey ordered a pitcher of ice water, too; she was planning ahead for the spiciness. She'd ordered two chicken-and-cheese enchiladas, I got one beef and one chicken. When our food was all set out, I lifted my bottle and said, "May a saber-toothed tiger materalize right out of the fog, so you can see that."

We clinked bottles and each took a swig. "Talk about getting into someone else's head," Grey said. "You got into mine with that toast, Tuttle." She leaned over and kissed me. "It was a thoughtful toast. I mean that. Totally unselfish."

"Well, there's not too many people I'd be truly happy for, if something fantastic happened to them."

"I'm happening to you, Tuttle."

"Yes you are."

We ate and talked about this and that, and Grey played five songs in a row on the jukebox, which we could barely hear over the surrounding conversations. Finally, Grey slid her chair close up to mine. "How'd you actually choose your profession, Tuttle?" she said. "I should have asked sooner, I know." She turned beet red. "God, half a beer and I'm slurring. What a cheap date, huh?"

We both laughed, and I could tell by the directness of her smile that we wouldn't be going to a movie. In fact, my heart actually felt like it fluttered in my throat, and I wanted to leave the restaurant right then. But Grey was relishing her meal, she wanted to talk, as did I, really. All of which composed the happiness I'd have been loath to ruin.

"I didn't go into the family business, if that's what you mean?"

"I suppose I meant, what keeps you being a chauffeur?"

"Mrs. Moro—I told you about her. She keeps me in it."

"On the practical side, sure, Mrs. Moro pays you well."

"Not just the practical."

"You like talking with her about the novels and so forth."

"Plus, I admire her overall character, I guess is the way to put it."

"Obviously, though, she's a wealthy lady."

"I don't know for sure. I've never set foot in her house. It's an old house, old for San Francisco, at least. She told me it's the only one on Russian Hill that was designed by the architect Maybeck, very famous. One morning, I saw a man, much younger than Mrs. Moro, standing in the front window, and when she got in the car, she said it was her son, visiting from Tokyo. Maybe I'm wrong, but just the way she said it, she sounded disgusted. Yeah, probably she's very rich. I don't think my being her chauffeur's her only extravagance."

"You really really like her a lot, don't you?"

"In a funny way—and I'm not asking for violins. And present company excepted, she's turned out to be my one friend. Sounds unlikely, I suppose. I mean, she's sixty-seven. But, she trusts me to drive her. She trusts me to share books. In the car, we either talk or don't. It's nice for me. One time, it was raining cats and dogs, I said, 'Now, Mrs. Moro, you're not really going to walk down to Sunset Beach in this monsoon, are you?' "

"What'd she say to that?"

" 'Tuttle Albers—' "

"Sorry to interrupt, but your Japanese accent is atrocious."

" '—Tuttle Albers, my hope is to one day see a white pelican.' Then she got out of the car, put up the hood of her parka, and just started walking. She travels pretty light, the backpack, thermos of tea, maybe an extra sweater. Her walking stick, notebook, binoculars. That's about it."

"That's nice, Tuttle. I like hearing about her. I like hearing about you and her together."

"I didn't realize how much I liked her, though, till you asked."

"You probably just never said so out loud."

"I bet that's it."

We went to Baskin Robbins for an ice cream, sat on the enclosed porch. It wasn't crowded at all. We each got double scoops of vanilla in a cup. "Truth be told," I said, "I've lost my taste for driving. Not my knack for it. Just my affection. I don't have another profession in mind yet. I used to work for this guy, David Tallen, at Airport Limousine, and he was a good employer. I don't like working for anybody, really, but I didn't mind working for him."

"You must've run into some doozies. Clients, I mean."

"I'll tell you a story sometime."

"Tell me now, Tuttle. We're just eating ice cream."

"Yeah? Well, okay—this one time. David Tallen calls me up, he says, 'A Miss Banaktian—' this was about five years ago. David says, '—her mother and father are from Armenia. And they're flying in via New York for her wedding. She's a student at UC-Berkeley, and she's marrying a guy she met in school.' Okay—so these parents have never been to the U.S. I'm supposed to pick them up at the San Francisco airport, right? Then drive them to the Mark Hopkins. The wedding's that night at the hotel. Then the next morning, I'm supposed to drive them—a group—to Carmel, where they've got a

house rented for a week. I'm supposed to wait a week, then pick
them up, the airport, and they go back to Armenia.

"It's pretty cut-and-dry. And it's a nice job, because, one, since
everybody's staying at the Mark Hopkins, I don't have to stick
around for the wedding in order to drive them anywhere else that
night. And, two, I get to see Carmel. And, three, I could take on
other clients during the week. I did some addition ahead of time,
and figured I'd come out with around six hundred dollars, plus a
tip, but do you know what I ended up with? Three thousand dollars."

"How'd that miracle happen, pray tell?"

"I pick them up at the airport, and the future bride is in the
backseat, and, Grey, she is very beautiful, very exotic-looking in a
way. I couldn't understand a word they said in the car, but it was
a teary reunion. The whole way to the city they spoke Armenian
and laughed and looked at photographs from the old country and
so forth.

"So. The wedding takes place. The next morning, 10 a.m. sharp,
I'm at the hotel, standing by the stretch. A very sunny day. And
out comes Mr. Banaktian, and he is looking highly agitated. He is
not happy. I thought, hangover mixed with jet lag. I saw the rest
of the family, aunt, uncle, mother, and the bride's brother, I
think—and then I see the bride and groom. He's holding the bride's
hand. But nobody—none of them—is looking in the least bit
happy. I say to myself, 'You're going to Carmel. The seals. The sea
otters. The beautiful scenery. Just roll the privacy window up, forget
it, no problem. Down and back, it's the beautiful coast highway.'

"When all of a sudden, the father, Mr. Banaktian—he's about
sixty—he comes up to me. His accent, mind you, is very thick. I
say, 'Congratulations, sir. The bellhops will put your luggage in the
trunk. I'm ready to go whenever you are.' I've already got the trunk
popped open.

" 'Wait a minute—driver,' he says. 'Wait a minute.' I can't do
the accent. He says, 'Tuttle—' because I've got my name tag on.
'Tuttle, look. Look. Look, there, there's my new son-in-law, and
what a piece of shit he is. My friend, my driver. I'm a *disappointed*

man. This piece of shit she's married. Dirty. Dirty hair. And no job. He's what we call—' and he said something in Armenian. The words twisted up his face. 'He doesn't eat. At his own wedding banquet, he drank Coca-Cola—he's a fucking *string bean*.' " Grey was laughing. " 'You call it here, a *string bean*.'

" 'Tuttle'—and now he places my hand directly over his heart. He had a silk suit on, I think" '—you can't feel anything, can you, because I'm *dead*.'

" 'I'll get the bellhops,' I said.

"But now he grabs my arm tightly. 'Tuttle, look at my daughter,' he says. 'Look at her face. In her face is not a happy future.' Now he steps up close to me and whispers, 'Tuttle, my friend. In my country, I have position. I come from an important family. My mother, she's ninety-three. Ninety-three years old. She's seen a lot. She's been through a lot. She deserves peacefulness. A peaceful death. She controls the family money—you mention this to anyone Tuttle, my driver, and I will run you over with this big limousine, eh? I'm smiling. I'm smiling. It's my big joke. Relax. But, Tuttle, my American friend, my goodwill ambassador.' He takes out a wad of American hundred-dollar bills. He peels off two thousand dollars' worth, stuffs it into my suit pocket, and says, 'In *addition* to your driving fee, Tuttle.'

" 'I don't understand,' I say.

" 'My mother,' he says, 'was too weak to come to America California for the wedding, her only granddaughter. I promised I would bring back photographs. We had hundreds taken. But no matter, no matter, because I promised her a special one, the bride, the groom, together—a photograph for enlargement—the groom stands next to the bride, eh? Tuttle, I look at you. I appraise you. You're a handsome man. I beg you—please.' He's actually got tears in his eyes. 'See that man across the lobby—our photographer. He's my cousin. He's going to take a picture of you next to my daughter. Just standing next to the impressive limousine. To my daughter, it will seem nothing, just a natural proud thing for her father, to show off the car, the driver. But I will personally see to it it is the only photograph of the bride and groom my mother ever sets eyes on, and she'll die in peace. Because you, Tuttle, are not a drug-head hippie string bean. Who somehow hypnotized my daughter.' He peels off ten more bills and stuffs them in. And he puts his face an inch from mine and says, 'To make my mother happy.' "

"And so," Grey said, "tossing chauffeuring ethics to the wind, Tuttle Albers accepts a whopping bribe."

"Weeks after it happened, you know what? I had very detailed, weird dreams."

"Such as?"

"It got pretty paranoid. See, this actual real event did happen, I *did* stand next to the Armenian bride in front of the limo. The cousin snaps maybe ten pictures. I drive them to Carmel and all the rest, no problems, no glitches, and I didn't hear another word from Mr. Banaktian. All that was real life. But then came these dreams.

"In dream number one, the ninety-three-year-old mother—"

"Oh, oh," Grey said.

"The old mother sees the photograph of me and her granddaughter together, and she completely recovers from her illness. She's all perky now. She's got the photograph on the mantel, and Mr. Banaktian's put in a fix, and the bride's not going back to Armenia so she can't say, 'That's not my husband!' One day—this is my dream, now—the old mother calls Mr. Banaktian to her side and says, 'I want to see my granddaughter and her new husband. If you don't bring them to me, I'll leave all the family money to a flock of crows.' "

"Crows?" Grey said, laughing.

"Grey—I'm just telling what I dreamed."

"Sorry—it's just that it's a Grimm's fairy tale, Tuttle."

"Anyway, that's dream number one. Dream number two. I'm sitting home in my apartment. I've got my chauffeur's suit on. I'm drinking coffee. It's late at night. The downstairs buzzer rings. I say into the intercom, 'Who is it?' It's a sultry voice with an accent— 'It's me.' I press the buzzer. I hear the elevator bell. There's a knock on my door. I open it."

"Of course, it's the Armenian bride," Grey said. "The bitch."

"She's got her wedding dress on. Oh, my God. Oh, my God. She pulls the dress right off and gives me the deepest warmest kiss, then she says, 'The airplane is waiting.' 'Where's your husband?' I ask. 'Oh, it was so tragic,' she says." I took some bites of ice cream.

"So naturally there's a dream number three," Grey said.

"Dream three. We're living in Armenia, I've fallen madly in love with her. There's no turning back. We have children."

"Bad ending for me," Grey said.

"You asked me to tell this story."

Grey and I finished our ice cream. She ordered a cup of coffee. She looked at me, shaking her head back and forth. "God, Tuttle, you mean you and this bride—actually, *real life* now, might be in a photograph, in an actual house in actual Armenia?"

"I'm certain of it. This *actual* Mr. Banaktian wasn't kidding."

"If I see any Armenian license plates around Inverness, Tuttle, I'm going to get upset."

Grey went to the ladies' room. When she came back, I was sipping her coffee. She sat down and I slid the mug over to her. "I'm shifting subjects here," she said. "But, Tuttle, how much do you like your apartment? Because you really only have to be in San Francisco Tuesday morning and Tuesday night, Mrs. Moro up and back, correct?"

"Are you asking me to be up here with you more?"

"Not live with me. Not yet. My grant's only good for another year. I'm under a bit of pressure there. I was thinking, we could see each other maybe at least one, two other days a week. Or at least steadily weekends guaranteed. The Holly Tree Inn has excellent off-season rates. You could start out there—it's ten minutes from my place."

"She likes me. She likes me."

"You drive home, okay? I'm still a little tipsy."

I drove the Land Rover back to Inverness. Beautiful starry night. I parked as usual in the lot of the Golden Hinde Boatel. I kept the engine idling, the heat turned low. We were looking at a few scattered house lights in the hills across the bay. Grey started to use a fake Armenian accent, much more on purpose exaggerated than mine, "Tuttle, Tuttle," she vamped, "we make love on the dock. We make love like mermaids under the dock. My handsome American love ambassador–driver chauffeur Tuttle." She draped herself over me and we kissed for a long time, a real drive-in-movie make-out session, replete with steaming up the windshield. When we took a breather, Grey said, "How many children did you have with her." She wasn't using the accent. "I'm just wondering."

In Grey's room, we put on KPXP, "all night country, country all night," as the deejay said. We had a good time.

Over the next month, I noticed that the books Mrs. Moro gave me to read were either about suicide or edited, incomplete novels by writers who had committed suicide, according to the "About the author" in back of the books. There was Akutagawa Ryūnosuke's *Hell Screen, Cogwheels, A Fool's Life,* which I found beautiful, but difficult reading. It was made up of three stories. The third was called "A Fool's Life," and it was like a diary. Each entry had a title such as "Laughter of the Gods." Though Mrs. Moro more and more chose to sleep and not talk, we still had animated conversations about the books, if noticeably briefer ones. She'd given me the Akutagawa book on a particularly glum overcast and cold day, which didn't help, or it might be argued was the perfect accompaniment to reading it. Mrs. Moro and I agreed—we said this in quite different ways—that the writing was powerful and disturbing (her two words), mainly about feeling puny and useless. "It's none of my concern, Tuttle Albers," she said, without a hint of sarcasm or even humor that I could detect, "but I wouldn't suggest reading it out loud to Grey Zamarkis in the bedroom." I glanced at her in the rearview mirror; she shut her eyes and fell asleep, and did not wake up until we were on Russian Hill.

Still, that day, Mrs. Moro had intrepidly set out along the Estero Trail in the rain. I walked over to the telephone booth and called Grey. The way I'd seen rainstorms lash the Tule Elk Reserve, I thought she may not have gone into the field. Besides, the night before, when I'd phoned, she said she'd come down with an achy cold, possibly the flu. It turned out she was at home. When she picked up the phone, I heard her teakettle whistling in the background. "Oh, Tuttle, it's you," she said. "One sec, okay?" I heard her turn off the kettle. "I'm back."

"You sound pretty awful," I said.

"It's full-blown flu. I was really looking forward to seeing you."

"What're you talking about? I'm coming right over. The deli section of the Inverness store's got chicken soup, remember?"

"I already bought some. But I still feel lousy. I've got all this work, and it's slow-motion when you're sick, right? Energy's real low. But call me tonight, okay? Plus, I might be contagious."

"Did you call a doctor?"

"It's the flu. I don't have to call a doctor."

"Did you at least take your temperature?"

"It's 102.5. Temperature's only alarming data if it's 105. In between that and 98.6, I figure it's just the flu."

"I could just sit in the kitchen with you for an hour or two."

"Not worth it, really. Because if it's going to stay the flu a while, it means precious time away from the elk, too. So, you *know* I'm not doing too well, huh?"

"Poor girl. I'll miss you, Grey."

"Me, too."

"Okay, I'm hanging up then."

"Tuttle?"

"Yeah?"

"Why'd you call from a booth? Usually, you'd just drive right over."

"I was going to sit in the car and read a little. I figured in this rain you'd be working on your notes. But since last night you said you were sick, I wanted to check up on you."

"Sweet, and thoughtful."

"And. I'm worried about Mrs. Moro."

"Why's that?"

"It's hard to explain. She gives me Japanese novels, right? Well, lately, the ones she's given me—. I don't know. I mean, there's this author, Akutagawa."

"That's like a knock-knock joke. Akutagawa *who?*"

"The guy's a genius, he wrote a novel called *Kappa*, which is about spirit-amphibians, or something like that, but he makes them seem human—more real than people you see on the street. Anyway, Akutagawa killed himself. Mrs. Moro gave me what amounts to his fifty-page suicide note. Besides which, for the last two weeks, she's been sleeping most of the way up and back from the city. Whereas before, she might take a nap, but mostly we'd talk, too."

"She's allowed to be a little depressed."

"I'm not explaining it right."

"You sound upset, though. You just haven't thought it through. How much of her personal life does she tell you?"

"Not much. Two weeks ago, she mentioned that her son canceled another visit."

"Mother-son. That's always a possible culprit. Maybe it's the son."

"Butt out, is what you're saying."

"Sort of, yeah."

"She gave me this author Mishima—he's a suicide. Kawabata killed himself. After he won the Nobel Prize, too. Five out of five books she's given me in a row, the writer—each and every one."

"Is she out walking as we speak?"

"I said, Why not have a cup of tea at Point Reyes Station, wait and see if the rain lets up? But off she went."

"She's got sixty-some years' experience making up her mind."

"You don't think, just this once, I should follow her."

"Breach of trust. Or something like that."

"Okay. You're right. I'll phone you tonight then."

"Kisses to you, Tuttle. I feel like shit."

"Hope that doesn't last too long."

Mrs. Moro was coughing the entire drive back to San Francisco that evening. Every ten or fifteen minutes, she'd doze off, but coughing would wake her up. She wrapped herself in the blue thermal blanket I kept in a wooden box on the floor of the backseat. The box also contained a first-aid kit. I had a flashlight stashed in

the glove compartment. I had a leather satchel for road maps. I had
a state-of-the-art coffee thermos. In the trunk I kept flares. Anyway,
the only thing Mrs. Moro uttered was so personal, I actually
checked the rearview mirror to see if she was talking in her sleep.
She was tented deep in the blanket, so all I could see was the top
of her head, white hair. I heard her cough. But I could barely understand her hoarse whisper above the windshield wipers and rain
on the roof. "Tuttle Albers," she said, "I've had the same dream
for many nights in a row. I walk to Sunset Beach. It is raining. I've
run out of tea. A beautiful flock of white pelicans is on the beach.
One of them speaks in the exact voice of my mother, in Japanese.
'People at home want to see you—here, have some tea.' Then, like
a magician, she makes a porcelain teapot appear. I taste the tea,
but it is too hot and I singe my tongue, and it makes me wake from
the dream." Mrs. Moro didn't ask what I thought of the dream.
Telling it to me seemed to exhaust her and she fell asleep. She
sank entirely down into the blanket.

The following Tuesday Mrs. Moro was not on her porch. This was
so strange that I checked the date in my appointment book, then
checked the front-page date of the *San Francisco Chronicle:* Tuesday,
December 14. I idled the car and waited, heat turned on, until
6:45. Morning traffic had picked up along Jones Street, fog was
thinning, and around Alcatraz tourist ferries were already out, and
an oil tanker moved slowly across San Francisco Bay. There was a
cluster of seagulls on Mrs. Moro's roof. I'd always wanted to see the
view from her window. Russian Hill was the section of the city I'd
live in if I could afford it. I turned off the ignition and waited
exactly another fifteen minutes. Finally, I drove to a magazine stand
on Jones, parked, jumped out, and telephoned Mrs. Moro from a
street booth. No answer.

I drove back to 1960 Jones Street. It was 7:30 a.m.

I stood on her porch, knocking. I rang the buzzer. Nobody came
to the door. I drove to my apartment. I telephoned Mrs. Moro,
letting it ring at least thirty times. I had a coughing fit out of

anxiousness, I guess, because I knew, then and there, that if she could Mrs. Moro would've answered the phone. I telephoned her every ten or so minutes throughout the morning. I sat at my kitchen table and tried to read *Thousand Cranes* by Kawabata, tried to stay as calm and focused as his writing, and not obsess that Mrs. Moro had been mugged, murdered, or whatever other ambushes of city life. At noon I went to the Mission Diner, ordered the meat loaf, mashed potatoes, and coffee special, and called Mrs. Moro twice during the meal. Back at my apartment by 12:50, I watched daytime TV. The movie channel. *The 39 Steps*, directed by Alfred Hitchcock was on. I kept telephoning Mrs. Moro. Around five o'clock, I telephoned Grey and explained the situation, why I hadn't had lunch with her as promised, or shown up at all. I related Mrs. Moro's dream to Grey.

"So, Tuttle, you think somehow she's, what—been called home, so to speak? By her mother. I'm honestly trying to understand."

"Grey, I don't think *anything*. All I know is she wasn't on her porch. And she's not answering her telephone. None of this is familiar. None of it makes sense. My question is, shouldn't I call the police?"

"I'd leave a note on her door."

"What about hospitals? Last week she was coughing like mad. Like she might've caught pneumonia."

"Then call hospitals. You should call hospitals, Tuttle. Otherwise it'll drive you nuts."

"I'll drive up to see you as soon as I can."

"Okay. Keep me posted."

And in fact, I did telephone the five hospitals, public and private, closest to Russian Hill, plus a private clinic; none had an inpatient Mrs. Moro.

I got in the Town Car and drove to 1960 Jones Street. In my apartment, I'd written a brief note and found a thumbtack, and was going to tack up the note, then keep trying to call until I got through. But I decided to knock once more. This time, an elderly Japanese man opened the door. He was dressed in an elegant black suit, light blue shirt, black tie with a silver tiepin. "How can I help you?" he said. He had a tight-lipped smile, almost a grimace, and a serious, kind voice.

"I'm Mrs. Moro's driver," I said. "Tuttle Albers. She wasn't on the porch this morning so I could take her to Point Reyes, and I was worried."

"I won't invite you in. I'm Mrs. Moro's brother. Mrs. Moro died last night. Peacefully or not, how can we know? I flew in from Los Angeles."

I sat down on the wooden bench.

"I'm sorry," I said. "My condolences."

"You may sit as long as you wish."

"Thank you."

"Tuttle Albers. Yes, my sister spoke fondly of you."

"I'm very pleased to know that."

"You may sit as long as you wish."

"Thank you."

"Well, then. Please. I'll go into the house. There's arrangements. I'll be taking my sister back to Japan."

"I see. Of course."

"Goodbye then."

"Mrs. Moro loaned me a number of books."

"Books."

"Yes. Japanese novels."

"You read Japanese?"

"No, they were in English. In translation, I mean."

"I see."

"I'll return them."

"No need. Please. I must go inside."

"My card. My telephone number is somewhere in the house, I'm sure."

"My sister was very organized. I'll locate it."

"Goodbye, then. I'm very sorry. If you need to be driven any-where—."

"No need."

.   .   .

I drove directly from Mrs. Moro's house and got to Inverness at 6:50. Grey was dumbstruck by my news. She made me spaghetti, but mostly we polished off a bottle of French wine. At about eleven at night, we were lying in bed. Grey had all sorts of new strength after her weeklong bout of flu. Across the room, her desk lamp was on, and on the table two candles were flickering low. Looking at the ceiling, she lay diagonally to me on the bed, her legs stretched over my stomach in such a way that I could massage her feet. "Maybe try and find another steady client," she said. "You can't replace her. I don't mean that. But the steadiness part, as soon as possible, might help."

"We spoke about you once," I said.

"You never told me that, Tuttle."

"The first time we—."

"Did what we just did, you mean?"

"Yeah—that morning, she'd given me a novel. By Kawabata, called *Snow Country*. Of course, I didn't do much reading that day. When Mrs. Moro got in the car, she noticed the bookmark. I had this fancy bookmark. It was only on page ten or so."

"Observant woman."

" 'You didn't stay interested in the story,' she said. So, I told her about you, partly to not hurt her feelings about the book. But mostly because I wanted to. Besides, she had an employer's right to know where I spent my afternoons. In case of an emergency."

"In case, sure."

"Another time, she said, 'How is Grey Zamarkis?' "

"You're pretty heartbroken about her, huh?"

"Heartbroken. I'm going to borrow that word."

"That's fine."

The next morning at 5 a.m. we sat at the breakfast nook table. We had orange juice, coffee, and toast. Grey was already dressed for the Tule Elk Reserve. I was wearing her oversized striped bathrobe. "I bought you a sweater," I said. "And I'm going to tell you something that's normally impolite. It cost one hundred fifty dollars, at Le Sweater. It's so rarefied an atmosphere in that store, when I bought your sweater, the clerk rang it up and said, 'Anything else?' One hundred fifty dollars plus tax, and she asks that."

"I like knowing the price. Maybe that's vice-versa impolite. Where is this mysterious sweater?"

I took the gift-wrapped box out of my overnight bag and handed it to Grey. She carefully undid the wrapping paper and put it on the table. She opened the box and lifted out the handmade sweater, black with a subtly pleated black pattern. "It's really beautiful, Tuttle," she said. "And it's very feminine. You must be sick of my field duds, huh? Thank you, thank you, thank you. I was thinking just now: can we go to your apartment? Tonight, I mean. Can we drive down to San Francisco after I'm done working? I haven't been to the city in a year. I'd like to eat at Kupelos. It's the best Italian. I'd like to see your apartment, too."

"Fine with me."

"Of course, I'll wear this," she said, pressing the sweater flush against her chest, then fitting the sleeves against her outstretched arms. "This is so nice."

"It's a good color on you."

"I've got to get going, though," Grey said. She kissed me, a better kiss than the Armenian bride—that actual thought came into my head. She put the sweater on her bureau. "What're your plans for the day?"

"I brought one of Mrs. Moro's novels. I might not get out of this robe till lunchtime. Maybe I'll buy some new slacks and a shirt, Route 1 Cal-Mart. It's just a twenty-minute drive. I can't go out with you tonight looking like a chauffeur. We won't want to stop at my apartment first. I might even splurge on a new sport coat."

"You okay, Tuttle?"

"When her brother came to the door, I peeked around behind him, and I saw this hallway full of family photographs. It was a long hallway, with a wooden floor. There were five or six Japanese people sitting in the kitchen at the end of the hallway, too."

I made a quick sobbing sound, but it wasn't actually crying; events had just suddenly caught up with me.

"I don't have to go right now," Grey said. "Want some company?"

"You go to work. If I get lonely, I'll drive to the reserve."

Grey took up her day pack, kissed me on top of my head, and went out the door. I watched her until she got to the other end of the dock.

By 5:30 there was a light drizzle. The wind had picked up, too. I could hear ducks muttering under the dock. After she took a shower and put her hair up in mismatched braids, Grey put on the new sweater along with a black skirt, high, lace-up felt boots. She looked tremendously pretty. I had on gray slacks, white shirt, and a dark, herringbone sport coat, sleeves a touch long. In the car, Grey said that I looked nice, and I told her I'd spent $250.

"Between that and what my sweater put you back, you might qualify for the Living-Beyond-Your-Means Award," she said. "Or are you holding out on me, Tuttle?"

"I'm spending the rest of my meager savings at Kuleto's, too."

"Oh, boy."

"My apartment's not as bad as I might've hinted."

"Is there a bed?"

"Of course there's a bed."

"Is there coffee? Is there bread for toast?"

"We can pick up some bread."

"Money in our pockets. We're all set, then."

We were trying hard, in a mind-reading kind of way, not to mention Mrs. Moro. Grey knew I was pretty torn up over her. We drove along Sir Francis Drake Highway, south toward Route 1. It was about six o'clock, dusky light over Tomales Bay, and the rain had stopped.

"Let's start talking about Italian food," Grey said. "Naming different dishes. That'll guarantee we'll be starved for it."

"You know anything about Kupelo's menu?"

"I've been there twice."

"Oh."

"Don't ask."

"I won't. I'm just glad we're going, you and me."

"You could be a tiny bit jealous, if you want."

"You didn't go with Eddie. Not from how you described him."

"Not with Eddie, no. No, I went with girlfriends, actually. The first time. The second time, I went by myself. Anyway, I'll start: Penne with a perfect tomato and chopped mushroom sauce, accompanied by an Italian Chianti."

"That's what I'm ordering."

Just past Willow Point, at the southern tip of Tomales Bay, Grey hugged herself and shivered. "Tuttle," she said, "maybe pull the car over, okay? You left the back window open."

"Must've been out of habit, to clear the air. Sorry."

"People don't think California gets cold—"

What interrupted Grey mid-sentence was a loud blur of white off the bay to our immediate left. Then the backseat was completely filled with noise. It was a squalling half cry, half-guttural moan, the combination of which was so bizarre and startling, I almost swerved the car. Grey somehow kept quite composed, though, and she swiveled around and said, "Tuttle, we've got a pelican in the car." As if to verify the fact, the pelican let loose a rusty pump-handle squawk, and I quickly pulled off to the side of the road. Grey and I both turned toward the backseat. The pelican was now hunched to the left-side corner. Its leathery-pouch beak was actually vibrating, clicking. "Jesus, *weird*," Grey said. "Interesting noises come out of that bird, huh?" The pelican feebly caped open its left wing, which drooped. "It might have a broken wing," Grey said. But then—the pelican lunged forward and I shouted, "Watch it!" Grey threw her hands up in front of her face.

Grey tumbled out her door, and I heard the splash of her boots in water. "Shit on a shingle—my boots, Tuttle, and I'm bleeding!"

Grey stepped from the shallow ditch and walked over to my side of the car. I was standing near the front bumper. She peered in through the front window, and her sympathies shifted. "Guess what?" she said. "That's a white pelican. Rare to get them bay-side. They like the wide-open sea."

"Let me see your forehead a second," I said. I examined Grey's face, touched the cut and slight bruise on her forehead above her left eye. "I doubt you'll need stitches. I've got a first-aid kit in the backseat."

"Some uninvited houseguest, huh?" Grey said, and started to laugh. "I didn't see it coming off the bay, did you?"

"We got blindsided."

"Well, I'm basically okay, so we have to figure things out now."

"Let's go to the Point Reyes Walk-in Clinic. We should find out if pelicans carry diseases to worry about."

"I don't think it was the beak. I think it was the wing. It has hard, sharp wings."

"Just a precaution, Grey."

The pelican lifted and squawked, then beat its good wing hard against the closed window. It produced a mournful baritone gurgle, then rasping barks. "It's in pain, Tuttle," Grey said. "I think its wing is broken. I feel terrible for it."

I crouched along the car and opened the back door. Grey and I stood across the road. "Come out, come out, come out!" Grey said, but the pelican kept to the car. Every so often it fluttered its wing, half toppling, but its movements and distress calls had become half-hearted.

"This is pitiful," Grey said.

"How about the police?"

"They might shoot it."

"I doubt it, Grey. They might have a net or something. You must know somebody in Fish & Game, or somebody else."

"Donnie Rush, the veterinarian's assistant! I've had coffee with her. Her boss is a large-animal vet, though."

"Come on, Grey, he's not going to turn down a pelican."

"Donnie'd be home, I bet. She has three young kids."

"And she'd contact the vet, right?"

"That's the idea."

"Okay. The Holly Tree Inn's a hundred yards from here. I'll go call this Donnie Rush. Is she listed under that name?"

"Rush, yeah."

"You stay with the car. I'll be right back."

A hundred or so feet up the road I turned and saw Grey toss her dress-up English raincoat over the pelican, then back away from the car and start to sing to the bird.

The Holly Tree Inn had a pay phone on the porch. A phone book was dangling by a chain. I decided to call the veterinarian directly. I looked it up, and found a Dr. James Glass. I dialed and Dr. Glass picked up, which surprised me because it was after usual office hours, though maybe not for a veterinarian. I explained about the pelican. He said to try and put a sweater or blanket over the pelican to calm it down. "What about singing to it?" I said. "See what works," he said. "I'm only a few minutes' drive from where you are." He gave me exact directions and I ran back to the car.

We drove to the veterinarian's. He lived just outside of Inverness, off Sir Francis Drake, up a winding road, in a house overlooking Tomales Bay. Grey's having put her raincoat over the pelican had in fact calmed it. On the way to the veterinary clinic, Grey looked into the backseat. "It's not talking," she said, giving a worried, nervous laugh.

The clinic was adjacent to the house. I ran up the stairs and knocked on the door. Dr. Glass answered right away. He was a tall man, about fifty years old, with the strongest-looking hands I've ever seen—wide, thick-fingered hands, not freakish by any means, no doubt hands comforting to an injured horse or cow, or a deer struck by a pickup truck. He walked down to the Town Car. Grey had opened the back door. Dr. Glass gently lifted the pelican, which was inside Grey's raincoat, and carried it up the wooden steps to his clinic. Inside, he set the pelican on an examination table. Grey and I stood against the wall across from the table. When Dr. Glass removed the raincoat, the pelican remained perfectly still. With slow, deliberate movements, he held the pelican firmly against his chest and administered a hypodermic. He'd had it filled and ready when we arrived. The needle made the pelican squawk open its mouth once, its only reaction. The air now smelled of fish. In a few moments, the pelican slumped like someone had cut the strings of a big marionette.

Dr. Glass began his examination. The pelican was anesthetized and Dr. Glass laid it down without its protesting. He lifted and examined each wing and leg, under its tail feathers, where he found a splotch of blood, and a little dripped onto the table. "Looks like a broken wing and some internal bleeding," Dr. Glass said. "We can x-ray right here. Fish & Game will rush an animal to Mill Valley Animal Hospital, if necessary."

He carried the pelican into the X-ray room, set it on the table below the machine, lowered the machine, calibrated it, turning two knobs. He then stepped into a small side room. Through the window, Grey and I watched the pelican get x-rayed. Dr. Glass then slid a thick metal plate out of the camera, if that's what you call it. We sat in the waiting room. Magazines were on the table. There was an aquarium with tropical fish in it. In about ten minutes, Dr. Glass stood in the doorway. "It's pretty well broken up inside," he said. "Internal bleeding, just as I suspected. A fractured left wing as well. It may be concussed. That's hard to determine. To be honest, this is my first pelican, and I'm not familiar with the literature. I had a heron in here two years ago. An owl sometime later. I think it's best to call Fish & Game, have it brought down to Mill Valley. That's my advice."

"How long will that take?" Grey said.

"Depends who's available. I'll make the call."

Dr. Glass went into his office. I saw four framed diplomas on his wall. Grey bent over, tilted her head, and looked into the aquarium. When Dr. Glass came out, he said, "Damn answering machine at Fish & Game. But I did reach Mill Valley Animal Hospital. There's a round-the-clock staff."

"We'll drive it there," Grey said.

"A good forty-five minutes, at least," Dr. Glass said. "I'll carry the pelican to your car. Keep the heat on. But don't suffocate it." He wrapped the pelican in a blanket. Then he helped Grey on with her raincoat; considering that the pelican had been inside the coat, and might well have bled on it, this was still so absentmindedly polite a gesture it made Grey blush and slightly stammer, "Thank you."

In the car, winding our way out onto Sir Francis Drake again, Grey said, "What we really need is a siren."

For at least ten minutes I was going well over the speed limit. But then, I'd guess four or five minutes south of Tomales Bay, the pelican died. We knew it had died, because it produced a classic kind of death rattle, which rolled up from deep inside its chest, unnerving kind of acoustics, really. It was the saddest sound I'd ever heard; Grey burst into tears, and that got to me, as well. We couldn't look at each other. I adjusted the rearview, and saw that the pelican looked like it was still alive, its eyes wide open. I noticed that Dr. Glass had fastened the seat belt around it.

Of course, San Francisco was long ago out of the question. I turned the car around in the parking lot of a seafood restaurant, and we drove directly back to the clinic. I carried the pelican up the stairs, Grey a few steps ahead. Dr. Glass was doing paperwork. He only had the small desk lamp on. He answered Grey's knock. "It died," she said.

"Bring it in," Dr. Glass said. "Just put it on the table, if you would."

I laid the pelican on the examination table, then joined Grey in the waiting room. "It doesn't surprise me," Dr. Glass said. "It took a hard blow. Pelicans fly pretty low and can build up good speed, as you know. Fish & Game will want an autopsy, even though it's clear *how* it died. The accident, I mean. There might be other information we can gain. Then there's taxidermy. For a community museum, or to bring around to elementary schools. Something along those lines."

"I understand," Grey said, as if comforting Dr. Glass. She was still sniffling and had swollen eyes. "I work at the Tule Reserve. Last spring, an elk slid off a muddy cliff. Fish & Game knew how it'd died but wanted it checked for all sorts of things, naturally."

"Yes, that particular elk was in my clinic, here. Small world,"

Dr. Glass said. "Look, you both seem upset. Can I get you a cup of tea? Or something a bit stronger?"

We both said no thanks.

"By the way, I'm Jim Glass." Grey and I each shook hands with him.

"There's nothing more to do, really," he said. "I'll take it from here. A little paperwork. That's about it."

"Thanks for your time," Grey said.

"Well, that's what I'm here for."

Grey and I didn't say a word driving back to her place. She sat at the kitchen table staring at her notes, or staring at the moonlight spread out on the bay, or putting her face in her hands, trying not to get upset all over again. We didn't have the radio on. I fell asleep on the sofa. When I woke up at 6 a.m., Grey wasn't there. I had slept in my new shirt, slacks, and sport coat. Grey's sweater and skirt were on the bed. Coffee was in the coffeemaker, and there was a note on the table:

Tuttle, darling. Needed to work. I just know you think the pelican has some connection to Mrs. Moro, but it doesn't. It was a sad freak accident. Don't be superstitious, okay? Hope you want to stay over tonight.

Pals with you,

Grey

But I didn't stay. I drove back to San Francisco, and I don't know all the reasons why. I suppose I fled something. And I didn't visit Grey for three straight weeks, though we spoke on the telephone every night. We were very loyal to this nightly appointment. I'd call at 10 p.m. Grey would answer, "Hi." But, then, so much went unspoken, in fact most everything of real importance. What we should've said to each other was very, very close by, like the silences between tappings of Morse code. But we didn't speak it. Instead, it was, "How's the thesis going?" Or, "I drove a client today—yeah, I'm working, nothing taxing, though. My heart's not in it, really." The barest hints of our day. And after we spoke I'd drive around.

And on Jones Street one night, I noticed a FOR SALE sign in front of Mrs. Moro's house.

One day, into the fourth week of not seeing Grey, I drove past a fairgrounds. They were dismantling the Ferris wheel. Across the field, two men were standing in front of an enormous helium-filled balloon, like a zeppelin. The men were holding the anchor ropes, but at the same time, the balloon, with its gondola and bright lettering, was being deflated. I stopped the car to watch. I thought that the zeppelin might thrash about, act like a desperate, panicked huge animal when losing air like that. I'm not sure that seeing one thing caused the other, but I said "Grey" out loud, and then felt like my very breath had been knocked out of me.

Two days later, February 11, to be exact, I telephoned Grey, and instead of saying, "Hi," she said, "You thought the pelican was Mrs. Moro's ghost, didn't you? I've been thinking hard about this, Tuttle. I know we're not going to see each other anymore. Real Sherlock Holmes, huh?"

"Grey—."

"I'm going to a conference this weekend in New York. I'm not going to call you, and don't call me, either."

"What ghost?"

"That dream she told you. With the pelican, the teapot, the whole thing, Tuttle."

"Okay. Maybe it's been haunting me in some way. Maybe you've just articulated it."

"Good for me."

"Let's start this conversation over."

"No, no, you listen, Tuttle. You've been so distant. I mean, weeks of phone calls. We could've been—. You could've been at the Holly Tree Inn at least two nights a week. We were doing fine. We were moving ahead.

"You know what's scariest? What's scariest is when somebody you love makes a private decision, but he doesn't tell you what it is. And the result of that decision—the privately held conclusion—

becomes like a ghost. It affects you deeply. It acts on you. But you don't get to fight back. It's very very very unfair, Tuttle."

"I haven't made any such decision, Grey."

"You haven't been here in a month. That's a decision. What we should address here, Tuttle—can you stop being such a fucking coward and own up to this? It's the pelican. After the pelican, something went wrong. It was bad luck is what it was, Tuttle. But you've purposely let us get estranged over it. You took it as some kind of omen. Look, I'm no shrink, Tuttle. I'm no psychiatrist. I've never been to one. But what I think—and I've been thinking a *lot* about us. I mean, I know you a little by now, right? You know what? Remember you told me Mrs. Moro was always hoping to see a white pelican?"

"That's what she said, yes."

"Well, she *didn't* ever see one, did she?"

"No."

"You liked her so much, didn't you? And you felt close to her. You wanted her walks to the ocean to go safely. You worried. When it rained, you worried. I mean, do you know how often her name came up in conversation? Very often. And I enjoyed hearing about her, don't get me wrong."

"What're you saying here, Grey?"

"I'm *saying*, Tuttle. What I'm saying. Is Mrs. Moro's dying got to you. You felt she gave you things in life, Tuttle. I'm not trying to be sappy or philosophical, but she did give you things. Those novels. All that conversation. The sweet opportunities to worry over her. I don't know what all.

"So maybe—this is just a guess. Maybe, in your mind, you've turned Mrs. Moro into the one thing she most deeply wanted to see. Because that way she'd become her own good luck, the kind of luck she didn't have when she was alive.

"See? See, Tuttle? Her suicide was bad enough. Now you have to go and make it twice as bad."

"Her brother never used that word."

"Come on, Tuttle. It's me you're talking to."

"Since you've come up with such a complicated psychological theory, maybe you're the one who believes the pelican was a ghost."

"I'd be willing to have that in common with you, Tuttle."

There was a silence on the line then. "Look," she finally said, "I'm sorry. Probably my thinking's way off. At the time—you know, when the pelican flew into the car? Between the two of us, I was the one most visibly upset. But since then, you've taken the incident and hoarded it from me, and you won't let me back in. Half the time, on the phone, it's been like we've just met."

We both didn't speak for another moment. I heard KPXP in the background, then heard Grey turn the volume down. "I hate this kind of talk," I said.

"Well, thinking about Mrs. Moro wandering some rainy beach was probably a torment."

"No, I meant us breaking up."

Grey gave a short sigh, then said, "This conference, Tuttle. It's all the bigwigs in my field. It's to interview for jobs. Research, teaching, you know, all the grant applications I've been typing. I bet you'll miss the sound of typing in the middle of the night, huh? Look up and see this naked girl typing. Anyway, I was going to grasp at one last hopeful straw, and ask do you want to come to New York with me, but I don't think it's a good idea anymore, truth be told."

"You'll be gone how long?"

"Probably a week. I have an open return flight."

"Which hotel?"

"I'm not saying."

"Well, it sounds mostly like a professional trip, a work thing, huh?"

"I might catch a Broadway play."

"Don't mind me asking. But do you want a lift to the airport?"

"The airport's got long-term parking. I'll drive myself, thanks."

"Just offering."

"I'm tapping my forehead, Tuttle. Tap, tap, tap. I'm tapping my forehead but pretend I'm tapping yours. Because I'm thinking, here

I'm going three thousand miles away from Tuttle, but he's already—
in his head—farther away than that."

Then the phone clicked down.

I kept on with my freelance chauffeuring, making ends meet, but
not much more. As I said, my heart wasn't in it, but I didn't yet
have the gumption to invent a new life. Then, eight months since
I'd seen or spoken with Grey Zamarkis, she sent the newspaper
announcement of her marriage to Dr. Glass. The envelope had the
veterinary clinic as her return address. A month after that, a package arrived at my apartment. It was plastered with Japanese postage
stamps. There was a customs receipt taped to the top. I opened the
package on my kitchen table; it contained Mrs. Moro's bird lists.
There were eighty-eight lists, in eight separate notebooks, all written in English, but with Japanese writing in the margins, too. Each
entry was dated, along with the name of each bird, and time of
observation, and brief description of where along the Estero Trail
she had seen it. The official-looking letter that came with the lists
was from the family's attorney. It was typed in Japanese, with the
translation below it. Part of which said, "You are bequeathed. . . ."
I knew that Mrs. Moro had employed drivers previous to me, to
take her to Point Reyes. I hoped that I was the only one who'd
been willed her bird lists.

I put the lists in my desk drawer. Another week passed, and I
decided to drive up to Point Reyes. It wasn't anywhere near the
anniversary of Mrs. Moro's death; it wasn't a morbid kind of sen-
timentality or anything. That is, I didn't want to try and please her
ghost. I just wanted to see if I could remember the names of hawks.
It was a crisp, sunny day, no traffic to speak of when I set out at
10 a.m., and I made good time. I got a coffee at the Inverness store,
then drove up Sir Francis Drake, past Grey's cottage—well, it was
no longer hers, of course, and she never called it a cottage. I turned
left and drove the few miles to the Estero trailhead sign. The
glassed-in display held a few stuffed birds and mammals, paintings
of local flora, a list of proper trail etiquette, a warning about deer

ticks, with an enlargement of a microscopic tick, and a dotted-line map of the Estero Trail.

I had on jeans, tennis shoes, a flannel shirt, a sweater, a parka. In my backpack, I carried a thermos of water. I had binoculars around my neck. I had the field guide in my pocket. In two hours, I was able to identify two kinds of hawks with certainty, but I didn't really care about anything, except to look at them. I got to Sunset Beach. It was a pebbly, wide curve of sand, zigzagged with shorebirds, dozens of them scurrying along the edge of the froth, like they were stitching each wave to the beach with their beaks. Though I knew that they were trying to find something to eat. I sat on the fallen tree. I took up the binoculars and scanned the horizon. Brown pelicans—I knew that bird. And seagulls diving just out past the whitecaps.

I stayed for an hour or two, I guess. I ate the tuna sandwich I'd packed. I drank some water. I may have dozed off for half an hour or so. When I woke, the sun was a sharp glare. Chill wind, sun, a clear view of the sea. I thought a moment about Grey. I missed her. I didn't forgive myself about her, didn't forgive myself in the slightest. Every worst maudlin C and W song would've wholly captured my stupidity and regret, then multiply by ten. "Sadness in severe disproportion to the opposite," as Akutagawa wrote. Other than about Grey, I don't remember what I thought. But I know this: what fixed me in that present time and place was my deep happiness at not seeing white pelicans. I was hoping that I wouldn't. This was my first time. They might've been indignant, knowing I hadn't earned such good fortune.

THE SNIPE HUNT

by Jill McCorkle

Caroline stood with her brother in the darkness of the woods, a large burlap sack held between them while their father disappeared down the path to the house. Though the lights from the house were hidden by the slope of the hill and the thick dark pine branches, Caroline knew that she was still within yelling distance, and now she had that impulse. "Daddy!" she called in a loud whisper, her high-pitched voice interrupting the incessant drone of crickets, Danny's elbow digging into her hip to silence her. "Daddy, where are you?"

"Hush now," Danny said, and she knew his teeth were gritted though she could barely make out the profile of his thin angular face. "We ain't gonna catch nothing if you act like this."

Caroline quieted with Danny's words as she usually did. After all, he was older; he was going to be in the fourth grade come fall and she would be starting school for the very first time. The thought of first grade and all the stories she had heard about how the principal would seize children in the hall and beat them burned through her body like a comet, causing her to wake nights all that summer to a wet bed or a dizzy feeling like she had been spun around and around like a june bug on a string. "The principal is a wonderful man," her mother would say, but Danny, somewhere in the vicinity, a doorway, beside her in the backseat of that old blue Rambler, would glance down with raised eyebrows, shake his head, sigh, and her mother's soothing words flew past as quickly as a Roman candle shoots into the sky.

"I'll watch out for you at school if you do whatever I say," Danny had told her with such forceful authority that she was able to go for thirty-minute stretches without even thinking about it at all. "You know, like, if I hear you've disappeared from first grade, I'll go down to that dungeon where he puts the bad children and I'll spring you."

But now, in the prickly darkness of the woods, even with him there beside her, the fears came back. What if they did catch a snipe? What if one of those huge brown birds all of the relatives talked about did fly from the woods to the hole in their big burlap sack? Caroline braced herself, determined not to scream when it happened, determined not to be a baby. Danny was already mad at her; he was mad at everybody and had been all day long.

She listened for her father's and Uncle Tim's footsteps but all she heard was the steady drone of crickets. She tried to think about how she had felt earlier in the afternoon, the excitement while waiting for the relatives to arrive. The kitchen table was covered with food, big cold watermelons on the back porch along with the box of fireworks that had been off-limits until that day.

The relatives had descended for the Fourth of July like a swarm of locusts, their old blue station wagon so overloaded with bodies and watermelons and Tupperware that it scraped concrete coming up the drive. The small house on Hickory Street was so filled with their shrieks and buzzing that it seemed the windows might pop out and shatter.

Caroline was straddling the porch banister when they arrived, holding a piece of twine tied around the post like reins. She had spent the entire day at the YMCA pool and her eyes were red and burning, the whole world a blur. The porch vibrated with the music from the living room, where the teenage cousins—three giggly girls, one of whom arrived with her hair rolled up in orange juice cans— were huddled around the phonograph. Two of them, Uncle Tim and Aunt Patricia's daughters, had arrived with little circular carrying cases filled with records. They sang "Where the Boys Are" and argued over who was the best-looking doctor, Ben Casey or Dr. Kildare. They marveled at the fact that Caroline's mother had a copy of "Moon River" and a Chubby Checker album, which the one in braces said was her *fave*. They argued over what was the best way to tease hair, and then they whispered about *Mark Eden* and laughed. Caroline was taking notes in her head. This was her assignment: *Hear all you can but don't say one word, not to nobody,* and she knew that somewhere out in the yard Danny was hiding and watching to make sure she passed the test. If she passed today, he would let her go to the pool with him again tomorrow and he would even admit to people that she was his sister. Today she had been an orphaned neighbor child whom he was being paid big money to watch.

Their neighbor, Mrs. Hopper, had been stretched out in her lounge chair even though it was after four. Her sprinkler arced and sprayed a fine mist over her ugly brown lawn and equally ugly son, who lay out in the grass with his big bare feet propped on the end of her chair. Occasionally Mrs. Hopper laughed and shook her head from side to side. It was just the two of them who lived there. Mrs. Hopper was a divorcée who had once lived in Chicago. Her son's name was Bo and her cat's name was Cat, after one in a movie she'd just seen. She wore big round sunglasses and colorful beads and taught biology at the community college. These were the facts Caroline had gathered for Danny on another assignment. Mrs. Hopper looked normal enough, but Danny said that at sundown her yellow hair stood straight up and her teeth grew long and mossy green. He said that her husband hadn't really left like all the grown-ups said; she ate him.

With this spooky thought Caroline was brought right back to the woods and the black moonless night. She shuddered with the image of Mrs. Hopper's teeth growing and then came the sick wave of school thoughts; the teachers with their paddles, the squat-necked man in charge of it all. She tried to shut out of her head all the stories she had heard by reciting things. She knew all of "This Old Man" and "When You Wish Upon a Star." She knew all the words to "Don't say ain't," which used to be Danny's favorite poem before he learned "Beans, Beans."

Don't say ain't, your mama might faint. Your daddy might fall in a bucket of paint. Your brother might die. Your sister might cry and your dog might call the FBI.

But, the thought of school and all the stories she had heard about how the principal would seize children and haul them into his office, where he kept the paddling machine still made her shudder. Just yesterday she caught herself needing to cling to her mother's bare legs as she stood in the yard and talked to Mrs. Hopper.

"Go on now, honey," her mother had said. "Let me talk to Mrs. Hopper for a sec."

"Lord, please let her call me Gail," Mrs. Hopper said, and lifted those big sunglasses to reveal wide blue eyes fringed in what might have been glue on lashes. "I was never cut out to be Mrs. Hopper." They both laughed. Mrs. Hopper said she couldn't wait to get a load of those relatives and Caroline's mama said that she could.

"I'll tell you about the relatives," Danny had said that very morning, his spoon poised over a bowl of Cocoa Puffs. "They all eat like hogs, and Aunt Jewell wants to hug and slobber all over you. Those *girls,*" he whispered the word as if it were a disease, "are just stupid, all of them. Uncle Tim is fat. The only boy cousin is Randy, who's okay except last time he brought a girl." Danny knew these things. If he said that Mrs. Hopper was friends with the devil and kept him in her basement, then it was so. It gave Caroline a shiver to think of all the secrets he told her late at night when their parents were asleep: hunks of hair from dead people found in the cafeteria ravioli, kids' fingers bent backward by the principal until the bones snapped, parents getting arrested and sent to prison when their children talked too much.

Caroline's mother referred to the relatives as the "dog people" because they spent their lives going from show to show with these big scary Dobermans. They were always talking about "the circuit" and such. They had wanted to bring along some of the "baby poochies" but Caroline's mother forbade it.

"I don't blame you at all!" Mrs. Hopper had said, her tanned bare foot swinging back and forth while she sipped a glass of tea. She had a thin silver chain around her ankle. Caroline was hiding under the bushes near where they sat, a cowgirl hat pulled low to disguise herself. "Just who does this sister-in-law of yours think she is?"

"Doris Day." Caroline's mother laughed and sat down. "Doris Day on the darkest night of her life."

"I have never missed my divorced relatives," Mrs. Hopper said, and then the two began talking about their yards. Mrs. Hopper said she'd like to pave hers and then paint the grass and flowers in place. Caroline's mother said she pictured something different altogether: new place, new town, new weather.

Not an hour after that the station wagon scraped an awful sound, the car horn blasting several short notes and Caroline's mother rushed past, her perfume sweet and clean in the still summer heat. Her father followed, the screen door slamming shut. Mrs. Hopper was out in her yard just as she had said she would be, "to catch a peek," her hair wrapped in a white towel as she sat in a lawn chair, her sprinkler spraying her bare tanned legs. Danny made a face and shook his head back and forth when Mrs. Hopper lifted her hand in a wave. Caroline was still looking for some sign of her being a witch but aside from the big purple beads around her neck and the black thumbnail, which she *said* she got when she accidentally hit herself with a hammer, couldn't come up with anything.

"Fat as ever," Danny said, and nudged Caroline when Uncle Tim caught their mother up in a big hug and lifted her right off the sidewalk. "Posse's coming," Danny said and sniffed the air, pointing to the walk where they all stood. There were eight of them if you count that bald-headed spit-up smelling baby.

"I smell 'em all right." Danny swung his legs over the banister. "You keep a watch while I blaze the getaway trail and set up camp." He pointed to the rubber tomahawk strapped to his belt. Then he jumped down behind the box shrubs and was gone, scrambling on hands and knees to the back of the house.

Caroline was on the verge of following when her parents called to her, all the relatives lined up and waiting, baskets of food and a box of diapers at their feet. It was like playing firing squad when Danny had tied a dish towel over her face and leaned her back against a tree, all those boys from his neighborhood club lined up and ready for the signal. "When you hear the shots, you gotta fall out and be dead," he had whispered, and then she waited. She waited until the whole yard was silent, bracing herself for the jump. "I'm getting tired," she finally called. "Go on and shoot, okay?" No answer. "Danny!" She screamed his name until her face felt hot and someone finally came by and removed the cloth. The yard was empty, and Danny and the Indian scouts were nowhere in sight. It was against all the rules to tattle, so that night she asked Danny why he had tricked her. He said it wasn't a trick it was a test. It was the first test, being still and being quiet, and she had passed.

The relatives got out of the car and stood there nodding like those spring-neck dogs that the man who owned the fish market had in the back window of his car. "I ain't having nothing to do with these *relatives*," Danny said last night when he crept in her room and knelt by the bed. He said the word "relatives" the same way he spit out "married" so it didn't linger in his mouth. "I'm pretending they ain't even here and you better do the same, Caroline." He pronounced her name with two syllables, Care-line. She could see by the yellow glow of the night-light as he knelt there, jaw clenched while reeling off the rules. "You gotta ask Uncle Tim how much he weighs. Ask Patricia how come she looks and smells so much like her dogs. Don't talk to the girl with the baby *at all*."

. . .

"Caroline." Her mother was smiling, but Caroline knew from the tone in her voice that she was getting impatient. "And where did Danny run off to?" She gripped the banister and stepped slowly onto the second step. This was test number two and she knew that Danny was somewhere watching, at the corner of the house or up the pine tree where he kept his secret information. But even worse than that was the fact that Mrs. Hopper was watching, her slick-covered magazine hiding her bare stomach as she wiggled her fingers.

"What have you done to your shirt?" Caroline's mother smoothed the wrinkled collar. "And where are your shoes? Where *is* your brother?" Caroline shook her head, shrugged. Danny was watching, and if she messed up, he'd never let her be the maiden scout; she'd have to represent the posse of white men for the rest of her life. Mrs. Hopper had her eyes closed now but that didn't mean anything. *She can cast a hex any old time,* Danny had said. *People might say her husband left her but I got other ideas. That's what I'll say for now. I got other ideas.*

"My my, grown like a weed," Uncle Tim said and shook his head. "You're a cute little boy now, aren't you?" They all laughed and Caroline stared at him, reaching down to her hip, where very soon she'd have her own tomahawk.

"Don't tease her. She's a pretty thing. Got hair like us, Jimmy." Aunt Patricia patted Caroline's father on the arm, and then she stepped closer, her arms swooping like the great white hawk as she caught Caroline in a cloud of high-smelling dog-flea cologne. Caroline pulled and twisted away before the Great White Hawk could begin to slobber.

"Caroline, can't you say something?" her mother asked, and she nodded, again fingering that imaginary weapon at her side. "You remember Cousin Randy." The tall one, long legs like a posse rider and hair hanging to his shoulders, stepped forward. He wore his hair long and beads around his neck to trick the *real* Indian scouts. He had round black eyes. "And this is his girlfriend, Sarah." Another trick, her hair in braids, feet in leather-strapped shoes. She wore the Indian jewelry and carried a Frisbee. "And this is Cousin

Sue and little Paul Jr." Sue looked like the Thin White Hawk and
Paul Jr. was a poor excuse for a papoose.

"Come meet little Paul."

"How much do you weigh?" she asked loudly, and pointed to
Uncle Tim.

"Caroline?" Her mother's arms were around her now and steering
her up onto the porch. "I'm sorry, Tim, who knows what gets into
them."

"The devil, I guess," her father said, and shook his head. He
glanced over at Mrs. Hopper when he said that, a sure sign that he
knew something about what went on in her basement. She had the
straps of her suit undone and the strings swung forward as she bent
to rub lotion on her legs. There was a moment when she was looking right at Caroline, a moment when their eyes locked. *It only
takes a minute for her to put the devil in you. It can happen so fast
nobody knows until it's too late.*

Now, Caroline was crouched down in the pine straw, trying not to
make a sound. She was looking for the devil, looking for a snipe.
She felt something brush against her bare legs, leaves or snipe feathers, snakes or mosquitoes. "Our mosquitoes are so big," her daddy
was famous for saying, "they roll up your pants legs to bite you."
She swatted with her hand and moved her feet away from whatever
was down there. The thought of Mrs. Hopper sitting up in a tree,
a long black cape blowing around her and wild-eyed cats sitting on
the limbs, made her jerk.

"Will you stop?" Danny whispered, his voice still deep. "How
are we gonna catch a snipe with you making all this noise?"

"You talked," she whispered. "I wasn't talking."

"You were moving. Moved your feet and moved your hand." She
knew the expression on his face as if they were standing in broad
daylight, his blue eyes glaring, the sharp bone of his jaw clenched
so that the pale purple vein in his cheek could be traced as easily
as if it had been put there with a ballpoint pen. "You let your hand

off the bag and messed up the hole. Snipe ain't coming unless it
sees a big dark hole."

"Yessir," Uncle Tim with the fat red face had said. "I bagged myself
five big snipe one night. Nobody ever bagged five." Instead of standing behind their uncle and making faces, Danny had sat on the
floor right by the man's feet, laughed and slapped his leg. Caroline
wasn't sure if Danny was pulling a trick or really liking these people,
and he wouldn't even give her a sign to let her know. He said that
he didn't think he ought to have to eat at any children's table with
her; he wanted to do what the men were doing.

"What's a snipe anyways?" Caroline asked, and waited, her face
going warm while they all laughed.

"She don't know nothing," Danny said. "She hasn't even been
to school. She doesn't even know what a snipe is." He rolled on
his back and laughed that deep laugh. "Tell her, Uncle Tim. Tell
her what a snipe is."

"All right." Uncle Tim stared hard at Danny and then looked
around the room. "A snipe, Miss Caroline, since you're the *only*
one here that don't know, is a great big brown bird. Well, it's so
big you don't even want to call it a bird. It's more like an animal
with great big wings."

"Yeah," Danny said, and turned to her, nodding with each word,
his face flushed and short bangs cowlicked by his mimicked gesture
of running his hand over the top of his head. "Jesus Christ," their
father often said and did that very gesture. Caroline had attempted
it herself, though with little success.

Now, she longed for the yellow lamplight of the living room, the
warm soapy water that filled the kitchen sink while her mother and
the other women talked and handed plates back and forth. "Jesus
Christ," she whispered, and ran her hand through her hair. She
waited for Danny to respond, but he kept his vow of silence and

simply pressed down on the toe of her shoe with his foot. "I said Jesus Christ, oh Jesus Christ, Jesus Christ."

"Call on somebody you know," he whispered harshly, another little saying he had learned at the school.

"Moon looks right for sniping tonight," Uncle Tim had said, and Caroline went to peek out the window at the thin sliver of a moon just above the trees. It was the fairy-tale moon, or so she'd always heard, never heard of a snipe moon, but there it was, thin, white, and waiting. It sent a chill over her scalp.

"Can't snipe alone," their father said, and Caroline froze, part of her wanting so bad to go; it was the same part of her that wanted to be in the first grade and have a book sack to carry. But then there was that other part, the school dungeon and Mrs. Hopper's nighttime teeth and a big brown animal like a rhinoceros with wings.

"Go with me, Dad," Danny said. "Let's me and you and Uncle Tim and Randy all go."

"Just the men, huh?" the girlfriend asked, and came to stand beside Caroline. "Girls can bag a snipe as good as a man. Right?" Caroline nodded with her, this grown-up girl, so grown that she carried a purse and put stuff on her eyelids. She had unbraided her hair and now it frizzed in perfect waves almost to her waist.

"She's too young to go," Danny said, and pointed at Caroline. "Leave her out of it."

"Can't be done," Uncle Tim said, and lit a cigar. "You see, you can't hold both sides of the bag when the snipe flies in, 'cause he'd knock your socks off. You got to have a person on each side."

"But you gotta have a strong person," Danny said. "Like you."

"Can't be done, son," their father said, and went to sit beside Uncle Tim. "You see, once you get to be a certain size, oh, I'd say about Randy's height, then you're too big to go sniping, because the snipes'll see you there holding the bag. They're smart, those snipes, they aren't gonna come if they think somebody's holding the bag."

"Yessir, Danny." Uncle Tim locked his hands behind his head and stretched his legs. "Take advantage of the fact that you're just the right age for a snipe hunt. It's one of those things you remember for the rest of your life, like catching a great big fish or hitting a home run." Uncle Tim looked at their daddy and grinned. "A few other things."

"I've done those things," Danny said, his face so serious. "Done both of those, caught a fish at camp and hit home runs all the time."

"Well then, let's get you out in the woods to bag a snipe."

"But Caroline hasn't. She hasn't caught a fish or hit a home run."

"But I can do it," she had said suddenly, her heart beating faster and faster with the thought of it all.

Now it seemed like she had been in the woods forever; a mosquito bit her on the leg and she let him without saying a word. It just wasn't a good night for snipes. Deep down, she hoped one didn't come. It was too hot and too dark; the snipes were going to fly into somebody else's bag. Again, something rustled against her leg. She tried to think of something good, the big box of fireworks; she was going to eat a slice of watermelon and sit on the porch rail and watch those fireworks sizzle way up into the sky. She was ready to go. "They ain't coming," she whispered.

"Not if you keep talking," he said, but this time his voice was slower, like he was getting tired of standing in one place, too. "This is the right spot," their father had said. "Don't move from this spot."

"I gotta pee," she whispered, but he ignored her. "Danny? Danny, I really do gotta pee."

"Shhh, one's coming."

She froze in place and sure enough she heard something way down the path, a rustling sound, and she imagined that big bird animal creeping along ready to suddenly fly up and into a hole just like they'd said. She could hear Danny breathing, her own heart beating up in those soft spots of her forehead. She couldn't stand it anymore.

"I can't wait. I gotta go."

"Go in your pants," he said.

"I can't go in my pants. Mama'll get me."

"I'll get you if you don't shut up," he whispered. "I'll tell the principal you been bad, too. I'll tell the witch to come get you. I'll tell you a lot of things you don't want to hear, okay?"

Caroline swallowed hard, blinked back the tears, and crouched forward to squeeze her legs together. "I can't wait. I can't hold it."

"Here." He took her side of the bag. "Go over yonder and pull down your pants. Pee out there, but be quiet."

"Come with me."

"I can't, you big baby. I gotta hold the bag. How do we know that a snipe ain't been watching this hole the whole time?"

Caroline took a step away and moved her hands through the air that circled her to make sure there was nothing there. She eased down the zipper of her shorts. "I talked to the witch today," she whispered. "She's planning to pour cement all over her yard."

"Yeah, right," he said. "Go on now. You're too close. Go away from here so the snipe don't see you."

She took another step and then squatted, feet apart, pants around her knees and held forward. Now she couldn't go, something tickling around her legs, another rustling sound from in the woods, closer and closer. "I talked to her the day you put me in front of the firing squad, too," she whispered, expecting him to tell her to shut up, but he was listening now. "She was right there in our yard and I never even heard her walk up. She's the one untied me." His silence scared her and she hurriedly pulled up and zipped her pants, relieved to take her side of the bag and feel him there beside her. "She said, 'Oh my poor darling,' not mean at all."

"She ain't a witch," he whispered now. "I lied about all that." She nodded.

"And I lied about first grade, nothing happens in first grade. Bunch of babies learn to say letters and crap."

"Really?" She turned now and stared at him, angry for the joke but so relieved she wanted to scream and dance.

"But now I know something real that's bad," he said. "I swear to God."

"Tell me," she whispered, not really wanting to hear; she was hoping her dad would come running down the path, but there was nothing beyond the darkness.

"You gotta cross your heart and hope to die," he said. "If you tell it, I'll kill you myself." That was something else he'd learned at school and their mother had told him not to say it. Now he was waiting for *her* to say it. "Swear to God."

"Swear to God," she whispered, and waited.

"Mama is about to leave us." He stared straight ahead. "I heard her tell Mrs. Hopper that as soon as school starts and you ain't scared anymore she's gonna take us and move across town, maybe even to a new town, but that all depends on how we're doing in school and how Dad is doing all by himself. She told Mrs. Hopper that she had had all she could take. She said she does not love him at all. She said the only good thing he ever did was have us."

Danny was about to say more, but there was a rustling down on the path, a sudden sound like giant wings rushing forward. It seemed the sound was getting louder, closer, the trees closing in.

"Shit, here it comes," Danny whispered, and Caroline froze to the sounds, unable to move, closer and closer, a rush of big brown wings, a head the size of a bear. "Snipe!" Danny called, his voice suddenly high with fear. It was coming; it was coming, racing up from the woods on its big long legs to jump in the bag, there, over there, out of the woods and right in the path. She straightened, her pants wet, down her calves and into her sneakers. She was too afraid to think of anything. The snipe ducked back in the woods and it was quiet again; Danny was breathing hard.

"I wet my . . ."

"Shhh!" There was silence and they waited again. Caroline moved closer to Danny. Now she couldn't even run down the path to their house because the snipe was out there, just there and waiting to catch her in his big brown wings and fly away. "You stink," Danny whispered. "Snipe ain't coming because you stink." But his voice had lost all anger now, and she knew he was scared.

"I couldn't help it." She was about to tell him that he was nothing but a baby, too, when up from the bushes sprang a snipe as big as a man. Caroline jumped toward Danny, getting tangled in the sack and pulling both of them to the ground.

"Daddy!" Caroline screamed as loud as she could, screaming and crying as a dim beam of light moved from side to side on the path and finally stopped on Danny's pale face.

"Can't catch a snipe that way." Uncle Tim said. "No sir, sure can't." And then they were all there, all the relatives laughing and stepping forward. Caroline ran and grabbed hold of her mother, momentarily forgetting that her pants were wet and what Danny had told her.

"I almost had one," Danny screamed. "He was right here, right at the bag and Caroline had to go and pee in her pants and scare him off."

"I didn't mean to scare it," she said. "Really."

"Come on, now." Caroline's father took her hand and led her down the path, her mother on the other side, while Uncle Tim reached way up in the limb of the tree above Danny's head until he pulled down a small microphone dangling from the cord of a mini recorder.

"We've still got the fireworks," their mother said, and patted Danny's back, pushing him along. "And watermelon and homemade ice cream." And then, loud and clear came Danny's voice from Uncle Tim's hand. "How are we gonna catch a snipe with you making all this noise?" They all laughed while he stood so still, so pale in that yellow glare.

"You talked. I wasn't talking." Caroline stared in amazement at the box where her own voice sounded so strange.

"You were moving. Moved your feet and moved your hand." Danny clasped his hands to his ears, his thin face with a look of horror while tears filled his eyes.

"Cut it off!" Danny screamed. "Cut it off. Why'd you go and spy on us anyway?"

"It's a joke, son," their father said. "It's just a joke we've been playing in this family for years. Besides you're one to talk about spying and eavesdropping."

"You mean there wasn't a snipe out there?" Caroline asked, and then turned to Danny. "What about all the other things we were told?"

"What things, baby?" her mother asked.

"Lord, these clowns have been wanting to pull this trick every summer since Danny was born," Aunt Patricia was telling Cousin Randy's girlfriend. Uncle Tim clicked off the machine and handed it over to their dad while Danny ran inside and let the screen door slam shut behind him.

"Let's start the fireworks," Uncle Tim said. "That'll bring that boy back out. Snipe hunt is *supposed* to be fun."

"But it wasn't." Caroline followed Danny into the house, the tape still on the front porch. She crept up the stairs and then eased open the door to his room. He was kneeling on the floor by his bed, the burlap bag still clenched in his fist. "Danny?" she called.

"Get outta here."

"It was a joke."

"Don't you think I got ears?" He turned toward her, and in the thin strip of light from the doorway, she could see his eyes and cheeks glistening. "It ain't a *damn* bit funny. You can go tell them I said that, too. Go tell I said it ain't a *damn* bit funny or a *damn* bit fair!"

She waited and then tiptoed close to the window, where she could see the first skyrocket soar up and over the pine trees, as high as the stars. He leaned against the windowsill, chin pressed in his hands, and watched the brief flares of light. "Don't you sit those pee britches on my bed," he said.

"I won't." She knelt beside him, his breath in deep sighs, as they watched the bright sizzling colors splash in the sky. They could hear their mother calling for them to come outside, but Caroline didn't answer.

"You stink." He shook his head, sighed again.

"I know it," she said, and then fell silent, relieved that he was talking to her at all.

"That was a dumb joke." He pressed his face to the window and stared down at where their parents were standing side by side, their dad's arm looped around their mother's waist. "I can't believe they tricked us like that."

"Danny?" She waited, wondering exactly what she was going to ask him while her mother stood in the yard and twirled a sparkler round and round. "Is what you told me a trick?"

He stared at his hands, then at the burlap bag for a long time before answering. Now Aunt Patricia and the cousins had sparklers and were writing their names in the sky.

"I told you that you don't have to be a scared baby if I'm there, right?" She nodded, wanting more from him, but that was all he offered. She inched closer and rested her chin on the burlap sack, a wash of comfort leaving her drowsy and looking forward to the feel of clean cotton sheets and the buzzing conversation of the adults downstairs.

In the following years there were two apartments, one house and two different towns, a stepfather, a stepmother, and graduations and weddings of various relatives. There were the high school years, when Danny chose to live with their dad, and in those years they sometimes experienced that shy formality reserved for distant relatives, a feeling that dissipated quickly but always served as a reminder of years that were lost. Still, when she thinks of family and home, this is the image that comes first: lights, Danny, a burlap sack; the summer smell of his cotton T-shirt and the pulse of his sticky wrist as she clung to him and his assurances while their parents stood together that last time in a dazzling glow of fireworks.

A BLACKFOOT RIVER FABLE

by Norman Maclean and Franz Kafka
as misremembered and retold
by David James Duncan

One blazing-hot afternoon this past summer I waded far out into the Big Blackfoot River and stood, fly rod in hand, studying the fishing situation. No trout rising, due to the heat; nothing on the surface but the occasional flotilla of beer-swilling inner-tubers. I began, between flotillas, to dredge the emerald depths of a granite-rimmed pool with a weighted streamer fly—a rabbit-fur Muddler, actually, tied by my friend, Bobby Powell, which fly I have since given away, in case it had anything to do with what followed.

I'd fished for perhaps half an hour and was about to give up, make a beer run, and join the inner-tubers myself, when my rod bent double, my reel let out a shriek, I set the hook to something rock solid—and up to the surface of the pool rose the enormous, thrashing bulk of what could only be a bull trout. I was shocked to hook such a fish at all, and doubly shocked by its behavior. The few big bull trout I've hooked had stayed deep, fighting a dogged battle reminiscent of chinook salmon. Not this beast. The instant it slammed my fly it shot to the surface, where it began not so much leaping as just raising its head out of the water, the way a seal does in ocean surf—as if trying to locate the son of a bitch who'd hooked it. And soon as it spotted me it charged, cutting a huge wake, its whole back and dorsal out of the water, its eyes locked on mine. I felt like prey. A six-foot minnow. I was about to panic and run when, in maybe twenty inches of water, right under my rod tip, the bull trout came to a halt.

The situation was weird. It got weirder. A little sculpin came swimming up alongside the trout, and the sculpin, too, grew still as a statue in the shade of the trout's mighty side. Both fish then peered up at me with almost human-looking scowls. "What the hell?" I said aloud.

"What the hell yourself!" came a voice right next to my ear. I whirled around. No one there. Nothing near me but my own fly rod. "Look at me when I speak to you!" said the voice, which seemed to come from the rod.

I gaped at it. It's an old Sage. I vowed to switch brands as soon as possible.

"Not there, you idiot! Down here!" the voice in the fly rod said.

I looked down at the bull trout. It glared up, Bobby Powell's Muddler still embedded in its jaw. It was an old man's voice I was hearing. A crotchety-sounding old man. It was just the sort of voice you'd expect a fish that size to have, if you expect fish to have voices. I don't. "As far as I'm concerned," I said aloud, "I'm hallucinating. Heatstroke maybe."

"Stop acting so *stunned*," said what could only be the trout. "It's annoying. You're in no danger. We're just faceless souls from the afterlife. But we've been given a dispensation to speak to you today, and have borrowed these fish as vehicles. Allow me to introduce us. I was known, until fairly recently, as Mr. Norman Maclean. And my friend here, all the way from Austria . . ."

I don't care to keep painting this scene in detail. It's all men-in-little-white-coats stuff. Suffice it to say that in the shallows at my feet hovered a bull trout of perhaps twelve pounds who claimed to be the author of *A River Runs Through It*, in my opinion the greatest fly-fishing story of all time. And in the shadow at its side lay a sculpin of perhaps five inches, who the trout claimed was Franz Kafka.

"We have an ugly story to relate," the bull trout said. "And we ask you, please, to relay that story to as many people as possible. If you'll do that, we'll not trouble you again."

I promised to do exactly as they wished. The fish ogled me approvingly. I have *never* looked so forward to an act of catch-and-release.

Norman Maclean, via the bull trout, began his "ugly story" by saying that after he died he'd chosen to cash in his one-way ticket to Heaven. By downgrading his Paradise ticket, Norman said, he'd been able to upgrade his brother Paul's ticket to Hell and squeak the pair of them into Purgatory. "Neat trick," I told the bull trout. The sculpin nodded its ugly noodle in agreement.

The chief drawback of Purgatory, Norman Maclean said, is not the near-endless, arduous hike up the stupendous Mount that leads to Paradise. The trouble with Purgatory, Norman said, is that it sits in such close spiritual proximity to *this* sorry planet that the pilgrims on the Mount are still privy to certain goings-on down here. Norman and Paul, for instance, had recently learned of the gigantic cyanide heap-leach gold mine proposed for the upper Big Blackfoot River. Their reaction to this awful news had been to sit down smack in the middle of the single-file trail up Mount Purgatory. "I'm not moving!" Norman had declared. "To take a single step farther toward the Paradise of a God who'd create a river so beautiful, make us love that river so hard, then abandon that river, the instant we turn our backs, to greed-crazed investors, poison-spewing madmen, and jewelry-wearing fools is not for me. I'm staying right here."

"*Long live the Blackfoot!*" roared Paul.

Angels, Norman informed me, are very powerful, stubborn beings, and they run the show there in Purgatory. But when one flew down the Mount, spotted the two-man sit-down strike, and told the Macleans to move it along, Paul hollered, "Save the Blackfoot, you big fairy! Then we'll think about it."

It turns out the Christians got it half right: the path up Mount Purgatory is anything but "straight," but it is "narrow"—so narrow that the millions of souls working their way up the Mount all had to stop, beg the pardon of the Macleans, and step carefully over them. "Long live the Blackfoot!" the brothers bellowed at them all. "Whatever," the pilgrims would reply, concentrating on their own salvific journeys. But the delay caused tremendous gridlock. In no time souls were backed up, butt-to-belly, all the way down the Mount to Limbo.

Among the pilgrims at whom the brothers bellowed their redundant slogan was a gaunt little fellow about Norman's size but with unusually large, sad eyes. After climbing over the brothers, this man stopped, turned, and inquired, "Vut is ziss *Blackfoot?*"

"Do I know you?" Norman asked, peering at him.

"I don't belief so," the little man said. "I vuss Austrian on Earth. My name zere vas *Franz Kafka.*"

Maclean grunted (a bit rudely, he confessed to me), and told Kafka that he'd never been fond of his surreal fables.

"Zuh surreal has its place," Kafka had calmly replied. "But perhaps you haff been fortunate never to live in such a place."

Norman was disarmed by this reply. A conversation ensued, during which it grew apparent to the Macleans that, where Kafka came from, smoke jumpers, grizzly bears, and fly-fishermen were surreal creatures in their own right.

Franz was delighted to learn that Norman had refused Paradise for the sake of his brother. "But," Kafka said, frowning, "ziss seems strange. Now you both refuse to climb zuh Mount for zuh sake of a mere *river?*"

For an instant Paul looked like he might shove Kafka off into the abyss. Then he remembered Franz's weird urban background. Turning to his big brother, he said, "Tell him, Norman."

"*Mere* river?" rumbled the elder Maclean, his rage and rhetorical power building. "*Mere river!* The Blackfoot is *the* river! The one cut by the world's great flood. The one that runs over stones from the basement of time! It is my father's and mother's and brother's river. River of grace, and of utter heartbreak. River where sunlight turned water electric, and a wand made contact with the world's deep magic, and a leviathan danced the dance of death as Paul created art that defeated that death, and my father and I watched and the sight seared our souls and the water and λόγος sang as hope, brothers, father and river merged so tight and true that, even in that world of sorrows, sorrow was forced, for a time, to flee . . ."

"And *now*," whispered Paul, when Norman's voice broke and failed him, "now, some low-rent sons o' bitches wanna kill the whole thing. Take away some gold. Leave behind a pit the size o' Hell an' a mountain o' poison an' the Blackfoot doomed to drink it all. 'Makes perfect sense,' they say. 'It's just a river, or maybe two.' An' while they're weaselin' around where we can't lay a finger on 'em, we're stuck clear the firp up here . . ."

"So we're not moving," Norman concluded.

"Hike's over," added Paul, who didn't really say "firp."

Kafka looked hard at the Blackfoot-crazed brothers. "I did not know," he said finally, "zat it vas possible to feel ziss vay about a river!" Then he too sat down in the purgatorial trail, the three of them blocking the path up the Mount completely.

An angel zoomed down at once, and called, *"What's this? Get up! Walk!"*

"Go play your harp!" Kafka hollered at it.

Norman wheezed with glee.

"Go watch John Travolta in *Michael,* you big Twinkie!" added Paul.

The angel flew off for consultation or reinforcements.

"As you haff assisted your brother," Kafka said, "I vud like somehow to assist you. How do I do zat?"

Norman's smile faded. "Save the Blackfoot," he said miserably, "though it remains on earth, and we do not."

"A man may only give his best, is ziss not so?" Kafka said. "Und you und I, Norman, tell stories. So let us tell a story for zuh sake of your river, zen agree to resume our uphill walk—*if* zuh angel agrees to zend our story down to help."

That was the deal. That's what they did. And there on the Blackfoot a bull trout and sculpin took turns speaking the story to me. I could never begin to duplicate the original telling—the fey terseness of Kafka; the surging river music of Maclean; the Blackfoot purling round us. But the basic fable, with a few flourishes of my own, goes like this:

One Cowboy's Knees

Ty Coburn was a Montana cattle rancher. He didn't go to church. Didn't smoke or drink to speak of. Didn't golf, or bowl, or even fish the Big Blackfoot River, though it ran right through his little spread near the prairie-dog-sized town of Ovando. He did shoot a couple deer each fall, usually one on his own tag and one on his wife Annie's. But that was work, not sport. Hunting by tractor (towing the usual cattle feed on the trailer so the deer wouldn't suspect), Ty took five or ten minutes to bag the two best bucks, and the rest of the day to carve, package, and freeze them.

He didn't mind the endless work, though. The fact was Ty had never wanted "sport" or "relaxation." His two kids, six horses, and varying-sized herds of cattle, his hay fields and water rights and addiction to Skoal were all he'd ever wanted. "This ranch is my country club, church, and whorehouse all balled up in one," he liked to say—when Annie was well out of earshot.

Lucky for the marriage, the ranch kept Annie satisfied, too, as long as she could add one outside ingredient to the mix: though she rose at dawn and worked the same double-shift days as Ty, every night she watched *CNN News*, over and over and over. "Connects me to the world" was Annie's excuse. "Disconnects her from re-memberin' our total economic dependence on a buncha stupid cows" was Ty's theory. "It's her mantra," opined their six-year-old daughter, Rhett (who was getting weird ideas at school). "It's *boring!*" roared three-year-old Russell with cattlemanly authority.

Whatever it was, seven in a row was Annie's CNN record, and three per night was her norm. She didn't doze while she was watching, either. Annie could tell you which newsclips were fresh and which were repeats from the past half hour; she noticed every time Lynn Russell changed hairdos or David Goodnow suits; she never stopped wondering why Bob Lozier (whom Ty called "Bob Loser") always wore the same smirky smile no matter how grim the news. Of course, Rhett and Russell threw fits about their mom's one-show obsession—especially after she tried to defend it by calling it "educational." But Ty had long ago noticed how Annie's mo-nopolization of the tube bored the kids into an early bedtime, which left him and Annie a quiet hour or two together. And to his delight Ty discovered that, twice a week or so, after he'd triple-checked the kids, Annie was not averse to having sex to a CNN accompaniment. He loved the crazy buffalo rug she'd take down from the shelf to lie on; loved the way her body looked in the flashing blue light; loved it that he was the one thing on earth that made her ignore her boring show. Hell, he even grew fond of CNN itself, if only by association—though he did sometimes wonder, when they were hard at it, whether he and Annie might be the reason for Bob Loser's smirky smile.

One night after Ty dozed off, Annie caught a CNN clip on the dangers of cholesterol. As head chef of a family that daily inhaled serious quantities of homegrown beef, the CNN story scared Annie the way tuberculosis-plagued elk farms scared Ty. The following morning she drove to OK Books in Helena, bought *The Next to No Cholesterol Cookbook*, hurried on to Wholly Foods (an establishment Ty would soon be calling "that goddamned hippie feedstore"), spent a small fortune, returned home, and proceeded to revamp the family diet.

"I blame Ted Turner for this!" Ty roared the instant he set eyes on the tofu-and-vegetable stir-fry Annie had concocted in lieu of his customary catcher's mitt–sized, drippingly rare steak.

"You should *thank* him for it!" Annie retorted. "I'll bet your blood looks like sausage grease. I want you to get it checked."

A modest request in most families. But the only medical problems for which Ty Coburn ever opened his wallet involved his kids, horses, wife, or events that knocked Ty himself unconscious and unable to resist. He agreed to check nothing. He said hard ranch work purged the blood. He did eat the stir-fry—hating every bite, feeling hungry again an hour later. It was a thankless act of courage: the next night Annie served up something called tempeh that had Ty looking back on the tofu as if it had been steak.

Things went from bad to worse. Bulgur-oatmeal burgers. Rice so wild it drove little railroad spikes between Ty's teeth. Four-pound loaves of bread that tasted like stagnant pondweeds. Soybeans that tasted okay drowned in ketchup but later produced enough methane to heat the house. The weird food began to terrorize Ty's dream life, too. He dreamed he went shopping for dangly earrings—for himself. He dreamed he joined PETA. He dreamed he changed the name of his favorite horse, Butkus, to Shakti. He dreamed he rode Shakti out into his fields, took a pair of bolt cutters to his own barbed-wire fences, and set his cattle free. He'd wake in a terrified sweat, usually needing to fart. It upset him.

Ty took action by trying to joke Annie's health kick away. The kids' pinheaded collie dog, Boofus, had been chewing up pine cordwood lately, and pugging splintery loaves of that. Ty sneaked out in the yard one freezing-cold night, picked up half a dozen Boofus loaves, stuck them in a Ziplock bag, hid them in the freezer, and after a trip to Helena a few days later, informed Annie, "I stopped by Wholly Foods. Decided to set eyes on the Enemy myself. But I found these—skinless soy sausage with toasted almond slivers. Thought they might be worth a try."

Annie was so pleased by Ty's sudden cooperation that she had the things frying in olive oil and garlic, and was quadruple-checking the kids' shoes for dog doo, before she figured things out. Ty, peeking in from the living room, was rolling on the floor by then. Annie was not amused.

Things went from worse to awful. A pair of four-wheel-drive ruts appeared on Annie's forehead every time she glanced at Ty. A mask of saddle leather replaced Ty's face whenever he looked at Annie. Russ and Rhett ate so little they began to look sickly. Annie started fixing them separate meals. Ty took to clearing the table, just to sneak scraps from the kids' plates. Boofus sulked miserably about, watching Ty steal what used to be *his* food. The TV-lit lovemaking went the way of the rare steaks. Bob Loser kept smirking at them anyhow.

"Two hundred tons o' cattle surroundin' me day an night," Ty finally bellowed over his string squash and Swiss chard one evening, "an' I'm *always hungry!*"

"A blood test costs *twenty damn dollars!*" Annie bellowed right back.

Neither wives nor husbands survive long on ranches without being heroically stubborn. The next time he drove to town, Ty showed Annie, Ted Turner, Bob Loser, and all the rest of 'em how real ranchers operate—by again refusing to see a doctor, toting home his first bottle of whiskey in years, and matching every CNN his wife watched that night with two double shots of Rebel Yell. But Annie knew a thing or two about ranching herself. Seeing Ty's game, she just sat back and watched CNN so many times in a row that Ty finally got the whirlies, dashed in the bathroom, and did some rebel yelling down the toilet.

The next morning Ty, looking as if he'd had Boofus sausage for breakfast, loaded up the hay trailer, climbed onto the tractor, drove down by the Blackfoot, watched the river flow as the cows chewed and crapped and lowed, and felt his stubbornness melt away. He missed Annie's smile something awful—not to mention her buffalo rug and kisses and the blue flashes of the *Hollywood Minute* and *Dollars and Sense* upon her body.

"I surrender," Ty told the Big Blackfoot, who thought no less of him for that.

So at age forty-one, feeling strong as a wild bull elk, Ty Coburn swallowed his cowboy pride, drove into Helena, and splurged on a complete physical for himself and a dozen red roses for Annie. Turned out he was right about hard ranch work, too: his cholesterol matched his weight at 195.

"Not bad for a decrepit ol' carnivore," Annie admitted as they lay in front of the tube that night, naked as the steaks they'd devoured for dinner, with Annie loving her roses and Ty loving Annie and Bob Loser's smirk making perfect sense again.

But when Ty woke to a ringing phone in the middle of the night, something did not make sense. It was his doctor, saying that Ty's blood tests had revealed more than a cholesterol level: they'd confirmed a condition known as "Miner's Knee." What's more, the doctor said, he worked for a corporation known as SurgiCorps International. "And on SurgiCorps' behalf," he informed Ty, "I'm staking claim to both your knees."

Ty chuckled at this nonsense. He thought his sawbones must be drunk, and off and running on some complicated joke. But there was no punch line. "SurgiCorps' corporate prep team will be out to see you in a few days," the doctor said.

In preparation for the SurgiCorps corporate prep team—whatever that might be—Ty drove down to Missoula and the University of Montana library and did some homework. Miner's Knee, he was appalled to learn, was a genuine condition: a mineral buildup that occurs on the kneecaps of maybe one in five hundred people. The condition caused no pain, no loss of mobility, and posed no health risks, short-term or long-, if the minerals were simply left alone. But way back in 1849, researchers at the newly formed National Institute for Profitable Surgeries (NIPS) began looking for ways to make money on Miner's Knee deposits. And they found one: a knee mineral known as "glod" could be removed and fired into a malleable yellowish metal, then fashioned into jewelry.

That a knee-borne metal had been discovered at all amazed Ty. That a glod wedding band, necklace, tongue stud, penis ring, or cuff link would become the desire of millions of otherwise sane men and women seemed preposterous. But within a decade of the discovery, glod lust became a national epidemic. Citizens suspected of having Miner's Knee deposits were being mugged in broad daylight, ripped open in back alleys, crippled for life. Doctors were gunning one another down over knee rights to a single patient. Indians, Chinese immigrants, poor whites, and Southern blacks were being herded by the thousand through glod-extraction facilities that were little more than slaughterhouses for human legs. Then in the 1870s, glod fever became government policy when President Ulysses S. Grant, venting years of pent-up battle fury, signed into law the Surgical Act of 1872—a piece of legislative inanity that allowed the holder of any type of medical degree, from any nation on earth, to journey to this country, locate Americans with Miner's Knee, and legally operate on them.

With a terrible case of psychosomatic knee pain, Ty read how glod had been gouged, suctioned, blasted, and drilled from tens of thousands of citizens by quasi-Hippocratic opportunists from all over the globe. Hundreds of Americans had died from glod surgery; thousands had contracted cancer from chemicals used in the extraction process; thousands more ended up in wheelchairs for life. And Grant's antique Human Butchery Law was still on the books! To this day, Ty discovered, any dentist, any ophthalmologist, any proctologist or boob-job specialist on earth possessed the right to rip open the knees of any American in which minerals had been discovered! Worse still, the glod industry had made a minuscule number of people so stupendously rich that they'd hired lawyers, public relations firms, spin doctors, politicians, and hit men: every time a scandal, a ballot initiative, or grassroots protest threatened the 1872 law, an election was bought, a PR brainwash took place, a key activist vanished, and the maiming of American knees remained legal and profitable. The new transnational knee-mining corporations even had the gall to call their butcheries "cures."

What Ty learned in a nutshell was that he and his knees were in surreal, yet perfectly genuine, trouble.

The SurgiCorps team came jouncing up Ty and Annie's drive in a lost-looking Lincoln Town Car with the words SURGICORPS: CUTTING-EDGE SOLUTIONS FOR YOUR GLOBAL GLOD NEEDS stenciled on the front doors. Ty had given thought to their arrival: early that morning he'd turned forty head of cattle loose in the yard. As he opened the front door to greet his guests, he was gratified to see fresh manure clear to the hubs of the Town Car's wheels. But the two posh-suited, briefcase-toting men and one smiling woman who stepped from the car proved nimble: they made it to the porch without greening their shoes.

Annie, too, had been thoughtful. After leading the reps into the living room, she served a triple-strength herbal tea Wholly Foods advertised as "instantly laxative." With huge thanks and broad smiles, the reps each downed a honey-laced mug. When none showed discomfort or asked to use the bathroom though, Annie felt her first rush of fear: these were three competent-looking, determined people, skilled at denying or squeezing in every kind of shit imaginable.

Ty decided to end the team's visit with a single sentence. "I just flat refuse to be operated on," he announced, giving each rep a slow, ominous stare. "End of discussion."

But the lady rep just smiled more brightly. "Yours is a common first reaction, Ty," she said, "but hardly a *legal* one. If you cooperate, your cure will take place in the private hospital of your choice. If you defy the 1872 law, it will take place in SurgiCorps' state-of-the-art, fifty-five-foot traveling operating room, outside your cell at the state prison in Deer Lodge. That choice is yours. But rest assured, the cure *will* take place."

Ty was stunned to silence. Annie took up the fight. "Those forms you sent about a compensation check. Are they *real*? Is the U.S. government actually saying that the payoff for Ty's maiming is *five dollars per knee*? With no funding for physical rehab? No assistance for wheelchairs, wheelchair ramps, bathroom alterations? Or is this some sick joke?"

"The five-dollar compensation," the lady rep replied, "is a proud American tradition more than anything else, Annie. The price was set by President U.S. Grant himself—one of the men, I'm sure you recall, most responsible for ending slavery in this country."

"But this law is a form of the very thing Grant fought to end!" Annie shouted. "Any half-wit can see that!"

"But Congress can't see it," said the rep with the thickest briefcase, who turned out to be one of SurgiCorps' army of lawyers. "If you don't like the law, Mrs. Coburn," he said, "by all means, fight! That's your right as an American. Of course it'll be time-consuming. And *expensive*. If you lose it could cost you this beautiful ranch. But feel free. And may the best team of lawyers win!"

While Ty was reeling at the thought of losing his ranch, the lady rep produced a pile of four-color brochures, spread them across the coffee table, and in the hushed, excited tone of a TV golf announcer said, "What these illustrate, Ty and Annie, what we really came to discuss, are some of the exciting new options in glod-extraction methods! Over the past two decades SurgiCorps' world-class research team has developed safe, efficient new ways of extracting glod from American citizens. Ask anyone. We're cutting-edge!"

The reps loved this phrase: "cutting-edge." Ty noticed how much they loved it, because every time they used it his anus seized up like the Blackfoot River in midwinter. One of the cutting-edge extraction methods turned out to consist of removing the patient's knees completely and replacing them with metal joints—made of "cutting-edge aerospace metals." A brochure photo showed a bikini-clad postoperative victim in a poolside lounging chair, smiling seductively at her own shiny titanium knees. Gaping at the gorgeously maimed legs in horror, Ty felt his anus *and* his penis contract.

The cutting-edge extraction method, which the lady rep said "we'd be *thrilled* to see Ty choose," was called Cyanide Knee Leach Extraction. Hearing the name alone, Ty grew faint. Opening another brochure, the lady rep showed Annie and a fast-fading Ty how two plastic bladders, like colostomy bags, were strapped to the patient's knees, and a hose running from each was attached to a powerful pump. The bladders were then filled with cyanide. ("Yes, the *famous deadly poison*," the lady rep tittered in response to Annie's question. "But what a way to put it! Let's see if the rest of the brochure can't help you feel a little trust.")

The patient was fully anesthetized. Then—in a series of illustrations that even the lady rep dared not describe—the caps of both knees were, as the brochure put it, "traumatized," with repeated blows from a hardwood mallet, until "trauma fluids" (commonly known as water on the knee) formed. Ty was so faint by now he had his head between his potentially doomed knees. But Annie was CNN tough. She paid attention.

Once the "trauma fluids" formed, a hole was drilled into each knee, a second hose was inserted in each hole, the opposite end of the hose was attached to the cyanide bladders, the electric pump was activated, and lethal quantities, stupendous quantities, *unbelievable* quantities of sodium cyanide solution were pumped through the pierced, smashed knees of the patient to draw out the glod. "But won't the cyanide just *kill* my husband?" Annie finally cried.

The SurgiCorps team let out a unison chuckle. "We're a cutting-edge outfit!" the technician cried as Ty's anus tried to burrow like a gopher up into his intestines. "There's no sense confusing you with complex terminology," the technician said, "but you'll be glad to know that kneecap fluids are what we call *discrete,* and that the only way cyanide can enter the bloodstream is through what we call an *indiscretion.*"

"And what in the name of *Satan,*" Ty rasped from between his knees, "is an *indiscretion?*"

"A burst hose would be an example," the technician said. "But, need I say it, SurgiCorps' bladders and hoses are absolutely—"

"*Cutting-edge,* yes, we know, we know!" Annie snapped. "But Ty read that SurgiCorps, operating earlier this decade under the name Knee Source Incorporated, shot cyanide from burst hoses into the blood of three hundred patients in one year!"

The reps enjoyed another group chuckle. "SurgiCorps International is *not* Knee Source Incorporated, Mrs. Coburn," the lawyer cooed. "SurgiCorps was built, from the ground up, with *public safety* as its *number one priority.*"

"Ty read that you just restructured Knee Source to dodge lawsuits," Annie retorted.

The lawyer turned pink as a ham and began groping through his brain wrinkles for a response. But the lady rep, smile unscathed, silenced him with a look. "Your husband," she told Annie, "no matter what extremist literature he's been reading, will receive the benefit of *millions* of dollars' worth of cutting-edge research. And you two needn't fret about all this much longer. We've scheduled Mr. Coburn's cure for next week."

Ty raised a bloodless face in protest, but had to drop down between his knees again. Annie began looking around for a weapon.

"One more thing," said the lawyer. "Miner's Knee *is*, of course, hereditary. We've staked our claims to little Rhett's and Russell's knees. We'll wait till they mature to operate. Don't mean to bore you, this is all in the claim forms, filed up in Helena. But I *do* need to mention that Russ and Rhett are required by law to sign those forms the day they turn eighteen. And if, God forbid, they become parents in the interim, our right to any legitimate or illegitimate offsprings' knee minerals goes into effect from date of birth."

Determined to throw them out despite his queasiness, Ty tried to let out a roar that came out as a groan, flopped forward off the couch, slammed his face into the coffee table, and sprawled out on the floor in a dead faint.

The SurgiCorps' crew stood as if choreographed. "Dear me!" the technician said. "Ty's having a time of it adjusting his thinking."

"Don't worry, Ms. Coburn," said the lawyer. "He'll come around."

"Thanks so much," cooed the beaming lady rep, "for the yummy tea!"

They weren't two steps out the door before Annie picked Ty's pockets for his keys, unlocked the gun cabinet, and began cleaning both deer rifles, both shotguns, the .22, and Ty's antique Colt .45. She then drove up to Lincoln for ammo.

Lyle Croft, the gunsmith, was an old schoolmate of Ty's—and when he saw the fury in Annie's eyes, he was worried for his friend. "What's with the fireworks, Annabelle?" he asked. "Gonna *Una-bomb* the Tyster?"

"If those SurgiCorps geeks think they're cuttin' *my* family," she seethed, "they got more than just another think comin'."

Lyle usually stared at those he spoke with—especially at Annie, who was easy on the eyes. But now his eyes darted away. "If Ty an' the kids got the Miner's Knee," he said, "them SurgiCorps folks got every right to cure it."

Annie gaped. "Could you repeat that?" she whispered.

"Let 'em operate," Lyle said, still avoiding her eyes. "Ain't the end o' the world."

Up till now the whole glod threat had given Annie a muffled, foggy feeling. Lyle's words cut through the fog like a hard slap. "Then is it the end of the world," she asked, "if they *don't* cut my family? Give me one good reason why we should let this happen, Lyle. So a fashion designer in Paris can wear a glod ring in his eye socket? So some already-rich shareholder can get richer? So Ty can sit in a wheelchair growin' fat an' suicidal while the kids take over the ranch at the ages o' six an' three? So our grandkids' lives can be ruined before they're born? Come on, Lyle! One good reason!"

"The law's the law," Croft said.

"Till *you're* ready to drive drunk or poach an elk!" Annie retorted.

Lyle shrugged. "I read in the paper," he said, "how there's enough undiagnosed Miner's Knee in the Blackfoot and Clark Fork Valleys to keep a dozen surgeons busy for ten years. Them surgeons make big bucks, Annie, an' spend it in places like this. I'm lookin' out for number one, I admit it. You'd do the same in my shoes."

"In the first place," Annie seethed, "your shoes *reek*! An' in the second, those surgeons aren't *from* here! They don't care about you or me! They'll cut us up an' leave! You an' Ty grew up together, remember? You rodeoed, hunted, worked the mill—hell, you stole Ty's slut of a high school sweetheart an' saved him for me, remember? An' we go way back as your customers, too. That ain't big bucks, I know. Ty's a good shot's, the problem. But is betrayin' us your economic answer? Do you want a little *glod* money more than your lifelong friends?"

"Annie," Lyle said, at last meeting her eyes. "You an' Ty are mosquitoes in a blizzard on this one. Me, I choose to be one of the snowflakes. This glod deal's way bigger 'n any of us. Now take your ammo an' go 'fore you make me mad."

When Annie got home with her pathetic bag of bullets, she collapsed on the couch. No sooner had she done so than Ty tore downstairs, grinning. "Made some calls while you were out," he said, a little self-importantly. "Turns out there's a Clean Blood

Initiative on next fall's ballot that'd make Cyanide Knee Leach surgery impossible in this state. So the fight with SurgiCorps idn't *international* after all. It's a *state* deal, Annie! An' think who I'm friends with!"

Ty left a silence so Annie could answer. But she was stumped. "Butkus?" she asked. "Boofus? Not Lyle Croft no more, that's for sure."

"Bobby Robocot!" Ty cried. "*Governor Robocot's kid brother!* Bobby an' me were the all-league keystone combo two years in a row, remember? An' there comes a time to play the old-boy game. Go grab the extension, Annie. Me an' Governor Robocot're gonna have us a little chat!"

Annie went to listen. What a nightmare!

"Great to hear from you, Ty, you bet I remember!" Mart Robocot began. "Like clockwork, you and Bobby, turning those double plays. An' I'll remember you next week, too, when you go to work with SurgiCorps on this exciting new glod deal."

"Whoa there, Guv!" Ty said. "I'm goin' to work on no such thing! They've staked claims to our *kids* for chrissake!"

"Now slow down," the governor said. "SurgiCorps doesn't cure anyone under eighteen, for starters. And think of the jobs you're creating. An entire *team* of surgeons, nurses, anesthesiologists, care-givers! Think of the income that brings this beautiful state! A lot of good people are depending on folks like you, Ty. And, hey! That's a nice ten-dollar comp check you're gettin' in the bargain."

"I don't want comp checks!" Ty roared. "I want poison-free blood! An' kids that can walk! Sorry for yellin', Guv, but there *is* a way to fight this thing. Comin' next fall. That's why I called. You've got to—"

"Ty, Ty, Ty," Governor Robocot cut in. "I've been *good* to cat-tlemen. Good to you and yours, partner. But I'm a public servant first and foremost. And you're saying, 'Side with the radicals, not the public!' Saying, 'Turn your back on the unemployed.' Saying, 'Reward me for playin' ball with Bobby twenty years ago.' Let's get the sentiment out of this, Ty. What good are knees upon which no one operates? How does that create jobs? My mind's open as ever, you know that. But your facts and figures, Ty. That's what we need. Great talkin' with you! Bye!"

Click.

"This can't be happenin'," Ty groaned as the anesthesiologist lowered the mask over his mouth and he opened his eyes to memorize the son of a bitch's face so he could kill him later and instead saw Annie drawing away from his mouth, her face blue for some reason, her body blue, too, and naked—not a stitch of clothes! "What the—" Ty tried to sit up and cover her, but the instant he moved the anesthesiologist vanished, he and Annie and a dozen red roses were on the buffalo rug in their own living room, Bob Lozier was smirking out of the TV, Rhett and Russell were undoomed, his ranch and knees were safe, his life was worth living again—and Annie was *still* naked. Ty could hardly believe his luck!

"We fell asleep," Annie whispered, "till you started whimperin' like a dog on death row. What on *earth* were you dreamin'?"

Ty tried to swallow. "Worst nightmare o' my life!" he gasped.

"Tell me," said Annie.

So they lay back on the buffalo, and Ty did tell her—beginning with the 195 cholesterol count, which was real, and the condition in his knees, which thank Glod was not. And with his ranch-bred eye for detail, and in his joy at being awake, Ty soon had Annie gasping with laughter. The absurd intricacy of the dream, the inane terminology—*cyanide extraction; cutting-edge anal cramps; 1872 surgical laws; Governor Robocot* . . . But Ty was still lost in his yarn—still spinning out the lawyer's cordial threats to Rhett's and Russell's unborn offspring—when Annie sat up and cried, "My God!"

She sounded so scared that Ty jumped to his feet, ready to defend her. *"What?"* he whispered, listening for sounds outside the house.

"It's *real*," Annie said, staring straight ahead into the dark.

Ty listened for coyotes, or troubled cattle. *"What's* real?" he asked.

"The whole thing," Annie said, still staring at nothing. "Only

you're not you, Ty. You're the entire Blackfoot. An' your knees
aren't knees. They're the giant gold mine proposed for the upper—"

"Oh, don't *start!*" Ty groaned.

"Upper Blackfoot," Annie doggedly said. "An' your blood isn't
blood. It's the water, the life's blood, of the entire region. So what's
at stake idn't just one little family's ability to walk. It's worse, Ty.
It's the health of every water-drinkin' human being, cow, horse,
wild animal, bug, an' bird in a whole huge watershed. So what's
really happenin', don't you see, is even worse than your dream."

"*Bullshit!*" Ty snapped. And he was pissed. Ty was a lifelong
Republican, same as his dad and granddad; Annie was a tree-
hugging Independent; and they'd already *had* this worthless argument. They'd fought for half a year over the proposed Blackfoot
gold mine, then in November canceled each other's votes on the
one related ballot measure. By Thanksgiving, though, they'd agreed
to bury the hatchet. And now Annie was using *his* nightmare to
throw *her* silly fears back in his face. "Bullshit," he repeated. "It
was *my* dream, Annie. An' I say it's random craziness, mixed with
a little fear o' doctors, maybe. I say my dream was about one cowboy's knees. But I'm awake now, damn it. Show's over."

"Have it your way," Annie said quietly. "The hammers an' pumps
an' cyanide they wanted to take to your knees had nothin' to do
with real explosives or two-hundred-ton earth-wreckin' machines
or two-mile holes in the ground or whole *reservoirs* of cyanide. An'
your fears for Russ an' Rhett or our unborn grandkids? Silly! What's
real poison groundwater or mountain-sized toxic waste dumps or a
river of heavy metals flowin' right past 'em got to do with them?
It's random craziness. Just ol' Ty an' his knees . . ."

In a quiet, extremely controlled voice, Ty said, "I see you're out
to wreck an evenin' I was countin' among the best o' my life. But
I won't cooperate. I just won't fight you on this, Annie. An' for
everything this evenin' up till now, I *still* thank you."

Annie took this speech in—it was a long one, for Ty—and
mulled it a full quarter minute. Then she said, "An' I thank *you*,
Ty. First, for your toughness, which helps us survive, though it also

makes you vote the straight macho ticket. But even more, for the love beneath your toughness. For me an' the kids, for this ranch, for that river out there. Love that, despite your toughness, made you dream the very craziness you just dreamed. You got a big heart, Ty, much as you hate to admit it. An' it's as scared of upstream poison spewers an' crazed investors an' jewelry-wearin' fools as *my* heart. It's why I can stand to live with you, Ty. Why I love you. So I thank *you* for that."

Ty's toughness had to stare at Annie a long time before his heart could break through enough to let him mutter, "Guess you're welcome."

They kissed then, a perfunctory peck of truce, and went up to bed, where through the wide open window they listened—in a long, not-at-all perfunctory silence—as the Big Blackfoot went on talking.

Now if only it will go on living.

POND TIME

Gretel Ehrlich

Tengmiirvik. April. Or was it September? She couldn't remember. Madeleine saw five cliffs come apart and fall away and the ice on Newhalen River breaking into railroad-car-sized chunks, all upended, and the willow-choked path leading down to the water ablaze with red leaves. The footings of reality were loose, this she knew. They had been given to oblivion by fluctuating glaciers whose snouts pushed gravel forward and back. She likened ice to a single continent whose moving edge dealt blows to geology all winter, and by spring ate rock and was eaten by sun until the whole world opened into water. But other days, the bad days, she thought of ice as a bedcover being lifted from the gaunt body of her dead husband.

The cliffs were made of birds and the falling away was the birds flying from their resting places in the small clefts of rock walls. In the same way, what had appeared to be one thing turned out to be quite another when the plane bringing her there had to make an unexpected landing at a time in her life when she thought no more emergencies were possible. The engine failed; the palms of her hands grew moist and her first thought was, I'll get to be with Henry again, but instantly knew nothing is ever that easy. The air went coarse, the black grains straining to shoot the rapids of life's hourglass, and the ground heaved out of its flat aspect, taking on the complications of topography. Geography is destiny, she knew that; she knew she was geography's ant being hurtled toward rock, and she laughed, harder and harder, switching off the headset so the pilot couldn't hear.

They descended in slow motion, first circling, as if outlining the opened body of an animal. Caribou drank at the meltwater pond, their strong haunches pushing through tundra heath, their backs dappled with snow. One bull was neck deep in water and others walked the edge of the pond, stopping to drink, then graze, their coats dark brown, almost black at the hips, and their manes, butts, and chests the color of cream. She thought about the lichens and mosses they were eating, dredging snow with the broad blade of their brow tines—how neither plant has roots, absorbing water when there is some, lapsing into a near-death state of dormancy, then coming back to life, how both mosses and lichens are anchored precariously to rock by hairlike strands too delicate to see. She wondered why humans aren't made that way, why they are so heavily anchored to things, even death, and why, with a splash of life-giving moisture, Henry couldn't be reconstituted.

The bull rose out of the pond, his neck dripping, his back glistening in cool Alaskan sun, asymmetrical antlers tipping this way and that like dowsing rods as he searched for what would keep him alive in the winter to come. The caribou had splintered off from a large herd. Soon they would re-join the others and travel together, stopping only for rutting season before continuing south. She said to the pilot, "I don't know where I'm going. Let's just follow the caribou." And he nodded.

Flying into the country, she had seen the jumbled Chigmit Mountains, hanging green lakes fed by cornices, and red brush lining white highways of ice. The plane roared over valleys that lay like vessels cut open; what the vessels had been holding was now lost. Valleys opened onto other valleys and celadon lakes turned aquamarine. Under them, a river oxbowed, making hard, hairpin turns. The plane aligned itself with a narrow cloud shaped like an arrow, pointing at what? She didn't know where to begin her search for a girl whose name she didn't know. Just keep going, she told the pilot, as if the plane were a taxi, and he laughed, because even if she'd wanted to stop, there was no place to land.

Below was the northern tip of Iliamna Lake, big and brutal as an ocean, and every rocky beach had its own bear rolling in wild rye, napping in sun and rain. Even the first snow, when it came, did not discourage the bears, the sparse flakes upturned and chaotic, lost in air.

They flew above thin, striated clouds through which she could see the reflections of other clouds in a long lake to the north, Lake Clark, and the old village site of Iliamna, abandoned when almost everyone there died of TB. Stunted spruce trees looked as if they had been pushed backward, off balance, but the land lifted up from valley floors like brown wings, and the gravel outlets of receding glaciers leaked floury water—streams seeking the sea.

Tengmiirvik means "bird place" in Central Yup'ik, a language she didn't know at all. She had come here because of the story Henry told her, and because of something she found out after he died. He had talked so softly she'd had to put her ear to his lips. His voice was faint because he was on his way somewhere. She had grown ravenous; before he left, she wanted to know everything he had to say.

"Attu," he whispered, and she nodded. He meant the Battle of Attu in 1942. "I had to kill someone," he said. "No, lots of men. We landed on the beach in a fog. Swirling fog and hundred-mile-per-hour winds. The Japanese were waiting for us. Only we couldn't see them. They'd dug tunnels in the mountains. Waited until we got real close—a few feet away. Then they attacked. Not guns, but bayonets. My face was cut with a point made from a piece of sharpened bamboo.

"I was taken prisoner and put on a ship to Otaru, Hokkaido. On the way, my appendix burst. A Japanese doctor on the ship saved my life. He operated on me secretly—he wasn't supposed to help the prisoners at all—and made me promise never to tell anyone. I haven't until now. After, he jumped overboard. Why did he have to do that? Now I'm jumping too."

·   ·   ·

The plane reeled, then smoothed out. Earlier she had opened the
Yup'ik dictionary and saw the words, *cella maliggluku*. "I'm going in
the direction of the universe." That's what Henry would have said
if he'd known the language.

The other story went with the photograph she'd found of a
Yup'ik woman and a small child. Accompanying it was a badly
written note: "She got borne in the spring of the year May 1944
after you been heer since then Im missing you plese come. —A."

The Yup'ik woman was once Henry's lover and the child was
his, though so many years had passed the child wasn't a child anymore. Madeleine wanted to see the girl, now a young woman, not
from jealousy, though she felt some, but because the young woman
was all she had left of Henry, the only flesh of his flesh anywhere.

Looking up from the photograph, she saw how mountains gentled
into pond-dotted, barren country and wondered what she was doing
there. Nothing would bring Henry back. No meeting would erase
the watery nothingness of living on without him.

The plane was going to crash. It had floats, not wheels, and they
made a beeline, a bear-line, really, following a grizzly trail toward
a large pond. Trails crosshatched rock. She thought of those lines
as grizzly script, directions in bear writing: this way to big trout,
that way to good den, the other way to recent kill.

"Never before, never again. Take a deep seat, darlin'," the pilot
said on the headset. It wasn't clear whether they would be hitting
rock or water, whether they would crash and die or survive. Out of
a perverse curiosity Madeleine turned up the headset to hear what
the pilot would say as they came close to the end. But he was cool,
as if the possibility of death had never occurred to him.

The plane was a Super Cub and her seat was directly behind the
pilot's, a tiny slot into which her small body barely fit. "I can land
this little bug anywhere," he said. "And you with it."

A bald eagle perched on a rock stared at them as they whizzed past and a grizzly loped out from under the noiseless plane, abandoning the trail, his back fat rolling. She spied the pond's glint ahead, flashing its Morse code: LAND HERE. Her knees pressed into the hard back of the pilot's seat as if pushing the plane forward. "You should see this place in May when the caribou are calving," the pilot had told her earlier. "It's ringed with grizzlies, wolves, and eagles, all waiting for one moment of carelessness when they can move in and snatch a calf." Now she thought of that ring of animals squeezing in tighter and tighter—like a noose—vanquishing life.

Carelessness was exactly what is bringing us down, she thought, this stranger and me. And the failed attention of a mechanic. Now she was falling through the hole he had created for them. The plane's angle was nauseatingly steep at first and death was the blunt point at the end of the dart, the ass on which you pinned life's wriggling tail. Death was always a kind of steepness, whether it was Henry's, or this pilot's, or her own, a vertigo whose free fall had no end.

What if her life was to be spared? She wasn't sure how she would feel about it. She was sure Henry was laughing at them, at the comedy that kept the pale human stories going, page after page, in helpless, endless variations on the theme of error.

It was error that had brought her here in the first place, error that Henry had been captured and taken prisoner of war, error that when he had come home to eat, sleep, ride, and rest he still died, because he had traveled too far into starvation and horror to come back.

"Henry, catch me!" she said. The windshield of the airplane went black with oil.

If they survived the landing, they then would have to survive the night chasing the bear away, a bear who would be curious about the plane. Perhaps it was only curiosity that lets us live, she thought. Error curbed by wanting to know.

The pilot opened the side window and stuck his head out to see. At the last moment he flapped the flaps and the plane rose, then floated down into the earth's blue iris that had been watching them. Pond.

.   .   .

No time for anger, false melodrama. No time for death wishes. They went about the business of surviving. The pilot gave her orders and laughed; being alive seemed suddenly robust. He was small and compact, blond haired, his skin blotched dark red from twenty-four-hour-a-day sun and sun on ice. "I get crazy if I don't fly every day," he had told her before takeoff. "I always like to be leaving a place and coming to a new one, and I like all the decisions I have to make every moment while flying. It's a way of being alive, I guess."

From the plane he retrieved his short-handled ax, a rifle, which he loaded quickly, matches, a tarp, emergency food, four sleeping bags, flares, and assorted camping equipment. He zipped the sleeping bags together two by two, stuffing one set inside the other, and laid them on a doubled-up tarp on the ground under the wing of the plane. "We'll have to sleep together to stay warm," he said matter-of-factly, almost as if he was sorry, and she nodded as if it were a commonplace she'd anticipated. But it wasn't. The idea frightened her.

His name was Archer, but she tried to think of him simply as the pilot. He was impossible to fathom. Maybe all pilots are like that, she thought. Maybe that's how they stay aloft, by not letting anyone puncture them with questions or truths. He wasn't hardhearted. Quite the opposite. His blue eyes twinkled, but his shell was thick—she was sure he was as buoyant as his plane—and no heartbroken woman was going to ruin him.

Balancing on the plane's float, the pilot peered into the engine. It was beginning to get dark. He knew the problem was an oil line, but he couldn't see where it had disconnected. The plane wobbled like a rocking horse as he shifted his weight from one foot to the other, and the pond was a piece of night squeezed tight by tundra.

The bear would come back and they knew it. She had heard about the old trapper who had survived a plane crash but was eaten by a bear. The pilot told her they would have to take turns staying awake. She nodded. It wouldn't be hard for her. She was a rancher and, from years of calving heifers, knew how to sleep lightly.

When they had organized their camp, they walked to a small creek. "We're going fishing," the pilot announced, though he had no rod. The creek was twenty feet wide with clear, fast water and a gravelly bottom. It twisted through the caribou calving grounds and emptied into the lake. The lake was black and roiling. She could not see the other side and was glad they had not landed on it.

The pilot lay by his side and inched his arm down into the water. "These trout are some of the biggest in the world and live to be twelve or thirteen years old. I'll get an old slow one for dinner." She saw the water churn, then his other hand went in and came out empty. He grinned. "Almost," he said.

"Don't you ever get discouraged?" she asked.

"About what?" His innocence was a wall that repelled her.

He slid to a place where the stream bank hung over the water and tried again. This time he came up with a wriggling fish. When he bashed the fish's head on a rock, she turned her head away and wondered if she would be up to the rigors of survival.

"The Yup'ik don't like white people coming here to fish. They say it is not good to play with animals unless you need them. We're okay this time. We needed this food."

They cooked the trout on a stick over a smoky heather fire. He told her about *ircenrraq*, small people who were half animals—wolves or foxes—and whose songs are sometimes heard.

"They live in those hills over there," he said, pointing toward the dry ruffle to the northwest that eventually rose into mountains. He was smiling as he ate chunks of trout with his fingers. "Watch out," he said, "because if you spend the night with an *ircenrraq*, it will seem like just a few hours have passed but it will really have been a year. Also, they can tell the future."

She looked at him but said nothing. Then, "How do you know these things?"

He shrugged and watched with pleasure as she ate. "I live here."

"How long are we going to be here?" He shrugged again, pulling another chunk of pale meat from fragile bones.

.   .   .

They heard a noise. A slightly hunched-over bear appeared on the trail not far from the plane. The pilot handed Madeleine the coffeepot and a spoon. "Bang on it. Hard." The noise made the bear stop. He stood, sniffing the air full of cooked fish. She kept banging and the pilot lifted the rifle up, aiming just over the bear's head. He fired. The bear chuffed then hit the air with one paw, chasing bullets. Confused by the din, he turned and ambled off into the darkness.

"That worked out pretty good," the pilot said. "The bear's young. He's more curious than anything. The trouble is they can really tear up a little plane like this." She was sure he cared more about his plane than about her.

It had begun to get dark at night and it was dark when she woke. She had dozed off sitting by the fire, her head resting against his shoulder, and she was numb with fury and bewilderment. Henry had called to her in a dream: "Wake up!" he said in a voice from before he had become so sick, tinged with anger. She jerked awake suddenly to find the pilot sitting up with a rifle across his lap and the same expression of bemusement on his face.

"Stop looking like that!" she yelled at him.

"It's time for your watch," he said, handing her the rifle. "If the bear comes don't shoot him, just use the gun to make noise. Do you know how to use it?"

"Hell yes," she said.

He slid under the double layer of down, pulling his wool cap low over his forehead.

"I'm sorry," she said.

He saw that she was crying. "My husband died of starvation because he couldn't eat. He lost the will to live."

The pilot looked at her, then closed his eyes. During Madeleine's watch she fell asleep sitting up and another dream of Henry came: he was lying on top of his coffin beckoning to her. He had a smile on his face, the sweet, ironic dimpled smile that never failed to lure her to his side. Then everything began rattling as though in an earthquake, and she couldn't get to him. The earth kept coming apart the way the wall of birds had disintegrated and there was no passageway to him.

When the pilot woke, Madeleine was looking through the rifle's scope, peering into darkness at nothing.

No animals came. Madeleine slept. She felt Henry lying next to her and tried to hold him, but could not. It was like grabbing thin air. When her eyes opened, all that was visible was the pilot's gold hair and the bright rim of hills in the distance. She slept again, and this time was able to hold Henry close because there was something sticky on her arms. But the tighter she held him, the deeper she sank, and feared she would drown.

The pilot touched her arm and she woke. "You were moaning," he said. "Are you all right?" She couldn't speak, just nodded her head. In the north the hard spires of the aurora were searchlights, as if someone were looking for them.

"The Inuit say you have to make the path clear, you have to open the way from the land of the living to the land of the dead," the pilot said.

"How do I do that?" she asked.

"It's easy. As easy as shoveling snow from your front door."

A herd of caribou came close. Madeleine and the pilot could hear the animals' hooves on rock and the rubbing of muzzles over lichen. "The Yup'ik say it's best not to brood, not to follow your mind too closely, not to turn bad thoughts inside," the pilot said. "I'll tell you a story about caribou: 'A young woman went out to get some wood. Soon she became tired and fell asleep. Upon waking, she felt a great change in her life. Later on she discovered she was to have a child. When the time came she gave birth to a caribou. When the caribou was old enough, his mother sent him away from home to go and search for his own kind. Finally the child discovered a large band of caribou and joined the herd.'"

.   .   .

Madeleine slept and the pilot kept watch. The northern lights faded
quickly. In the winter they would undulate in the sky like curtains,
but it was still too early in the year and too warm for that.

The pond where they'd landed had begun to ice over. Now she
knew it wasn't April, but September. Had she made a mistake or
had she been there a long time? The pilot spent the morning trying
to repair the plane's engine. At noon they caught another large
trout—larger than she had ever seen.

He took the fish to where the creek emptied into the lake and
cleaned it there so the guts would not attract the bear. There was
no wind and the lake was as still as a window. But Madeleine didn't
want to see out. She was happy being where she was. They added
heather to the smoking fire and cooked the trout. Eating its flesh
was like eating pure water.

After, Madeleine showed the picture of the woman and child to
the pilot. He scrutinized it and turned it over as if the back might
say something about when and where it was taken, but there was
only a blank. He looked up. The ponds were half closed with white
ice, half shaking in sunlight.

"When was this taken?" he asked. She told him. He was silent,
then said, "The little girl—it's been a long time since she was a
little girl—she was my wife. We lived in Newhalen."

"Where is she now?" Madeleine asked.

The pilot looked away, then spoke. "She and her mother
drowned under the ice three years ago. The old woman hated snow-
mobiles and drove her own dogsled. It was spring and the ice wasn't
good enough. Usually the dogs know and won't go on bad ice, but
there was too much snow on top and it had formed a hard crust.
They went down through the crust and kept going."

Madeleine's eyes traveled the sinuous route of the creek travers-
ing barren lands whose ponds had no inlets or outlets, where black
fish froze into the ice and lived, thawing out in spring. Everywhere
she looked there was action going on, hand in hand with inaction:

lichens dying from thirst and reviving in mist, Henry's dead hand in her live one, and Henry's child mixed with the seed of this man.

She found the tiny bottle of brandy from the airplane in her jacket. She poured a thimbleful into the bottle top and handed it to the pilot. He drank. She filled it again and drank the portion herself. They did this until the small bottle was empty.

The caribou that had been grazing near the pond had joined the larger herd. Madeleine and the pilot saw them trotting across the rock barrens, up into the hills where the *ircenrraq* lived. Clouds had covered the sun and it was cold. Madeleine crawled into the zipped-together sleeping bags and the pilot crawled in after her, once again apologizing for the intimate arrangement. The wing of the plane stuck out over them like sculpture, casting an elongated shadow that extended beyond their bodies. She lay stiffly in the soft cocoon.

In the old days women wore bird-skin shirts sewn with bird-bone needles. Madeleine wondered what the shirts felt like and whether they enabled a human to fly. The pilot put his arm over her shoulder because she was shaking—whether from cold or from sorrow he never knew, nor was she about to tell him. All she knew was that they were both alive.

For a long time they lay under the plane. On the hills that curved around them the red fire of autumn spread through brush. The plane was a shadow. It was a man hovering over her, a bird, like a condor, or maybe death. She liked best the story the pilot told her about the small beings called *amekaq*, who can travel through land as if it were water and leave no hole when they come out of the ground. She wished she could be one of them.

She dozed. Sometime later, claustrophobic and sweating, she struggled to free her arms. Her breathing came fast. The pilot lay beside her on his back. Was he the plane's shadow, arms out-stretched to hold her, fallen to the ground? She knew she had been selfish, thinking she was the only one with a claim on sorrow. The pilot, this stranger with gold hair, had lost someone, too. In her sleep she had called out for Henry, and the pilot had said in a clear voice, Henry is dead. He had soothed her, stroked her neck, finally and wordlessly entered her, and she remembered that it had been amniotic, as though the rock ground and fiery hues of autumn brush had turned to water.

The bird cliffs fell away and no new ones came into being. The pilot was still asleep beside her. She touched the back of his neck, where his hair shone, and wondered if he was an *ircenrraq*, if he had made a whole year go by. She wondered if she could love him and what exactly that meant. She didn't know if she could stay with him; she didn't know if she could leave. Either way, it would be the same.

"I feel as if a lot of time has passed," she said. He jerked awake. When they sat up, they saw that the place where they had fallen to earth, with its lacework of lichen like memory's intricacy, had gone white with snow.

GLASS MEADOW

by Richard Bausch

A shady mountain road in early summer. 1954. Dappled sunlight
on tall pines, the lovely view of a valley with a bright river rambling
through it. And here comes a lone car, its tires squealing a little
with each winding of the road. A lime-green '41 Ford, with a finish
that exactly reproduces the trees in its polished depths. In the front
seat of this automobile are the eccentric parents of Patrick and
Elvin Johnston, brothers. I'm Patrick, twelve and a half years old.
Elvin is a year and a half younger. We're monitoring how close we
keep coming to the big drop-off into the tops of trees. We're subject
to the whims of the people in the front seat, whose names are Myra
and Lionel.

To their faces, we call them Mom and Dad.

Myra is thirty-six, stunningly beautiful, with black hair, dark
brown eyes, flawless skin, and—as we have heard it expressed so
often by our ratty, no-account friends at school—a body that will
make you cry. Lionel is younger, only thirty-four—tall, lean,
rugged-looking, with eyes that are the exact light blue of a summer
sky, and blond hair just thin enough at the crown of his head to
make him look five years older. He's sharp, confident, quick, and
funny. He makes Myra laugh, and her laugh has notes in it that
can alter the way blood flows through your heart.

Elvin and I have come to believe they're both a bit off, and of
course there's plenty of evidence to support our thesis.

But we love them, and they, in their way, love us. It is very important that one does not lose sight of this.

This is not a story that asks for tolerance for anyone, particularly. So.

We're on this mountain road, wending upward in the squeal of tires and the wail of radio jazz, while back home in Charlottesville lawyers are putting together the necessary papers to have us evicted from our rented house. The rental is our seventh in the last eight years. Our destination today is a hunting cabin owned by a child-hood friend of Myra's. We haven't packed a scrap of food, nor very much in the way of clothing or other supplies.

We woke up with Myra standing in the doorway of our room. "You're not ready yet," she said. "Are you."

It was still dark out. "What?" I said. "What?"

"Who is it?" Elvin said.

"We're leaving for our vacation this morning."

"Vacation?" I said. She might as well have said we were leaving for a life of missionary work in Pakistan.

Myra and Lionel have never been the type of people to take vacations, per se. They've always had a way of behaving as though they were already in the middle of some kind of—well, furlough, let's call it.

One Sunday morning as we were coming out of church, we saw Father Bauer backing out of the rectory door with a big box. Myra hurried over there, we thought to help him, but she stood silent behind him as he slowly backed through the door, groaning with the weight he was carrying in the heat of the summer day. She seemed merely curious, watching him. As he got free of the door-way, she leaned into him and said, "Hey!" loud, as if he were a long way off. Father Bauer dropped the box on his foot. Then he hopped in a small circle, holding the foot, yowling, "Merciful Heaven," at the top of his lungs.

He said this three times, as Myra, smiling, strolled away from him.

"I saw him hit a boy in the back of the neck yesterday," she told us. "He's not a very nice man, even if he is a priest."

Of course, we never went back to St. Ambrose Church. And she never went back to her job there, as a secretary in the day school. Myra likes going to new and different jobs, and we've already been to many different churches. We've attended services for every denomination of the Judeo-Christian South, and two or three of the Middle Eastern and Oriental variety as well—these in Washington, D.C., only seventy miles north and east of us on Route 29. Myra doesn't seem to be looking for anything either. She wants to experience the ways people find to celebrate having been part of creation, as she once put it. She isn't really batty in that way. Not religious, I mean. She doesn't think about it. The term "creation" is a convenient rather than a necessary expression. Her religious feeling is all aesthetics.

Lionel is less impulsive. His lunacy is more studied. He loves orchestrating the impressions of others. Once, with Myra's help, he got a real estate agent to show us a house that was for sale in our neighborhood; the name he gave the agent was Mr. and Mrs. Phlugh. ("That's P-h-l-u-g-h." Lionel spelled it out for the trusting agent. "Pronounced the same as the virus.") As the poor man walked them through the house, Myra began coughing and hacking like a tubercular victim in the last throes of the illness. "Is she all right?" the real estate agent asked.

"She's done this since I've known her," Lionel said, then coughed himself.

By the time the agent ushered them out of the house, he, too, was coughing, perhaps in sympathy, though it might also have been the result of anxiety and embarrassment. "Thank you so much," Lionel said to him, coughing. "But I think we'll keep looking. I want my house to be a place I can retreat to, you know—like a— like a sanatorium." He turned to Myra. "Don't you think, dear?"

"Yes." Myra coughed. "Like that. Something quiet as a clinic."

"Right. A clinic." Lionel coughed so deep it caused the agent to step back from him. "This is a great house," Lionel went on, coughing, "but not for the Phlugh family." Lionel is a qualified accountant, but he's currently between jobs, waiting to take up a position with the State Planning Commission. It seems to Elvin and me that they are both perpetually waiting for a new job to start. Lionel's real passion is playing mandolin in the hillbilly band he started up the year my mother was pregnant with Elvin. One of the other men in the band, a banjo player named Floyd, recently got married and moved to Tennessee to take a job in his father-in-law's distillery. No one has replaced him, though Lionel has auditioned several players, and so the band hasn't performed in months, and that source of income is dry. The woman Floyd married is a few years older than Floyd, and once Lionel brought her into the house and introduced her to Elvin and me as our real mother. Elvin divined what he was up to almost immediately.

"I knew that," he said, nodding at the woman.

I was momentarily flustered. Lionel saw it in my face, and reached over to take me by the wrist. "Well, we got Patrick any-way."

Elvin has always been skeptical about everything. When Myra developed appendicitis that year, Elvin thought she was joking, and ignored the moaning and crying from her bedroom.

At the hospital, while she was in surgery, Lionel paced up and down the corridors, muttering to himself. No one could approach him, or speak to him. And poor Elvin was as miserable as I've ever seen a kid be. Finally, Lionel came into the waiting room, where the two of us were sitting, and scrunched down in front of Elvin. "Don't you worry," he said. "They call this guy Buttonhole Smith. He'll get that old appendix out and he won't leave but the tiniest little scar, and Mommy'll be just like new."

"Yes, sir," Elvin said, and started to cry.

"Hey," said Lionel. "It wasn't your fault. You hear me, kiddo? Nobody's at fault here. Every now and then life gets serious on us."

We knew about the serious side, because of course we'd been privy to—or shall I say, we had been treated to a selection of—some of their more epic quarrels. Grandiose affairs, these were—with bro-ken dishes and threats of suicide, impossible shows of public temper. There was the time Myra chased Lionel through the aisles of a

sporting goods store, wielding the golf club he'd decided to buy
with money they evidently didn't have, or at any rate couldn't agree
on spending. Her aim, she later said, was only to wing him, bruise
a shin or an ankle, to make it hard for him to walk.

I remember an afternoon spent looking for the Antietam battle-
field. We got lost, and they started arguing about it. Lionel finally
stopped the car with a screeching of brakes and told her to shut up
and let him drive. As though she had been thinking about it all
afternoon, she opened the door and got out, and quite casually
marched into the trees. The coolness with which this was done
caused us all to hesitate: we watched her, as if there were something
we wanted brought back from there and she was the one we'd
chosen to get it for us. And then Lionel got out and followed her
into the deep green shade, calling to her—I'm sorry, please come
back, don't do this, answer me, Myra, Myra, come on now—his
voice getting farther and farther away.

"It's above Glass Meadow," Myra says now, looking at some instruc-
tions she's brought out of her purse. "Past a place called Brighton
Farm. Apparently there's a sign just past the nine-mile post."

"Whoa," Lionel says, as we surge down a narrow hairpin curve,
and then shift again, heading skyward once more.

Lionel was a gunner on a B-25 during the war. There's a small,
star-shaped scar on the fleshy inside part of his left forearm and an
oblong indentation on the outside of it, near the elbow, caused by
the path of the same tiny piece of shrapnel. Lionel deflects questions about it, usually with other questions: Why do you want to
know about the scar? What interests you about it? Do you like scars?
Is it the war you want to know about? Which war? Does war interest
you? He is capable of making you decide you don't want to ask
another question about anything ever again.

"Glass Meadow. One mile," says Myra, sitting forward to read
the sign as it glides by us.

"I never saw the milepost. Or the farm."

"It said Glass Meadow. That's what we want."

"Maybe there's more than one Glass Meadow."

"Don't be ridiculous, Lionel."

We drive on. We're quiet now.

On the left, as we come around another curve, is a novelty shop. There are bright tapestries hanging from a rack along the front. On the lawn are a lot of statues, looking like a gathering of little gray people and animals. Lionel pulls in.

"Oh, no," Elvin murmurs.

"Stay together," says Lionel. "No wandering off."

"Where would we wander?" Elvin asks, sitting back in the seat. He's apparently going to stay right where he is.

"You don't want to come in, sweetie?" Myra says. But she doesn't wait for an answer. She's out of the car and moving swiftly across the lot, in the direction of the statues. "Oh, look," I hear her say.

Lionel has followed her, keeping a small distance. He's between the little stoop at the front of the place and Myra, who has crouched in front of a stone angel.

"I want one," she says. "Lionel?"

"Where the hell would we put it, sugar?"

"The bedroom. All around the house."

"What house?" he asks.

She ignores this.

"An angel," Lionel says. "Any idea what we'll buy it with?"

"Good looks?" she says, standing and putting all her weight on one leg, so that that hip juts out.

Lionel walks into the store, and I follow. "How are you," he says to the man there, in a voice that is not his natural voice; there's a heavy, sonorous music in it, a sadness. It causes me to stare at him. "Nice place you have, sir."

And here comes Myra, lugging her heavy stone angel. She sets it down on the stoop, and comes up to where I am, in the doorway. "What's wrong with Elvin?"

"I think he's carsick," I say.

"That's the thing to do when you're carsick," she says, shaking her head, "sit in the car." She goes inside, and speaks to the proprietor in a soft Southern accent—slightly more pronounced than her ordinary speech. "It's such a lovely day to be up in the mountains."

I walk over to the car, and Elvin gets out. "They're cooking something up," I say.

He says, "Shit."

We walk up to the far end of the lot, near the road, and look back down the mountain. There's a cut in the side of the farthest bluff, in the shape of a giant human ear. It makes me feel as though we should whisper.

"They don't have any money," he says.

"Maybe they're gonna rob the place."

He says nothing for a beat or two. Then we laugh. It is my conviction that seldom has anyone else on this earth ever laughed in precisely that way, with precisely that amount of ironic agreement and rue.

Myra comes out of the shop and bends to pick up the angel. She makes her way across to the car and sets it down, opens the trunk, and, with a great deal of effort, lays it in. Lionel hasn't come out of the shop yet. She turns and waits, leaning on the open trunk as if she were propping the lid up with one hand. "Honey?" she calls.

Lionel comes to the doorway and waves at her.

Elvin and I walk down to her. She glances at us over her smooth shoulder, and smiles. "Where've you two been?"

"I'm hungry," Elvin tells her.

We watch as she closes the trunk and then crosses the lot, makes a little leap up onto the stoop, and, with her hands set to block light on either side of her face, peers through the screen in the door. Then she strolls back out to the little gray crowd of statues.

We watch her decide on another one, a deer bending to drink or gaze. She picks this one up and starts toward us.

"We don't have any money," Elvin says. "I don't know what she thinks she's doing. I heard Lionel talking last night. There's not a penny. We came up here to get away from being served something. 'They can't serve them to us if we're in Glass Meadow.' That's what he said."

The proprietor comes out of the shop, with Lionel, and together they walk out to the statues, Lionel protesting all the way. Myra reaches us with the deer, and opens the trunk again. Elvin and I get into the back, as she struggles to get the deer into the trunk with the angel. Coming toward us, with a statue of a Madonna and child, are Lionel and the proprietor, a man who we can see now has tattoos on his forearms. Myra has got the deer packed, and she closes the trunk, then turns to face them. "I guess we can put it in back with the boys," she says.

Elvin and I look at each other.

"Okay, boys," Myra says, "scootch over." She opens the door, and the two men step up with their burden. The Madonna looks like Doris Day, and the baby has the face of an old glutton. They get the thing on the seat, and then the men shake hands. Myra closes the door and says, "I don't know how to thank you."

"Think nothing of it," the man says in a voice out of the Deep South. He smiles at her, and there is a sorrowful light in his eyes. Myra has that effect on men. But this time, the sorrow I see is for other reasons.

"What're we gonna do with these?" Elvin says.

Myra waves and smiles at the man, as Lionel starts the car. "Thank you," Myra says. "And God bless you."

We pull out of the lot, and they start laughing.

"I couldn't believe he went for it." Lionel says.

"A sweetie," says Myra. "A tenderhearted man, I could see it in his eyes." She lights a cigarette, and hands it to him. They look at each other and laugh.

"What did you do?" I say.

"I had him going," Lionel says. "Didn't I?"

Myra looks at me. "Your father told that nice man I only had a year to live," she says. Then she addresses Lionel. "Did you cry?"

"I did," Lionel says. "Just a touch."

"Poor man felt so sorry he gave us the statues," Myra says. "Wasn't that sweet?"

If this were fiction, I might be tempted to say here that, as she sits laughing about the kind man who believes she has a year to live, Myra is indeed only a year away from the end of her life. But it wouldn't be true.

"We'll come back and put some money in his mailbox," Lionel says, glancing at me in the rearview mirror. "Soon as the new job starts and I get some pay." This is something they will do, too. Quite gladly, and maybe with a bonus of considerably more than they would have paid. It will be another one of their adventures together. Worth the trouble and the expense. And the man's life will be different; he'll have a day when he can tell people he found a fifty-dollar bill in his mailbox.

"I thought he was going to give us the whole store," says Myra. "Didn't you?"

"What're we gonna do with the statues?" I say.

"Sell them," Elvin says. "And buy some food."

We come to the sign: Glass Meadow. Lionel makes the turn. It's a dirt-and-gravel road, and a column of dust rises behind us. The back of the car is sunk down like the hot rods I've coveted at school in the afternoons, and the Madonna with her ugly child in her arms rocks with our motion, as if she's alive for those few seconds. I've got one hand on the rough, stone shoulder, trying to steady it. The head is an inch from my ear.

"What's she telling you?" Myra asks me.

"What about food?" Elvin says.

"Plenty to eat when we get there," says Myra.

At the end of the deepest part of the shade is light—an open, blue space. We come out of the trees into a wide field, dotted with yellow flowers. The cabin is at the other end of the field looking as though it's about to sag into the tall weeds that have nearly engulfed it. We pull off the dirt road and into the grass, right up to the porch—briefly, I think we're going to hit it—and when we stop, Lionel turns the engine off and seems to listen. We all watch him. Slowly, almost as if the motion causes him pain, he turns to us, and smiles. "Well?" he says. "What're you all waiting for?"

We leave the Madonna on the seat, and file up onto the porch, which is bleached to a tan in the sun, hot and creaky and rickety, with cobwebs everywhere, and signs of rodent infestation. Myra produces the key from the bottom of her purse. She opens the door and walks in, and Lionel steps in behind her. It's hot, airless, tenebrous; the floor sounds as if the wood might break.

"Get some windows open," Myra says. Lionel does this, winding a squeaky crank. He's got a look on his face, all concentration.

There's a ladderlike stair opposite the front door, with silky webs blocking it. The kitchenette contains a small icebox. The door is standing open.

"Great," Elvin says. "No food."

"That's no way to talk," Lionel says, finishing with the window. "We gotta get into the spirit of things."

"Oh, for God's sakes, Lionel," says Myra from the other side of the room. "That *is* ridiculous."

"You said there'd be food up here," he says.

"I was wrong." She starts opening and closing cabinets in the kitchenette.

"You know you might've checked with Betty about the food."

"When I came up here with her that time, we didn't pack food. The place was stocked."

"That was three years ago."

"Well, I'm just saying there was food here."

"There's no food here *now*," Lionel says.

"She and Woody were just here in June."

He repeats the phrase. "There's no food here *now*."

"I thought there'd be food," Myra says. "When do you want the divorce?"

"Today," he says, loud. "Let's make a big ceremony out of the whole thing, and invite a lot of people with food."

I take Elvin by the arm and we step out onto the tumbledown porch.

Myra mutters a few unintelligible words, and then we hear the chink of dishes clattering against one another.

"They're not your dishes, Myra." There's a pause. I turn to see that Elvin has his hands over his ears.

But Lionel comes to the doorway, and speaks quickly to us. "Bring your stuff in from the car if you want."

"It'll keep," I say. I have no idea where I learned the phrase— it might have been at the Saturday matinees—but in the moment I say it I feel very grown up. I feel, in fact, older than Lionel and Myra, as Lionel closes the door, and the shouting begins.

"Shit," Elvin says, and spits into the dust.

We walk out to the car. We hear glass shattering, their raised voices. It continues for a minute or two, and then is quiet. We are old enough, and experienced enough, to know that this furor means nothing. We are not even upset by it; it's an annoyance, something in the way of whatever is next.

Lionel comes storming out of the house, his hands shoved down into the pockets of his jeans. He comes over to us. His lips are white, his cheekbones flushed, looking blotched. "Boys, I want you to do me a favor." He reaches into his pocket and brings out a small folding knife, and holds it toward me. "We're on our own, boys. So I need you to go out and rustle up some grub."

"What?" I say.

"Food," he says. "Grub."

"Yes, sir."

"Here," he says.

I take the knife.

"Go out and find something we can cook. Do it."

I can only stare at him, and that is what Elvin is doing, too.

"Well?" Lionel says. "What're you waiting for?"

"Oh, come on, Dad," I say.

He takes the knife from me and gives it to Elvin. "We can eat squirrel and rabbit, or quail, or even pheasant if you can get close enough."

We stare at him.

"Go on," he says. We start off toward the line of trees at the edge of the field.

"Oh," Myra says from the doorway of the cabin. "That's wonderful—what're you doing, blaming it all on them?"

"No," Lionel says, as Elvin and I move off. "I'm sending them into the woods. They're going to do some *foraging*."

We head toward the woods, and I hear the stuttering of Elvin's breath, the thing that sometimes happens to his mildly asthmatic lungs when he's agitated. We come to the first row of trees and pause together, hearing the storm go on behind us, the voices carrying across the field.

"I suppose you think I *planned* it about the food."

"No, it was the *lack* of planning that I'm concerned with."

"Oh, you mean like quitting one job before you have another one?"

"I thought there'd be money from the band. I didn't know Floyd would fink out on us."

"Well, *I* didn't know there wouldn't be any food."

The cabin door slams shut. There's more shouting, but the words dissolve in distance now, as Elvin and I make our way into the trees, finding a thin path that winds through heavy undergrowth and around boulders the size of cement trucks. On one jagged, wall-sized stone, someone has carved the words GLASS MEADOW, 1946. We pause there, looking around.

"Wonder if there's bears up here," Elvin says.

I'm beginning to feel the sense of adventure, being in the woods, on the hunt. I think of it that way. We're on the hunt. We're after food. I can picture the look on Lionel's face as we trudge out of the trees with a string of killed squirrels and pheasants, a week's worth of meat.

"We're going to take it slow and careful from here," I say.

"Let's just go back now," Elvin says. "I don't like it here. There's too many trees."

"Shut up," I tell him. "Give me the knife."

"What're you gonna do with it? You know they're not serious."

"I'm gonna kill something to eat," I say.

He looks at me. I *am*, after all, the older brother. When he hands me the knife, I open it, crouching down—a Cheyenne, setting myself for the hunt.

"You're kidding," he says. "Come on, Patrick."

I don't answer. I head off along the path, keeping low—complete stealth. He follows. For a few minutes, there's just the sound of being in the woods. We traverse a small running creek, and climb a steep, rocky embankment, where we encounter a few birds. I put the knife in my belt and pick up a stone.

"Oh, right," Elvin says.

I'm concentrating. It's as though he's merely along as a witness— a referee or judge. I try to hit a blackbird, and something smaller with a dark tawny coloring in the wings. I miss, of course. At the top of the embankment we find a barbed-wire fence. We have always called it "bobwire," because that's the way we've heard it said. I hold it up for Elvin to crawl through, and then I get down and he holds it for me. On the other side, the ground rises gradually, as we come out of the trees up into a sunny field of tall grass swarming with flies.

"I don't know," Elvin says.

We head around the perimeter of the field, and I make a couple passes at squirrels, who are too quick and alert to be stalked by someone like me. They chatter at one another from opposite branches of a tree, as if they are talking about us, exchanging opinions. At the far end of the fence, in a little shaded area of tall old apple trees, is a black-and-white cow standing in a cloud of flies, tail swishing, slowly chewing, staring at us with the placid, steady expression of the species, hardly seeming to mark our approach through the grass, along the wide curve of the woods and fence. We come to within about ten feet of her and stop. Somewhere, crows are getting up a racket as if they have divined our purpose and mean to sound the alarm.

"What," Elvin says, and I realize that he hasn't understood why we've halted here.

"The cow," I say.

"What about the cow?"

"She's not fast. She won't run."

"What?" he says, looking at the cow and then at me and then at the cow again.

"She's too stupid to run."

"So?"

"We can get close enough," I say.

He merely stares at me.

"We have to kill the cow."

He looks at the cow again, and seems to be trying to translate what he's heard into a language he can more readily understand.

"It's a year's worth of meat."

"Yeah, but—" he surveys the field for a second. "Doesn't he belong to somebody?"

"It's not a 'he,' " I say.

"It's somebody's cow," my brother says.

"There's nobody here," I say.

"You're serious?" he says.

"We have to kill the cow," I tell him. "We were sent out here to get food. The cow is food, right? A couple thousand pounds of beef."

"Couldn't we just—*milk* her?"

"Come on," I say, and start toward her, through the grass. She takes one heavy step back, watching us, blinking in the swirl of flies, still chewing. We walk slow up to her, and she lets out a snort, shaking her head. The tail swishes against her swollen-looking side. I reach out and touch the tight curve of it. I wonder if the knife will penetrate; if there are any vital organs close enough to be struck by it.

"How're you going to kill this," Elvin says. "You gonna milk her to death?" He laughs.

It makes me angry. "I don't know," I say. "The knife?"

"You'd have to stab her six hundred times. She must weigh a ton. You think she's just going to stand here and let you work on her?"

"I have to find a vital spot. An artery."

"Where? Come on, Patrick."

I'm beginning to feel odd, discussing the slaughter of this cow under her very gaze. But there's something almost patient about the way she seems to listen to us, as if she has heard all this so many times before. "You got any better ideas?" I say.

He says nothing.

The cow tears some grass from the ground and looks at us again, chewing. The pink tongue makes me take my eyes away.

"What if we hit her over the head with something," Elvin says.

We're thinking about it, worrying it in our minds. I walk to the edge of the woods and begin going over the ground there. He calls to me from the field. He's found a branch, windfall. It's too heavy for him to lift. I make my way to him, and together we lug it back to where the cow still stands, quietly chewing, watching us. I can just lift the branch myself. I can get it up to my shoulder, a crooked bludgeon, with a white ripped place at the end, where it must have been wrenched from the tree. The cow takes another step back as I draw near.

"How will we get the body back to the cabin?" Elvin says suddenly.

His voice startles me, my concentration has been so complete. I turn and look at the field, with its crown of blowing grass, the peaceful swaying tops of the surrounding trees, and for a brief space I feel dangerous—no, murderous. The brute fact of what I have been playing with and may now do runs through me like a thrill, and before I can think about it anymore, I turn myself back to the task.

"What about it?" Elvin says. "How will we? It's too big."

"This isn't the time to worry about it," I say. And I raise my club.

"Wait." Elvin says. "Don't."

"We have to," I say. "Lionel said go get food." There's a relish with which I say this, though at the time I don't have the words to express such a thought. It runs through me like extra blood, a pounding in my ears and face and neck.

"This isn't food. It's a cow. We can't drag it past the fence. We couldn't even move it. It's a useless killing."

"We can cut it up and take it back in pieces."

"With that little knife? It'd take a year."

I don't want to hear logic anymore. "Just stand over there and wait, will you?"

"No," Elvin says. "I mean it. Don't."

The cow stands there, waiting. It's hard not to believe she knows what we're saying, the way her eyes take us in and *in*.

I step closer, and manage somehow to swing the branch. It misses, of course, and she bolts backward, with a deep-chested grunt, and lopes a few feet out into the field, her tail whipping high. She snorts, shakes her big head, lowers it, then seems to stumble a few more paces away. She makes a sneezing sound, and coughs.

"Come on," I say, feeling that I can do it. I am fully capable of it. Some part of me hungers for it. I have an image of Elvin and me, dragging the carcass right up to the cabin door and knocking on it, killers, with the week's supply of meat. "Here's your goddam food for you," I'll say.

"Lionel didn't mean a cow." Elvin begins to cry. "I don't want to kill anything."

"We *have* to," I tell him.

"No we don't, either."

"Aw," I say. "You baby." And I stagger with my weapon out into the field, where the cow has stopped and apparently forgotten how she came to be there. Her head is down in the grass, and the tail swishes her sides.

I become stealthy, lugging the branch, striving for the silence of predators. When Elvin tries to tackle me, he scrapes the side of his face on my belt buckle, and rolls over on his side, legs curled up, crying. The cow, disturbed by the commotion, lopes away a few more feet, and looks back at us. Elvin cries, holding his hands to his face. And then I see that he's bleeding. It's only a scratch, but the blood of my brother there in that field takes all the heart out of me. I drop the branch, and then, as if to protect the cow from my own freshly discovered savage nature, I run at her, waving my arms and screaming. I want her to run far away from me, and of course she only travels another slight distance, looking back with that placid, faintly consternated air. An expression almost of reproach. The sad steady gaze of the morally superior.

Elvin has got to his feet, and is wiping his bloody face with the tail of his shirt. "I don't care," he says. "I won't eat it. I'll starve before I eat one bite of it."

"Relax," I tell him. "She got away."

We walk back to the edge of the woods, down the steepness, into the shade, to the wire fence. He's crying and sniffling, and when he looks at me now, it's as if he's uncertain what I might do next. It unnerves me.

"Stop it," I say.

"I can't." He stands there bawling.

"Do you want them to see you like this?" I say. "Do you?"

This convinces him. As I have said, we love Lionel and Myra, but we can never let them know us, not really. To do so is unthinkable.

"Careful," I say, holding the barbed wire up for him to crawl through. He's on all fours below me, and I see the red-splotched softness of his neck. It is laid bare, his shirt pulling back, caught on one of the teeth in the wire. I am aware of a pressure under my breastbone, a sense of possibilities I don't want to allow into the realm of my thinking. I reach down and unhook the cloth, and I'm compelled to pat him on the shoulder, a caress. Somehow, it's a gesture I make to reassure myself. He scurries through, and I straighten and look back at the field, at the cow watching us from its safe distance.

"Come on," Elvin says. There's something grudging in his voice.

I throw the knife as far as I can into the field, Lionel's knife, and then I get down on my belly and pull myself along the ground to the other side of the fence.

We go back to the cabin. Myra and Lionel have made up, and are sitting on the porch steps, holding hands. They've been necking, Lionel tells us, and then he asks what we've brought back from our safari.

"I'm hungry," Elvin says. "I hurt my face."

Myra hurries over to him, and walks inside with him to wash the scratch. "Well, son," Lionel says to me. "No luck?"

"No luck," I tell him.

"Tough out there." He smiles, turns at the sound of Myra's voice, calling from the cabin. "It's just a little scrape. It'll be fine."

"Good," Lionel says, seeming to watch me. "You okay?"

"Yes," I tell him, though I feel as though I'm going to start crying. I have an urge to tell him what I did with his knife. I want to hurl the fact of it at him like a curse. I walk back to the car and around it, to where we left the dirt road. I'm walking in the tire tracks, crying a little without quite understanding why, managing to keep it quiet. Something has been stirred up in my soul; it confuses and frightens me, while at the same time making me feel weirdly elated, too. I look back, and there's Lionel, hands on his knees, clearly content, listening to his wife's voice from inside. Myra's singing to Elvin.

I don't remember what happened the rest of that week, or what we ever did with the Madonna, the angel, the deer. In the time since then, I've been married twice. One wife left me to pursue a career in broadcasting and wound up living with a doctor in California in a big ranch-style house with an Olympic-sized swimming pool. Our son spends his summers there. Regarding the second marriage, I confess I'm the one who did the leaving, for reasons that would take too long to explain (and indeed it seems that we are all always explaining these things to one another, as if we might somehow charm our failures out of existence by the sheer volume of words). We had a daughter, before we dissolved ourselves in acrimony and silence. We're both so much better apart: there is air to breathe again. My daughter lives with her mother in New York. Elvin, who keeps a small house alone in Bedford Hills, runs into them now and again, on his way into the city, to his job with Macy's department store.

Elvin has been in and out of relationships over the years, and at times we joke about how they seem always so tangled and troubled and nervous. Wound up like a spring with discontent and worry. When he talks to me about these complex and frangible connections, I listen, I sympathize, and I remember how it was all those years ago with Lionel and Myra, when we were growing up. Often, I receive an unbidden image of Lionel sitting in the sun on that weed-sprung porch at Glass Meadow, as he listens to Myra's voice, her singing. It was so long ago, and I see it so vividly. He smiles, shaking his head. This ordinary day in their lives is ending.

There will be more serious troubles, of course.

In five years they will open a business—a Cajun food store on a busy street in the city. Neither of them knows a thing about running a store—nor, really, much about Cajun food, and it will fail within a month. They are destined to lose everything three separate times over the next twenty years. We'll live in six other rented houses; and they'll mortgage and lose two more. In their late sixties, when Elvin and I are long gone, with our separate troubles, our two sets of complications, they'll decide on a disastrous move to Seattle—this one the result, Elvin and I are fairly certain, of a professional con, which misleads them into thinking they can get started in the computer industry out there.

Elvin will travel to Washington State to bring them home. We grow in admiration for them, even as they continue to trouble us.

They sail through each disaster as they've sailed through all of their other predicaments—the same, always: humorous, passionate, odd, still in love, and still completely innocent of the effect they have on us with their indulgence in each other's whims and dreams, wishes and fantasies and impulses, their jokes and idiocy. Their happiness.

BOTANIZING UPON THE MOUNTAIN: TWO STORIES

by Lee Smith

I. Gray's Lily
*Notes of a Botanical Excursion to the
Mountains of North Carolina*
Asa Gray, 1841

We botanized for several days upon the mountains in the immediate neighborhood of Jefferson, especially the Negro Mountain, which rises abruptly upon one side of the village, the Phoenix Mountain, a sharp ridge on the other side, and the Bluff, a few miles in a westerly direction. The altitude of the former is probably between four and five thousand feet above the sea; the latter is apparently somewhat higher. They are all composed of a mica-slate; and, we should remark, we entered upon a primitive region . . . The mountain-sides, though steep or precipitous, are covered with a rich and deep vegetable mould and are heavily timbered, chiefly with chestnut, white oak, the tulip-tree, the cucumber-tree, and sometimes the sugar-maple . . . besides many of the plants already mentioned, we collected or observed upon the mountain-sides, Clematis viorna (Leather Flower) in great Abundance; Iris cryostat (Dwarf Iris) in fruit; Ligusticum actoeifolium (Love), the strong-scented roots of which are eagerly sought and eaten by boys and hogs; the Ginseng, here called sang (the roots of which are largely collected and sold to the country merchants, when fresh for about twelve cents per pound, or when dried for triple that price . . .

And perhaps this was her mission, that young woman who rises even now in my mind's eye as she was then, that bright summer day, appearing precipitously, all of a sudden, upon the windy ridge that is Bluff Mountain's northwest side.

I was alone, I was most assuredly alone. I had carefully scanned the entire rocky cliff but moments earlier. Over the valley to the north, I viewed the three-topped mountain across a vast gulf where sailed three ravens and a broad-tailed hawk; I drank in the pure fresh air as if elixir, filled with *that general awe with which a man must contemplate this fair world and all these mysteries which appear before him on every side.* Giddy, then, with reverent possibility, I had turned my glance downward to the rock beneath my feet, an unusual hornblende gneiss, as any such lofty description of the universe sends me straight back to the thing itself. *For to see a plant vividly, to seize the essential features, and to describe them aptly* offers me far more than a sufficient purpose in this world. I do not espouse philosophy. I have ever been *determined to know no theory, but to see what the facts tend to show, when fairly treated.*

Thus was I struck by the tiny pioneer plants upon that stern promontory, which offered me the unusual chance to see the various successional changes that can take place to create a forest upon bare rock, given time—and all the time in the world has been given here. Only lichens and mosses grow upon the rock at first, but, as weathering creates crevices and pockets in the rock, other plants become established. The three-toothed leaves of the cinquefoil indicate the narrowest cracks with the least soil, and silverling invades slightly larger cracks, which offer a bit more. Then come those hardy explorers, the stiff-leafed asters, silverrods, and grasses . . . then the huckleberries mixed with mountain laurel where shallow crevices occur. I was all eyes (mere seeing is for me an exquisite art) when suddenly, from nowhere, came her voice.

"Mister," she said.

It was as if my very plants had spoken! I leaped into the air, stumbled, and half fell.

"Who is there?" I said, the words themselves carried off by the wind but redundant, of course, the moment I turned to behold her.

She had come quite close, upon the rock behind me—a young mountain female in apparent good health, of fair complexion and sanguine mien, with astonishing yellow curls that tumbled down her back and blew all about her face. I say "astonishing." I confess that those curls astonished me, expecting, as I said, no human form upon that stern rock cliff, no human being for miles and miles around, much less this lovely creature all cream and gold, a vision of loveliness despite her poor crude clothing, the thick men's shoes upon her slender feet.

"Mister," she said again. A voice like bells. She stepped closer. I saw the dimple in her cheek, the tiny mole at her throat.

"What is your name?" I finally asked.

She shook her head as if to say, I do not understand. And perhaps she did not understand, or perhaps more likely chose not to tell me. In any case, she shook her head (ah, those tumbling curls!) and blushed, and looked away, out upon the windy air. She owned that air, that place. Yet she turned back to me. Her eyes a lupine (*Lupinus perennis*) blue.

"Mister."

She wanted something. There was an urgency I then perceived in that intense blue gaze, in the little fingers plucking at her skirt (a kind of folded homespun apron), in her uptilted face like a flower following the sun. I do not mean to say I am the sun! I grow confused now, as I attempt to record this moment in tranquillity in my rooms at Harvard some months later, working from my notes. These notes read:

she

yellow hair

red lips (Indian paintbrush; painted cup *Castilleja coccinea*)

closer

closer

so much skin

I shut my eyes

And that is all! All! All!

I curse myself today for the fool I was, ever the observer, too busy classifying to stop and seize the moment, grab the girl who offered herself to me (yes, this was her intention, for whatever reason, or lack of it, I do not know). Yet she *could* speak, she said "Mister," that single word which told so much about the differences between us, huge as the great space of air between the bluff and the three-topped mountain there beyond: class, education, experience (she, evidently; myself, none).

She did this: unhooked the buttons of her frock, slowly and deliberately, one by one, staring at me all the while with that intense unfathomable blue gaze, then spilling forth, white open arms, came to me, came to me, I saw blue veins on the inside of her arms, I saw shy breasts, like lilies.

I shut my eyes.

I curse myself today.

How is it possible to be so foolish?

Did I think, I wonder now, to save her from herself? Or was I simply paralyzed by ignorance and fear? unable to comprehend that which I could not grasp and classify? Oh, many are the mountains I shall traipse, as endless is the bounty and wonder of God's world. My work shall never end. A happy thought, as this work is my life entire—and yet, and yet—what are these tears, that spring from no apparent source? What is this cloud that rests so heavy on my heart?

There now. The door is locked. I must compose myself. Perhaps I should marry. In any case, these notes shall be filed away with the notation, LILIACEAE, BLUFF MOUNTAIN, 1841.

[*Asa Gray was appointed professor at Harvard University in 1842; his marriage to Jane L. Loring in 1848 was happy though childless. His life's great work,* Synoptical Flora of North America, *remained incomplete at his death in 1888.*]

II. Blazing Star

An Interview with Willard Campbell
by
Jeannie Dressler

American Folklore, sec. 3
Appalachian State University
Mr. Richards
March 12, 1996

I was born in the back room of this house where you're sitting today, and I growed up right here in the shadow of the Bluff, and buried Mama and Daddy and Lorrie and Daddy's second wife, that no-account Naomi, up on the hill there, and I reckon to be there someday myself. Me and Lorrie side by side in death as we was in life, and it's been a good life, make no mistake about it. Raised four boys, two girls, and don't owe a penny to any man.

Though they was a time when I couldn't see it, and damn near chucked it all. I was ready to run, I'll tell you, run as far and as fast as I could. I was headed for Alaska, don't ask me how I had got Alaska fixed so firm in my mind. Something Miss Wright had told us about in school, I reckon, or some picture she had showed us in a book. I had my heart set on distance. I was always a fool for distance, and wild places, the wilder the better.

This is how come I was to spend so much time up on the Bluff as a boy. Ever time I could get out of the house, there I'd go, lickety-split. Took me a day to do it. Billy and them didn't like to go up there with me neither—they said it was hanted—but I never cared if they went with me or not. I didn't give a damn. I knowed that mountain like the back of my hand, ever trail, ever cave, ever cool spring of water. And I wasn't scared of nothing.

Oh, I had heerd the story, mind you. I growed up hearing it, and I'll tell it to you in a minute, honey, just hold your horses, and you can catch it in that little machine iffen you please. That's what you come for, ain't it? The story of Perkins Rock.

But let me tell you, there's other stories too, for it was a lonesome and singular race of people that lived over there on the mountain. Daddy called it *over yander*. Said, *They do things different over yander.* It was like they was still living in the old-timey days, and it was like going back in time to go over there. I used to try to come along by Polly Stutts's house of a early morning or an evening, for then here she'd come like a lady popping out of a clock, and preach a sermon to the cow. After which she would clap her hands and sing *Oh happy day, Oh happy day, When Jesus washed my sins away.* Then they was Granny Walton what lived in a little house by the hairpin curve, she cured disease by cupping, she was famous for it. People come to her from all around. Or that old man and old woman that'd set off walking to town ever day. Taken them all day to get there—half a day going, half a day back, regular as clock-work. And never a word to a soul. Some said they was going after liquor, but some said they was going after medicine, that they had some kind of a sick child up there, but then some said they was brother and sister, so I don't know. Never did know. But I'd jump out of the road to let them pass, believe me! All hatchet-faced and stern-looking, the way they was. They give me the creeps! And Old Marsh Roark, he strolled everplace eating dinner. "Don't care if I do have a little bite to eat," he'd say. He'd eat at two or three places ever day. Then there was Tommy Whaley that everbody used to call "Dummy," he was retarded, I guess you would call it today. And anyway he'd chase us, and throw rocks, and not stop till we got to the tree line. And they was a girl named Rosie, that claimed to have saw Jesus in the road . . .

Well, *I'm a-getting to it,* I am, I just want you to understand that what Old Man Perkins saw was not so much out of the ordinary as you might suppose, considering that he lived *over yander,* where anything might happen, and did.

The way my daddy told it to me, Old Man Perkins kept a con-siderable number of sheep over there on the other side of the Bluff, and one day when he was chasing a couple that he had lost, he got lost hisself. And he was most terrible lost, and a storm was coming up in the distance, lightning and thunder everwhere, and he was near out of breath when finally he come upon a little spring that he had never seen before. He couldn't hardly figure how it was that he had not seen that spring, as good as he knowed the mountain, and as much time as he had spent upon it.

So he was leaning way down over it to get a drink when here come the awfullest hit of lightning yet, splitting the sky in two like a big jagged rip down the middle of it, and the thunder was terrible. And Old Man Perkins, peering down in the water at that moment, saw something so scary that he leaped up and ran like crazy straight down the mountain, and caught his death of cold, and died eight days later without ever speaking a word. They say that when he died, the whole cabin shook. My daddy seen it, he was there.

What was it? What did Old Man Perkins see in that pool of water? you're asking.

Well, there's some that claims he seen the face of the Devil. And that may be. But I've got another idea.

I'll tell it—I'm a-getting to it—yet it's all mixed up in my mind some way with another story. Now this-un's *mine*. It goes back to that day I was telling you about, the day I was fixing to leave home for good and all, *forever*, but yet I had determined to go up on Bluff Mountain one more time.

For I knowed the blazing star would be in bloom, and it was my pleasure in them days to lay flat out at this one particular place and see it blooming all around that big old swamp up there. The funniest feeling would come creeping over me then, it was not like anything else, it felt like them dinosaur days. For I had also found a dinosaur track, a great big old one, up in the swamp there, which I had not showed to a soul. It was my pleasure to lay up there and look out at the swamp through that rosy-colored blazing star and think on them big old creatures moving along so slow—brontosaurus, stegosaurus, I could see them so real in my mind—and I was the only one that knowed they had ever been there. Miss Wright had give me a lot of extry books to read about them, on account of I was so interested.

The other thing I thought to do that day was look my last off Perkins Rock.

So I hightailed it on up there, and yet no sooner did I fling myself down flat among the blazing star than I heerd a rustling noise back in the trees, and then some more rustling. The hair on my arms stood straight up, I'll tell you! Oh Lord, I thought, it is Mr. Perkins or the Devil, one, but then the bushes parted and here they come, a town boy and a girl so pretty it was like she had stepped out of a magazine. I knowed the boy from school, though he was some several years older than me.

"Are we finally there?" she turned around to ask him. "Is this it, then?"

He said they were. He had got himself a job over at the golf course, and had bought him some two-tone shoes. She was a summer girl. I had seen her before, driving a little red car too fast, red hair flying out behind her. I had never seen the likes of them two up here before, I'll tell you. I laid low, feeling real put out that they was spoiling my last time up on the mountain, the very day I was fixing to leave forever.

"Give us a drink then, Dicky-boy," she said. She talked real soft and slow. She came from someplace else.

He pulled a little flat silver bottle out of his pants and unscrewed the top and she tilted her head back and poured it straight down her long white throat. She was a tall skinny girl with dead white skin and these big old baby-doll eyes. Legs like pipe cleaners. He come up behind her then and started putting his hands on her and trying to kiss her but she pushed him away playful-like, still drinking.

"Come on, come on," he said.

She was still drinking. When she finally got done, she hauled off and threw that little silver bottle as hard as she could. It sailed away up in the air, turning end to end, catching the sun, and it seemed like it hung there for a full minute afore it plunged down into the swamp.

"Goddamnit, Hadley," he says, making a grab for her arm, but it was too late. The silver bottle was gone forever, down in the swamp with the dinosaur bones, and she was laughing and laughing, a silver sound like bells.

"Look here, that wasn't even mine," the boy said. "I had kind of borrowed it from the club. I reckon I'll be in for it now!"

"Well I don't care," she says. "I don't care about anything anymore." She took a little round mirror out of her purse and looked in it, putting her lipstick on. Her fingernails were long and painted, bright red, not a thing like Lorrie's hands, which were strong and square, a man's hands nearabout, and freckled. Lorrie didn't have a mirror neither.

"I said, we can get married," the boy said.

"Don't be silly," she said. "I've got to go now, okay?" Already she was as good as gone. I knowed it and that town boy did too, that Dicky. "Come on," she said. He shook his head and cussed and followed her back into the trees and when I was for sure that they was far enough gone, I stood up there amidst the blazing star, which appeared to have lost its color some by then. And then I walked on out to Perkins Rock and stood for a while and this is when it come to me, what Old Man Perkins saw in the spring that scared him to death.

It was his own face, of course, which he had probly never saw before. I could understand that. I stood looking out on distance. I seen fog in the bottom and ravens in the air and night coming on like it does. I had the powerfullest will to jump, but I did not. I stood right there till the sun set and it come pure dark and the stars come out and then a little sickle moon come up over Three Top Mountain.

I seen my whole life stretched out in front of me then like a silver chain, ever link in it hooked to the next one. So I went on home. I didn't need much light.

I went on home and woke Daddy up and told him what I was going to do, and the next day I done it. I went and got Lorrie and took her into town and married her, and that was that. I quit school and gone to work. I been working ever since. And it's been all right, I reckon. A woman don't need much sense to make a good wife. Nor to make good kids neither. Our kids was all smart, and gone to school—I seen to that—and has all made something out of theirselves.

So you can turn that thing off now, honey. I don't know if this-un's the story you come after or not, but this here is the end of it. I never did show nobody else that dinosaur track. I never did go back upon the Bluff neither. Didn't want to. Nor did I get to Alaska, nor learn whatever happened to that fancy girl. Dicky Musick ran a grocery store in Jefferson until the cancer got him, must be twenty years ago. Don't seem like it. I swear, the years seem to rush so swift now, crowding in on a man like chickens coming to feed. I ain't been well myself. No, that's all right, honey. Fact is, I was glad to talk to you. Lorrie, she never did talk much even when she was living. I'm glad to have some company. For I have done gone over yander, and I ain't got nothing but time.

HUSH

by Eric Lustbader

The first thing I saw when I fell off the rock was the hard blue Alaskan sky. It was the color of the glass eye my father handed me the first day he took me into his taxidermy workshop. Brawny clouds shouldered their way across this sky, massing along the broken-arrow ridges of the Alaska Range. The mountains seemed alive, watching without judgment. While time seemed to stand still, an iridescent insect hovered so close I could make out the astonishing complexity of its head. I could hear the peaceful, sleepy drone of the insects, the wind soughing as it caught the tangle of underbrush guarding the wide riverbank that snaked into the interior of Katmai National Park.

Then the clean, crisp air of early summer took on a peculiarly bitter taste, like gunmetal. A vast shadow reared up, and the massive, hairy muzzle of the she-bear abruptly loomed over me. Sunlight blazed an aura of saintly gold around the crown of her head. Her enormous mouth gaped, and she roared. Her small, myopic eyes were fixed on me as she drew in my scent. A paw big and heavy as a medicine ball flew at me. I had the briefest glimpse of yellow claws unsheathing. Stupefied by the gleam of sunlight refracting off their curved, translucent surface, I failed to react and was whacked into unconsciousness.

.   .   .

When I was a little girl and came running home from school crying, my mother would gather me into her arms, hold me tight, and say: "Hush . . . hush." In my mind she is always wearing a calico apron—I remember her forever cooking. She smelled of flour and butter. Crystals of sugar clung in the damp spaces between her fingers. She'd rock me back and forth and kiss the top of my head. "Hush," she'd say, even while I was brokenly telling her what had happened, "hush," until my tears dried and my heart stopped its pounding, and I'd silently open my mouth for whatever small treat she'd stick into it.

He said I was lucky to come away with a mauled shoulder. The doctor I mean. His name was Doug Fisher and I could tell he was trying hard to be charming. "Don't worry about a thing, Nina," he said, smiling as if he'd just make a joke. "I'll have you fixed up in no time."

The nurse was less amused. "How could you be so foolish?" She was a young woman, nearly my age, with a short cap of auburn hair and eyes the color of the water back home in the Florida Keys.

"Hey, all I did was sit down, okay?" I snapped. "I was tired. I thought I'd rest on a rock."

The doctor gave her a warning look. "Joanne, you've no right to talk to Nina that way."

"That's okay, doc," I said. "I can take care of myself."

"The bear could have crushed her skull like an eggshell," the nurse said stiffly.

"But it didn't." Dr. Fisher gave me a big smile. "Joanne will finish the dressing. We're going to keep you here overnight just for observation."

"I don't think so," I said. "I'll go back to the hotel as soon as you're through."

He seemed a bit taken aback, but then, I suppose doctors are used to having their suggestions followed like orders. "It would be better if you stayed, but I can't force the issue," he said. "I'll see you on the way out, okay?"

I nodded.

The nurse worked in silence for some time. When she was done, she said: "They should have warned you, your guides." She was checking my vital signs now, her words as clipped and sure as her motions. "Brown bears sometimes sleep curled up. They look like a boulder to someone who doesn't know better." Her fingers were warm against my wrist. "I can tell by your body that you like the outdoors," she continued. "But this is Alaska. It's like no other place you've ever been to. You've got to keep your wits about you here."

She thought I was stupid or careless or both, and that pissed me off royally. What can I say? Misjudging people is one of my pet peeves. "You ever go out gator hunting?"

That gave her pause. "Gator? You mean as in alligator?"

"Right. My daddy used to take me. You go at night, pushing out on a pole boat in the Everglades. The water's shallow and rust-colored, like very strong tea, from all the tannin leaching out of the mangroves. The mosquitoes are as big as 747s. You use a strong spotlight to find the gators where they're feeding. Then you stand at the front end of the boat, brace your legs, and jab a spear attached to a gig down into the spot behind their long flat skulls."

She gave me some pills with a paper cup of cold water to drink. The little plastic identification tag on her starched green hospital blouse read: JOANNE LAW. "Aren't they an endangered species?"

"You're thinking of crocodiles." I swallowed down the painkillers. "Times of the year the numbers need to be thinned. They have a lottery to see who'll hunt them."

"You sound as if you actually liked it."

There she was, judging me again. "You bet I did. I was sixteen. With my daddy teaching me, I could do anything."

"Gators are one thing, bears are another."

"Tell me about it. That she-bear scared the hell out of me."

"The feeling was mutual, I'm sure."

"Don't for a minute expect me to feel sorry for that beast." I already felt like a fool, sitting down on the bear, she needn't have rubbed it in.

Maybe she understood this, because then she said: "I can tell what you liked best about the hunting was being with your daddy. I was the same way."

"You mean you had a daddy?" My eyes were closing just as the room began to swim like a grouper around a coral reef. The pain-killers she had given me were definitely kicking in.

She laughed, which pissed me off even more. Her voice floated across to me as if from a great distance. "I think it's time I left you alone."

That was okay by me. She should've done that in the first place.

My mom always said that my smart mouth got me into all kinds of trouble. But the truth of it is, inside, where it counts, I've been inarticulate all my life. I guess I inherited that from Daddy—for him, putting two words together was like trying to strike a spark from wet sticks. He loved me, I have absolutely no doubt of that: the look of satisfaction on his face when I brought those gators in close enough for him to crack their skulls was complete. Still, I can't help wishing that just once before he got real sick he'd told me as much.

It wasn't just my daddy who made those nighttime hunts so special, it was Sunny. Her name was Sandra, but everyone called her Sunny. We were best friends when I was sixteen. We did everything together: spoke for each other, dressed identically, laughed and cried at the same things. On those nights out in 'glades we both breathed the heavy, brackish air as Daddy poled the boat through the narrow waterways between the mangroves, what the native Calusa called walking trees, on account of the way they put down roots. And by morning, exhausted by exhilaration, we'd be curled up together fast asleep, arms and legs locked in a loose, comfortable knot, while Daddy took us home across still waters the color of a flamingo's belly.

Daddy taught us about the gators, and we were avid students. We were strong, too—as strong as a lot of boys our age—Daddy had seen to it. They'd had some words over that, Mom and Daddy, because she said at sixteen it was past time I turned into a lady, but Daddy just said to her, "Lord, Marty, let her be a girl for a while longer, would you? She's got plenty of time to be a lady." Which more or less ended the argument. But I know Mom couldn't have been happy about it. She had a thing about being a lady. Living where we did and all, I guess she felt a need for me to have some what she called "normalcy" in my life. Looking back on it, I think all she wanted for me was to have a comfortable life somewhere other than the end-of-the-world Keys where there were neighbors to share things with, occasional block parties, and nice restaurants to go to on a Saturday night.

Anyway, out in the 'glades, with the spotlight full on, Sunny and I would crouch one behind the other, waiting. The black, shimmering water purled from the lip of the boat's prow, bringing to the surface little iridescent bubbles as water spiders skittered away. Except for the cone of intense light, everything was pitch-black. But that blackness was teeming with life. I hefted the spear Daddy had made himself. It was as long as I was tall. Sunny whispered to me, her chin on my shoulder. I could feel the heat of her body, and I could almost imagine us as one person, some great mythical hero setting out on a holy quest to slay a fire-breathing dragon.

Then Daddy would call out softly, suddenly switching the direction of the boat without ever seeming to move his arms, and there was the gator caught in the cone of the spotlight. Sunny and I would stand one behind the other; together we'd grip the spear and, lifting it high, strike downward with all our might.

That sound as the tines went in, just before the violent thrashing started and Daddy would rush forward with a baseball bat to deliver the coup de grâce, stayed with me a good long time. Often, I heard it in my sleep.

Katmai National Park, where I'd gone by floatplane to take a look at the brown bears—what the cowboys and militiamen in Montana and Idaho call grizzlies—was across the water from the Kenai Peninsula, a lozenge-shaped spit of land sticking out into the end of

Cook Inlet south of Anchorage. After the she-bear attacked me, they flew me to tiny Homer, on the southern tip of the peninsula, and then on to Anchorage.

Anchorage was an odd town: it had the look of a base camp people stopped at before pushing farther on into the wilderness. Every structure seemed like it had been slapped together in about three minutes. In many ways, though, this made perfect sense. The state motto was "The Last Frontier," and most Alaskans lived and died by it. If I had seen a gun-toting Wyatt Earp or Doc Holiday walking bowlegged as all get-out down the street, I swear I wouldn't have been surprised. The Alaskans seemed forever pissed off at the government, chafing like a bridled bronco under the burden of rules and regulations. That was an attitude I could relate to. I'd spent the last ten years getting kicked out of schools and jobs because I was such a goddamned rebel, because it pissed off my mother until the day she died, and because I was so unhappy with my life I just plain didn't know how to live it any other way. This rage I had inside me—this flame, this buddy—burned bright in these people who were so damn ornery they spent more than half their lives in darkness.

I thought about all this while I was walking back to the hospital for my first outpatient checkup. It was a week since I'd been patched up. Nurse Joanne was waiting for me. She carefully took apart the dressing Dr. Fisher had put on and peered at the stitches. Sitting there on the examining table, I felt cold as stone as she worked on me. And when Dr. Fisher came in, checked his work, talked to me about the weather, the salmon fishing, the influx of mosquitoes in Fairbanks, where the mercury had hit ninety degrees, anything to take my mind off him pulling out my stitches, I felt Joanne's blue eyes on me like a pressure in my chest.

"If there's anything I can do," she said as I left, "please let me know."

That night, I saw her sitting at the bar of the restaurant I'd stumbled into. She was alone, one leg crossed over the other, sipping a drink and talking to the female bartender like they were old friends. In this small town, it was likely they were. She was wearing a short skirt that showed off her legs. An athlete's long and powerful legs. As she moved, I was aware of her white man-tailored shirt pulled tight across her back, outlining every muscle. I took one step into the restaurant, then turned around and walked out. All the way back to my hotel, I felt that pressure in my chest. I started to pack the moment I got back to my room, but halfway through I sat down on the bed and stared into my suitcase. Was this it? I asked myself. The sum total of my life until now? It wasn't worth shit and I knew it. I also knew I had nowhere left to go.

I spent the next couple days wandering aimlessly around town. It was laid out in a grid, just like a military base, which wasn't surprising, since Alaska had been more or less the sole province of the U.S. armed forces for many years. In fact, the state had first been populated by retired World War II vets who had been given homesteading rights by the U.S. government—free land if they could put up a habitable structure and stay the course for six months. That would have been me, if my mother had anything to say about it: staying the course, getting it done. My mom, hiding from life down in the Keys, didn't know any other way but the straight and narrow. She was convinced that rote protected her from the chaos of life. All the decisions, all the wrong turnings you could take terrified her. She fought so hard against these things that, in the end, she just wore herself out, had an aneurysm five years ago, and buckled over into the brilliant Florida sunlight that had been her enemy for as long as I could remember.

The architecture of Anchorage was so nondescript that you ended up looking at everything else: the watchtower mountains, the immense sky with its soaring clouds, and the water of Cook Inlet, shining metallic in the flat sunlight. Not that there wasn't a certain unique beauty to the city, but that beauty really belonged to the land. This time of year—late June—the days never ended. The sun set near to midnight and rose again about three in the morning, all in the eastern horizon. There was a joke among Alaskans that you could tell the newcomers in summer by the aluminum foil they taped over their windows. It was the only way they could sleep during the short, twilit night. I welcomed the premature dawns—it had been a long time since I had slept through the night.

The first time I'd traveled west, I thought I would never see anything so massively beautiful as the Rockies, but these Alaskan mountains were more. More what? More *everything*. They seemed older, more jagged, a deeper, purer blue. Approaching them in the floatplane, I'd felt a kind of fear as the intervening years since my teens peeled away like sunburned skin, until I was left with the thing underneath, the essence of my youth that I'd tried not to think about since the morning after my high school prom when I'd come running back home, sobbing hysterically, when Mom had held out her arms, and I'd buried my face against the calico fabric, felt her slowly beating heart, while she said to me over and over: "Hush now, Nina. Hush."

One morning, Dr. Fisher showed up out of the blue. He was waiting for me outside the hotel when I came back from my daily run. I was sweaty but he didn't seem to mind.

"You missed your follow-up appointment. I wanted to see how you were doing since I pulled out the stitches," he said, but I knew better. Doctors don't make house calls anymore, leastwise not these kinds, and not at seven-thirty in the morning. Besides, I knew that look. He asked if he could take me to breakfast, and I said, okay, why not?

He was a hunky kind of guy, maybe thirty or so, athletic and handsome in a button-down, careful way. It looked like he'd spent lots of time deciding what to wear. Where I came from, he'd no doubt be playing tennis in his off-hours; here he said he did a lot of cross-country skiing.

"What brought you up here in the first place?" he asked over strong black coffee and oversized corn muffins at a fast-food joint that had the kind of bad oil- and cheese-soaked food you could find anywhere in America. At that hour, it was the only place open downtown.

"Actually, I came for the salmon fishing." I toyed with a piece of muffin. "But I didn't find it all that fascinating, standing shoulder to shoulder with everyone else, elbowing for room in the river. Give me an afternoon of bonefishing in the Keys any day. When I saw a fistfight break out between two fishermen over territory, I was out of there. So I wandered down to Homer and got talked into taking that damned floatplane to Katmai." I touched my shoulder and smiled ruefully. "I never should've gone. I don't think bears and I get along."

"Join the club," he said with a laugh. "I don't know why, but people have this thing about bears. They think they're all warm and cuddly."

"Like the teddy bear they had when they were little."

"Right." He gestured to the waitress. "The truth is bears are big, nasty beasts. They're either hungry or pissed off. My advice is to keep a very safe distance."

"You won't get an argument from me."

After the waitress refilled our coffee, he said: "I wonder, how would you feel about dinner tonight?"

He'd slipped the invitation in there so smoothly I had to laugh. "Do you always proposition your patients?"

He got red in the face, which was nice. "Before you came along it would never have entered my mind."

That was also nice. "Sure," I said, "I'd like that," even though I knew it wasn't what I wanted. By then I was really scared, and the fear drove me to do the safe thing, the conventional thing, so that I could hear again my mom saying to me, "Hush, hush."

After he dropped me back at the hotel, I went up to my room, took a shower, then got myself lost in the tourist throngs downtown. It seemed that everything I'd said to Doug was a lie. The lure of salmon fishing was just an excuse I'd used to kick myself off the Keys. The truth was I'd become bored with the ragged tank tops, the tropical drinks, the lazy, shimmering days, the listless nights back home. I figured I needed something new; maybe I just needed to get away. Life in the Keys can feel awfully small. But that wasn't the truth, either.

Then I turned the corner and saw Joanne. There was a certain stillness about her that made her movements liquid, like mercury in a test tube that's slowly turned upside down. And this quality had about it a translucence that seemed to me the opposite of the annoying opacity that comes over men when you start to talk about what's really important to you.

I was about to turn tail as I'd done in the restaurant the other night, but I couldn't. I followed her without thinking. How could I not? There was that rugged walk, the memory of her reassuring voice, her warm, competent hand on my wrist. And in a flash Sunny was beside me. Sunny as she had been with me during those nocturnal hunts, when we breathed the same air and, together, saw the moon daubed like paint on the surface of the water. Sunny as she crouched behind me, her body warm and close as the old army blanket Daddy always took with us to the beach. Sunny as she curled up against my back, sleeping deeply, contentedly in the heart of the swampy Everglades. Sunny, whose lungs had, finally, filled with carbon monoxide fumes from the tailpipe of her father's car.

Dinner was a disaster. Not the dinner so much, actually, which was delicious, but everything that came afterward. I should have known.

He took me to a posh restaurant called the Crow's Nest on the top floor of the Captain Cook Hotel. He knew the maître d', natch, so we got a choice table by a picture window that overlooked Cook Inlet. The bartender brought us cocktails and the headwaiter plunked down a platter of something "the chef had whipped up especially for us." I could see Doug was going out of his way to impress me, but all he had accomplished was to remind me of the boys I'd known in high school.

We made small talk while we nibbled on the finger food. A squadron of squat, repellent Army jets ripped apart a corner of sky, on their way back to base. The restless water, reflecting the ferocious orange and red fires of the blowoffs from the oil rigs, seemed as thick and solid as lead. I had no trouble imagining that these flames were the shadows of trolls and witches and spirits moving within the flinty heart of the mountains.

We talked about where he went to school, what sports he played, how he was thinking of going into a specialty—what guys always want to talk about—while the plates of shellfish, blush-pink salmon, and halibut appeared, were eaten, and the remains taken away. All the while Doug was talking about himself, his greedy eyes seemed to eat me alive. How I ended up at his place I'll never know; I can tell you I never had it in mind. Then I compounded the mistake by going to bed with him.

Just as with every man I'd been with, I remained aloof and detached while he labored industriously for both of us. This in itself would hardly have qualified as a disaster; it was much too familiar. As his hands slid over my bare flesh, as I was locked with him, into my mind swam the image of Joanne. In a flash, I was imagining that Doug's hands were Joanne's hands, that his groin was hers. Instead of the carefully rehearsed fake responses I'd used with my previous boyfriends, I found my body responding. Oh, my God! I squeezed my eyes shut and saw Joanne. I shuddered deeply in response.

Needless to say, that was the end of my thing with Doug. When I refused to see him again, he was surprised and hurt. He thought our sex had been stellar, but then, poor boy, he hadn't a clue the whole time I'd been thinking of Joanne. I tried to be as kind as I could, told him I had a boyfriend back in the Keys. What else could I do? The prospect of those old feelings surfacing again was too much for me. I sure as hell wasn't going to tell him the truth.

Instead of allowing myself to think about what had happened with Doug, I threw myself onto the tender mercy of the land. I was quits with the city, even a rough-and-tumble place like Anchorage. I rented a car and drove back down to Homer. The approach was spectacular. The sky was purplish, and it was raining in a series of blue-gray veils. My mother had an odd notion about such storms, which, in the Keys, were often associated with hurricanes. She'd come looking for me, certain if she didn't get me home I'd be struck by lightning or swept away by the angry sea. Her father had been killed in a lightning storm and I suppose she never got over it. She had a fear of many elemental things. Needless to say, there were always serious words between her and Daddy when I went out gator hunting with him. It took me a very long time to understand how my mother could be frightened by the things that fascinated me.

No one actually stayed in Homer itself. It was a weird little place that tried so hard to be touristy it had lost its soul. Rather, they drove or biked down the long, low tongue just past the town that jutted out into the south end of Cook Inlet. Due west, across that shining body of water lay Katmai, and the brown bears.

Along both sides were set shoulder to shoulder the tiny wooden cubicles from which you made reservations for sight-seeing ferries, fishing trips, and floatplane charters. There were also a couple of dank bars, one ratty convenience store, and two truly awful fast-food joints. I stopped by to say thank you to the owner of the floatplane service, who very generously had paid all my hospital and doctor's expenses. He was so glad to see me safe and sound he offered to take me back to Katmai free of charge. I said that wasn't necessary, but he insisted, and finally I said, What the hell, and let him book me a seat for early the next morning.

At the very end of the spit, just past where the commercial fishing fleet anchored, lay Land's End, a cozy hotel where I'd booked a room. I spent the evening walking the shoreline, watching the long day turn into an even longer twilight. Sharply angled sunlight spun off the wave crests, and white-winged gulls called shrilly as they skimmed the rocky beach looking for handouts. Fishing boats chugged into port, their holds filled with salmon. The light lent everything the hard, precise edge of colored paper cut with a razor blade. I wrapped my arms around myself against the chill of evening and wondered what the hell I was doing. Did I really want to return to Katmai and confront those bears? I didn't know. I only knew that my daddy always said you had to go back to that hard, scary thing and try again till you got it right. "That don't mean winning, necessarily," he'd said in a rare moment of articulateness. "It just means getting it so it feels okay—*here*." He poked my breastbone with his bony forefinger. It was stained like all the rest of his fingers by a lifetime of working with his taxidermy chemicals, like the roots of the tannin-rich mangroves. On the other hand, Mom's skin was white as milk. She never stepped outside without a wide-brimmed hat and a skirt that came down to her ankles. But to those hard things that scared both me and her, she'd say: "Hush now . . . hush," and fill my mouth with a warm just-baked cookie or a forkful of key lime pie.

That night, I dreamed of Sunny. I could smell her just as she had been on those humid nights in the 'glades, her clean sweat smell mingling with the citrus of the bar soap she used and the vanilla of her shampoo. My heart constricting, I began to cry. As I turned to look behind me, I noticed a gaping hole in the bottom of the boat. In the purling water I could see Sunny's reflection wavering and shimmering like a mirage at the height of day, so that she seemed to dance. I started awake and was immediately back at our high school prom. I was dancing with Andy Beckwith, a sandy-haired twerp only too anxious to hold me tight enough to urgently grind his overactive pelvis into mine. As we moved around the room, I looked over his shoulder to keep my mind off him and his lustful thoughts. I saw Sunny. She was dancing with Mickey Kaye, another one of those endless pinheads who had the hots for me. She had whispered to me sometime before that he was only dancing with her because she was my best friend. When I said she was nuts, she told me he'd already asked her to put in a good word with me. "As if that would do any good," I'd scoffed. "What a creep."

When I glanced her way again, I noticed that she had swung around. She was gazing at me over Mickey's shoulder in an odd, almost dreamy, manner. After some minutes, it occurred to me that she was maneuvering Mickey so that she could keep me in sight. What, was she worried that Andy's pelvis would suddenly whirl out of control and nail me to the wall? I looked back at her and saw her lick her lips. That must have been some kind of signal, because as soon as the band took a break, we rushed toward each other, and while sharing a Coke in a dark corner, giggled nastily over the slack-jawed hunger of our respective dates.

For a long time, I lay in the darkness of my hotel room, listening to the pounding of my heart. The images from my memories of that night rose like steam, fanning out across the ceiling until the room seemed far too crowded. Suddenly overheated, I threw the covers off me and padded over to the picture window. Pulling aside the thick drapes caused the pearly night to bleach my face. The disc of the sun hung low in the eastern sky as if pinned there. I thought about my dream, the hole in the boat where Sunny should have been. The reflection of her in the black water seemed to be calling to me. Feeling exhausted, I rested my forehead against the cool glass, and repeated to myself over and over, "Hush now . . . hush."

By six, I was showered and dressed in the layers I would need as the chill of the long morning gave grudging way to the heat of afternoon. I went down to the dining room with every intention of eating a hearty breakfast, but when the eggs and bacon arrived I couldn't even look at them. I settled for some black coffee with a ton of sugar, but my stomach wasn't happy with that, either.

At the lake where the floatplane would take off, I parked alongside several other cars. The plane was tied up at the end of the short dock. I saw a middle-aged couple getting their backpacks together, and a father helping his young daughter put on the hip waders we'd need when we landed in the river at Katmai. The girl seemed more excited than all of us combined. Farther off, nearer the floatplane, a young woman with waders already on was talking to the pilot. She turned as I slid a pair of the huge rubber boots off their hook, and I stopped dead in my tracks.

"Nina," Joanne said, with a big, easy smile, "I saw your name on the reservation list. What a coincidence."

"Yeah, isn't it," I managed to get out. Improbably, my heart, beating a painful tattoo, seemed to have taken up residence where my vocal cords should have been.

In a weird kind of trance, I took the hand she offered and pumped it.

"So how are you feeling?"

"Fine," I said. "Really good. Not too much pain since Doug took out the stitches."

"I'm glad. You still seeing him?"

I let go of her hand as if it would burn me.

"He talked to me about you."

I cocked my head. "Really?"

"Just . . ." She shrugged. "He wanted to know whether he should ask you out."

"What are you, his mommy?"

She gave me that disarming smile. Even when I was trying to piss her off, it seemed, I couldn't get anywhere. "It was advice he was after, that's all."

Behind us, at the end of the dock, the pilot was helping the child into the cabin of the floatplane. In went her father after her. The couple with the backpacks were stamping their booted feet, champing at the bit like racehorses.

"And what did you tell him?" I asked.

"That I didn't know, that it was up to him." She paused a moment while the pilot hurried by us. "He gave it a shot, didn't he?"

"That's just what he did," I said. "He gave it a shot."

She squinted at me through the morning sunlight. "Have I done something? Offended you in some way?"

The pilot returned and, at his behest, we began to move toward the floatplane. He handed a pair of binoculars to the woman with the backpack after she had boarded. Then, he helped her husband, pointing out a seat for him to take. That left us. Then we'd be off.

"Nothing I can't handle. I'm often misjudged."

"Hmm."

" 'Hmm'?" My hackles started to rise again. What was it about this woman? "What do you mean, 'hmm'?"

"It's possible . . . You know, if you misjudge yourself, it's easy for others to do the same."

"Where d'you get off talking to me like that?"

"My mistake."

"Damn straight."

I was angry the pilot sat us together, our legs jammed one against the other in the cramped cabin. I thought about complaining, but there seemed no alternative. The father and daughter were in front, the couple in back. We taxied to the end of the lake, turned around, and he revved the engine. We skimmed the water. Birds rose in our wake.

The sunlight seemed to rise with us, bearing us aloft. It struck the curved plastic windows, piercing me like an arrow. I felt like a prisoner, strapped into that tiny cabin with Joanne. Being so close to her made me jumpy, and I couldn't calm down. God*damn* her.

The still lake fell steeply away, then Homer itself, its unlovely buildings clinging rather precariously to the cool brown cliffside. Smoke from a brick chimney rose in a silken spider's thread, as if trying to draw the village up into the sky. Then we left the land behind, as we nosed out over Cook Inlet. Ahead lay the Aleutians, their crests mantled in white.

Because I didn't want to look at Joanne, I closed my eyes. The thrumming of the engines lulled me into a kind of hypnotic state where the present bent back in a circle so that I could touch the past again.

I was walking up the worn coral steps to Sunny's house. It was three weeks since we'd had our fight. It seemed like three years. I noticed that the plants were dry and the lawn needed mowing. The fat, aggressive blades tickled my bare ankles. I remember looking down at my new sandals, thinking how much Sunny coveted them. I'd even let her try them on, just before the fight, and she'd laughed in delight, twirling like a ballerina. They were expensive; her parents couldn't afford to buy her a pair of her own. The front door opened to my knock and Sunny's father appeared.

"Hello, Mr. Robbins. I heard Sunny was ill. We haven't spoken in a while."

"I know. Sunny told me."

"Can I see her?"

He glanced at the bouquet of flowers I was holding, but a moment later he sidled away, deferring to his wife. Right before he disappeared into the dark, cool interior of the house, he gave me an odd look, his eyes weary, the way people's are when they haven't slept in a while. I had the fleeting impression that the house was full of people, and yet that couldn't be right because there was a certain hush, like the slight rustle just before a bird is about to take off from its hiding place inside a bed of reeds.

Then Sunny's mother stood looking down at me. She was dressed in a simple black shift. Without makeup, her face had a hollow appearance, like an unfinished doll. She said nothing. After her eyes had registered who it was on her front stoop, her gaze rose over my head.

"I'd like to see Sunny, Mrs. Robbins. I miss her and I'd like to tell her I'm sorry. I brought these for her. See? Orange and yellow gladiolas, her favorites." I held out the flowers, now as much a peace offering to her as to Sunny, but she recoiled as if I'd thrown battery acid in her face.

"You can't see her." I remember thinking how weird it was that she'd almost choked on the words.

"Is she that mad at me? I mean, I really want to tell her . . . To make up with her. Friends always have fights, but it's not right to stay mad at each other."

"I told you, you can't see her."

"Well, okay. What about tomorrow?"

"Tomorrow," she said with a tremor, "will be the same as today."

"Please don't say that. I wish the stupid fight never happened." I waited a minute, hoping that the iceberg might melt.

"Was it a stupid fight?" She said it in the kind of hushed voice people use to say their prayers in church.

"Well, sure. Look, will you tell her how sorry I am?"

"How sorry *are* you, Nina?"

"What?" It was the oddest question, and I wondered why it made me shrivel up inside. "I want us to be best friends again, just like before."

"Best friends." She somehow made those words sound disgusting, evil. "Go home now, Nina."

Feeling confused and more alone than I'd ever felt, I threw the glads away. I slipped off my sandals and pushed them at her. "Would you at least give these to her? Tell her they're from me."

Had she heard me? I'll never know, because right then she closed the door in my face.

Whatever foodstuffs we were carrying—lunch and snacks, even breath mints and cough drops—we left on the floatplane. Bears may be as nearsighted as the Nutty Professor without his glasses but their sense of smell is top-notch. The water felt cool as we waded to the east bank of the river. In the soft purling, it seemed as if I could hear the voices of the people and animals that had stood here in years past. At that moment, they seemed no different—the people and the animals speaking one ancient language.

"Can we call a truce?"

I turned around to see Joanne looking at me, and for a moment I freaked. That look was just like the one Sunny had given me the morning after the prom, just before it had happened, just before we'd had our fight.

"You don't give up, do you?"

"Not often."

We were all in the process of pulling off our waders.

Joanne had a pair of sturdy hiking boots she was lacing up. "I must say I admire you, coming back to the place of the accident."

"I'm quite all right."

"I'm sure you are." She seemed thoughtful. "That being the case, I wonder if you would mind if I stayed close to you? These bears sometimes give me the willies."

"They do?" I didn't know whether to be skeptical or intrigued. "Then why are you here?"

"Oh, you know, it's like going back on that roller coaster that's big and fast and scary as hell. It makes you dizzy with fright, but it also gives you a charge you don't soon forget."

I knew just what she meant. That was how I'd felt about the gator hunt.

She ducked her head almost shyly. "Anyway, I'd enjoy the companionship."

I swallowed hard and nodded.

In a double line, we headed north along the wide, flat dark-brown bank, into Katmai. To our left, across the river, felt-leaf willow and balsam poplar gave way quickly to steep slopes that rose like bared knuckles into the mountains. On our side of the river, though, only low, brushlike alder and willow rambled over the humped backs of gentle rises that gradually petered out at the waterline of Cook Inlet. There was a constant droning of insects.

Joanne identified the foliage for me. For someone cooped up in a hospital all day, she knew an awful lot about the outdoors. It turned out she was something of an amateur musher, one of those people who guide the sled dogs in the Iditarod, that crazy, exhausting wintertime race across the frozen Alaskan wilderness.

Our guide led us away from the riverbank and up a narrow path beaten into the underbrush. At the crest of the low rise, the path curled around into a small meadow studded with wildflowers—red fireweed, blue chiming bell and lupine, white dwarf dogwood. We were now behind an almost semicircular clump of gnarled dwarf birch trees, Sitka alder, and diamond-leaf willow: a perfect blind from which to hunker down to watch the brown bears as they lumbered south along the river looking for berries or salmon. The sun was already warming the air and we stripped off the first of our layers. I could smell a light scent coming off Joanne like perfume from a flower.

"I brought a pair of birding binoculars," she said, showing them to me. "They let in a lot of light and things don't seem as two-dimensional as they do with the regular kind. We can share them. Here, take a look."

Whatever I trained the glasses on leaped into sharp focus, the colors bright, not washed-out like they normally were with the cheap binoculars I'd used. I could see the ripples in the water, and here and there what looked like dark creases. They were salmon shooting just above the slick gray-green surfaces of the rocks on the riverbed. How long had I been like them, struggling upstream?

Just then, the guide touched my shoulder, the way my daddy used to wake me for school, and pointed silently through an opening in the underbrush. Upriver, the brown bears were coming.

A week after Sunny's mother slammed the door in my face, I ran into her father at the supermarket.

"Hey, Nina, I been thinking 'bout you."

"How's Sunny?" I asked him. "I really miss her."

"We all do," he said, shifting a plastic string bag of grapefruit from one arm to the other. "She's dead."

He had to drop the grapefruit and grab me under the arms to stop me from staggering into a pyramid of canned cling peaches. As it was, one can spun away, cartwheeling down the aisle, looking explosive under the glare of the fluorescent lights.

He took me to the cemetery where she was buried. How had they kept the incident so secret? As if reading my mind, he said: "The sheriff and I go way back, played high school basketball together. Seems so long ago, like another lifetime." He scratched his cheek, which I saw was woolly with more than a couple days' growth.

We stood in front of her grave. It was hot under the blazing sun, but I could've used a parka. My knees were clacking together so hard I could barely hear my teeth chatter. I couldn't get my mind around this. Any minute now Daddy would shake me gently awake, I'd roll over in my bed, pick up the phone, and speak to her like we always did before school.

Sunny's father held me while the tears streamed down my face. "Now, honey," he said, "as time goes on, you might hear some funny things. The thing is Sunny—she had, well, you know, problems."

I sniffled, and he gave me his handkerchief, which I blew into. After that, I was able to say: "What problems?"

"She was troubled, you know? Poor thing, couldn't seem to shake the feeling." His head wagged sadly from side to side. "Took her to the doctor, of course, and he sent her to a specialist up in Miami. Psychiatrist at Jackson Memorial, who put her on medication. Anyway, she was better for a while, then it was like a big black funnel cloud would settle over her head and she'd sink back into herself." He squeezed me. "Kinda helpless feeling, you know? Stand around and watch someone you love beat her head against a wall till it just squeezes your heart."

"She never told me," I whispered.

"She was embarrassed, I've no doubt." He sighed. "Her mother's doing. She's a good woman, but she's got some wrongheaded ideas. Never should've treated you like that."

"I'm ashamed of how I treated Sunny. When we fought—"

He spun me around. "Now don't you go feeling like that, hear? The times Sunny spent with you, they were the happiest of her life. I know 'cause she told me straight out." He grimaced. "Pity of it all was it made her mother angry to see Sunny happier with your family than at home, made her heart ache, she'd tell me. I told her, 'God sakes, hold on there. Be happy for Sunny, she's got so damn little of it.' "

We saw a male bear first, ambling down to the water. He was huge; Joanne said over eight feet tall. With one casual swipe of his forepaw, he plucked a salmon out of the river. Snapping off the head, he left the rest of the fish behind. Joanne said the head was the only thing the bear was interested in eating because it was the most nutritious part. "If only humans were half as smart," she joked.

By the time he'd moved past us, a female with two cubs had come into view. Because of them, she was initially more wary, rumbling our way so she could give us the once over. I felt a bead of sweat crawling down my spine as she approached. Sensing my discomfort, Joanne shifted slightly so that she was between me and the she-bear.

I looked at her. "You're not afraid of them, are you?"

"Oh, I've got a healthy fear of them all right."

"Like I have of crocs," I said. "But that's not what I mean. You told me—"

She crawled closer to me and dropped her voice. "I could feel your fear, Nina. Knowing what you'd gone through, I thought it would be easier out here if someone was with you."

"Why didn't you just say that?"

"You would have bitten my head off."

That made me smile. "Yeah. I guess I would have at that."

The cubs were busy at the water's edge, good-naturedly batting each other around. They tumbled head over heels like acrobats and came up with their teeth bared. When mama joined them, it was apparently time for lunch because she rolled over on her back so they could climb aboard and suckle at her teats.

Watching them, I realized how the largest predator mammal on earth had become a favorite children's toy. In their movements and their play, as well as in their elongated bodies and far-reaching forelegs, they seemed uncannily like a species of great ape. In fact, when they sat up, those forelegs seemed more like arms. The only thing missing was a sense of family. Yes, there were mothers with their cubs, but the males were loners, coming together with females only during mating season. When I mentioned this to Joanne, she agreed: "They're like outsiders in the usual familial animal world. They don't roam in packs or form family units. The mothers stay with their cubs only long enough to give them a start. Then they drive them off."

"It seems sad, somehow."

"Feeling like an outsider always has an element of sadness to it," she replied.

"Bears don't seem to need or want friends."

"Maybe." The sunlight seemed caught in the auburn web of her short hair. "Or maybe they just have a different standard of friendship, one we have to look real hard to see and understand."

I thought about what she'd said, then looked back at her. "Listen, Joanne, there were some things I said back at the hospital I didn't mean."

She cocked her head. "Like what?"

"For one thing, I said I was surprised you had a father."

She laughed softly. "There's something very appealing about you when you're pissed off."

I turned my head away.

"What's the matter? That was a compliment."

I got up and walked down into the meadow. A breeze had sprung up, ruffling the lovely heads of the lupine, the brilliant spikes of the fireweed. The wild grasses brushed against my calves. I stood looking at the bright spots of color for some time. Amid the waving grass, they looked like a finger painting I'd done as a child. I felt the cool wind on my face, the hot sun on my shoulders. Even when I sensed Joanne come up behind me, I didn't turn around.

"Is it always this difficult for you to make friends?"

"I arrived in Anchorage already dead." I could hear her shift behind me. Or maybe it was the wind plucking at the corner of her vest. "You see, it's easy now for me to imagine the kind of effect victims of awful tragedies often speak of: a white light at the end of a dark tunnel. That's what I'm in now, that dark tunnel. Only difference is there's no white light at the end of it."

"That sounds like an awful state to keep yourself in, like being frozen in amber. Don't you think it's time to take a sledgehammer to your prison?"

"If only I could," I whispered in despair. Then I felt her hands on my shoulders, turning me slowly around to face her.

"Your pain is all over your face. I want to help."

"Why?"

"Because no one should be in this kind of pain."

"And . . . ?"

"And what? Does every act of kindness have to have an ulterior motive?"

I found I couldn't speak. At last, I managed to say: "I know what I feel."

"I wonder," she said. Then she added softly, "Tell me what happened."

.   .   .

"The prom had broken up late," I told Joanne, "later than my curfew, that's for sure."

Sunny had already managed to ditch that pinhead Mickey Kaye, but I was still stuck with Andy and his amazing whirling-dervish crotch. When Andy said, "Let's split," I looked around for Sunny, but he pulled me away before I could pick her out of the throng of kids. By that time, I'd had it with crowds myself, so I went with him. We walked for a time down Bayside. The lights from the fishing boats winked and nodded like old men dozing. The water lapped and purled softly through the black fingers of the mangroves, the tree frogs chirped from their hiding places, and the silver moon surfed on the bright crests of the scudding clouds. I pointed out Orion and the Big Dipper, but Andy was too busy drooling all over me to notice. I suppose the whole scene would have been major romantic if I'd been with the right person.

"Hey, Nina," he giggled as he threw me to the hard, lumpy coral, "come to Papa, baby." I felt him hard and hot on top of me and told him to stop goofing around and get off, it wasn't funny. When he paid no attention, I lifted my knee into his groin. I felt the short, sharp exhalation of his breath.

"*Sonuvabitch!*" he gasped.

I pushed him off me and began to run toward the building where a local company processed and canned fish and the conch they flew in from the Bahamas. He caught me in its inky shadow and threw me down again. He lay crosswise so I couldn't knee him again, and began to pull off my clothes. I was strong, maybe even as strong as he was. But he was bigger, heavier, and, more important, he had those male hormones pumping him up like one of those old ads for the ninety-pound weakling that turns into Mr. Universe in ten seconds.

The air stank of dried fish and I could hear the buzzing of the overhead power lines that snaked all along the thin crescent of the Keys from Homestead on the mainland. Those power lines were our lifeline, but they were of no help to me now.

He pushed up my dress and hooked his fingers into the waistband of my underpants, gave them a violent jerk down, and I could feel him rubbing up against me. It hurt and by this time I was really frightened. I began to cry and, ashamed of that, I slapped him across the face. That hardly deterred him. By the time he got my legs opened wide, he was panting. He stank of beer and a queer, heavy musk that nauseated me. He was heavy on me and I couldn't catch my breath.

Out of the corner of my eye I suddenly saw a black blur rearing up like some animal. Then Andy was yelling, rolling off me, and yelling some more as Sunny sank the toe of her shoe into his soft belly. He fetched up against the side of the building, staggered to his feet, caught a roundhouse right full on the jaw so that the back of his head bounced off the wood planks of the warehouse. Tears welled up in his eyes and he started to bawl as he hightailed it down the dusty road in a kind of awkward zigzag path.

Sunny crouched beside me. She put her arms around me and lifted me tenderly so that my head was cradled in her lap. I felt a great heat welling up from her. "Nina," she whispered, "Nina, are you okay? Did he hurt you?"

I was still so paralyzed with shock and fear that I just concentrated on breathing, as if it was something I had just learned to do. I started to shiver big time.

"I never should have left you," she crooned from just above me. "I shouldn't have let you go off with him."

"Sunny," I said when I found my voice.

"He didn't hurt you? He didn't . . . ?"

"No."

"Thank God." She held me close and rocked me, and ever so slowly the deep chill that had invaded me began to dissolve.

"Don't worry," she whispered. "I'll never let anything bad happen to you again."

"That's not the end of it," Joanne said. "Why did you stop?"

I bit my lip and remained silent.

"She sounds like a good friend. A wonderful friend," Joanne continued. "But something happened between the two of you, didn't it?"

I wished she'd stop pushing. I felt terrified and elated all at once, as if I was standing on the brink of a chasm. I went farther away into the meadow, and when she came after me, I whispered: "What do you want from me?"

"I want for you what you want for yourself—I want you finally, absolutely to stop lying to yourself."

"How do I do that?"

"Say what happened between you and Sunny."

"You mean confess."

"I don't mean anything," she said softly. "This is for you, Nina."

I closed my eyes and, taking a deep, shuddering breath, told her what happened afterward.

I was still shaking when we got to Sunny's. She called to tell my mom where we were; I couldn't trust myself not to break down when I heard her voice. When I took a shower, I turned the hot water way up so I was almost scalded. I closed my eyes and heard the soft slap of the water against the coral, the sweaty slap of flesh against flesh. I must have used a whole bar of soap. Just before I shut off the water, I pressed my back against the slippery tiles as if I could rid myself of the hateful impression of the coral sand. Sunny was right there when I stepped out, wrapping me in one of her parents' thick, oversized bath sheets.

There were two beds in Sunny's bedroom—she used to share the room with her older sister, who was away at her first year of college—but we both climbed into her bed, and I pretended that we had just been out on the pole boat, exhausted after a gator hunt. I curled up against Sunny, our limbs entwined in their familiar pattern.

"I kneed him once between the legs, but you got him good, didn't you?" Sunny told me in detail how she'd kicked the shit out of Andy, how she'd do it again if it would make me feel better. We talked for a little more, making up more and more venomous and outlandish schemes of getting back at Andy. I smiled into the darkness, feeling warm and protected. "My hero," I joked.

I dreamed that I was being ground down into the coral by a rough weight. It scraped my back like claws. I tried to scream but no sound came out of my mouth.

I awoke with a start. In a panic, I shook Sunny awake, begged her to look at my bare back. I had to know whether the coral had scarred me.

"Everything's fine," she said, running her hand over my back. "Your skin is as beautiful as ever."

I slumped over, so relieved that I began to weep. I felt her arm around, pulling me close.

"It's okay. Oh, it's okay."

Her lips were so close to my cheek I could feel their movement like a butterfly's kiss. I turned my head toward her. There was a breathless moment when neither of us moved. I stared into her eyes.

She whispered my name as if it were a question.

My brain had turned to sludge. Not a single thought flowed. It was as if the two of us had been removed from the real world. All that existed was Sunny and me and her naked look.

"Sunny," I said softly, "what's happening?"

"Don't you know? Oh, but you must, Nina. I love you." Then she put her lips over mine and I felt the quick adder's flick of her tongue seeking entrance.

I jerked my head away with a deep, unnameable fright climbing my spine. "What—? What the hell are you doing?"

"Nina, don't be mad. You know I'd never—"

"I trusted you," I screamed at her. "I thought you were my best friend . . ." I wiped the back of my hand across my mouth.

I paused, and Joanne wiped the tears from my eyes. Near us, a huge dragonfly darted, as if trying to stitch the sunlight into a spider's web between the flowers and the leaves, as if it saw a beautiful pattern lost to me. "Sunny longed to keep talking, to try to explain, but I wouldn't let her," I told Joanne. There was a bitter taste in my mouth. Like I'd bit down into tinfoil. "She couldn't bear the thought of losing me, but the horror and disgust on my face snapped her mouth shut. Three weeks later she killed herself."

"Listen to me, Nina, because I know these things. It's part of what I do. People take their own lives for many reasons but not because they have a fight with their best friend."

"But I rejected her. She revealed herself and I humiliated her."

"Now, at last, we're coming close to the truth," Joanne said. "I understand how you could feel guilty, no matter how misplaced that guilt might be. But there's something more, isn't there?"

The breath caught in my throat, just as if I'd swallowed that darning needle. "Don't." My voice was barely a whisper. "Don't make me."

"It takes so much effort, doesn't it, to push it away, and to keep pushing. Sunny couldn't own that part of herself and look what it did to her."

"You're wrong. I did that to her."

"The truth, Nina. Look at the truth, not the story you made up to protect yourself."

There was a vibration inside me, like a piece of crystal struck by a tuning fork. I felt my thighs trembling with the force of it.

"The truth is . . ." At the very edge, I faltered. I was engulfed by what-ifs.

"Say what you have to say." Joanne held me as the tears streamed down my face. "Whatever it is, I promise you it'll be all right."

I felt her heart beating slowly and evenly as she held me and then it came out in a rush, like a long-held exhalation. "The truth is Sunny knew me better than I knew myself. She was right. I am like her." For a crazy moment, I was sure Joanne would pull away from me in horror or alarm, but nothing like that happened. And deep inside me was an assurance that it wouldn't. So, at last, I said what I'd been terrified to admit, ever since that morning after the prom. "I remember her mouth on me, the taste of her tongue. The forbidden longing . . . I was so ashamed of those feelings." I held on tight and, true to her word, Joanne didn't let me go. "I loved her and, oh, God, I said such terrible, hurtful things to her—things I didn't mean. I told her she wasn't my friend, but she was, she was my best friend."

"But you weren't the cause of her death." She put her knuckle under my chin and lifted my head up. "You finally understand that, don't you?"

"I went back, you know. I didn't know she had died and I . . . I had decided to try to be her friend again, to erase the whole incident from my mind like it never happened. The pain was . . . I missed her; I so very badly wanted things to be the way they were before." I thought of Sunny's father and what he'd said to me that blistering-hot afternoon at her graveside. I nodded. "Yes, I'm beginning to understand."

"Good. Now all you have to do is stop trying to kill yourself."

"It was brave of you to come back here," Joanne said as we walked up the slope to where our group was watching the bears. "That was a nasty encounter you had. Either you're the luckiest person on earth or the bear pulled her punch."

It was a relief to talk about more mundane things. I felt drained, almost woozy. Also, it seemed incredible to me that Joanne was treating me no differently than she had before my confession. "What d'you mean?"

"Look at it this way. If that had been a black bear, she would have had you for lunch. Black bears may be smaller than brown bears but they're carnivores. Brown bears are strictly fruit and fish eaters. They don't see you as prey. On the other hand, you startled this bear at such close quarters she should have shattered your shoulder, not to mention mauling you but good."

I peered through a gap in the alders at a male bear happily munching on a clump of berries. He rolled over on his back. He seemed to be staring up into the sky, as if daydreaming. About what? I wondered.

"But she didn't."

"No," Joanne said from right behind me. I could smell the clean clover scent coming off her. "She whacked you just hard enough to land you in the hospital." She laughed softly. "Just think, without her you and I probably would never have met."

I turned to glance at her. "You make it sound like she had a purpose in attacking me."

"Are you skeptical?" She plucked a blade of beach lyme grass and put it between her lips, tasting it just as Sunny and I used to do when we were kids. "The Native Americans hereabouts have a saying: 'Not even God knows the mind of a bear."

"Yes, but . . ."

"You came to Alaska for a reason. Maybe she was the reason."

Now it was my turn to laugh. "Yeah, right. Like she knew me in another lifetime."

"No, you're right," Joanne said, "probably not." She looked thoughtful. "But, you know, the Aleutians revere the bear. They say bears are higher beings, the creatures through which the gods speak and, sometimes, act. There are many stories—"

"Legends."

"Yes, from long ago."

"Tales invented to frighten children and make them behave."

"Or to teach them important lessons." She took a last look at a cub scampering after its mom. "Like everything else, it's all in your point of view."

"And what's your point of view about me," I asked her as we wound our way slowly along the riverbank toward the floatplane, "now that you know what I am?"

"Should that change anything?"

"Of course. Everything's changed."

"No," she said. "Everything's just as it was this morning. I am who I am and you are who you are. You've just become aware of it."

"Then you're still my friend?"

She stopped. We were the last in the single-file line that kept moving steadily downriver. To our right was the river, to our left, just beyond the wide, rock-strewn bank, a softly waving field of high grass.

"I'm glad you consider me a friend, Nina," she said. "Truly glad."

I blushed, grateful that the rest of our party was now out of sight around a bend in the river. "I have no right to say this, but I had a fantasy about you." My heart was hammering wildly in my chest. Why was I saying this? I asked myself. I thought of Sunny opening her heart to me, and now I began to understand the enormity of the risk she had taken. But I couldn't stop myself, as I'm sure she couldn't stop herself. "When I was with Doug, I wanted to be with you. And thinking of you, picturing you in my mind, I was able to let myself go in a way I never could before."

A breathless moment went by. I was sure that she was going to reject me, just as I had rejected Sunny. Maybe she'd even tell me how I'd ruined what could have been a beautiful friendship. Part of me even thought darkly that it would have been poetic justice. But that's not what happened.

"When you were brought into the hospital," Joanne said, "I felt so protective of you, so . . ." She shrugged. "I think that's why I was so harsh. I felt afraid for you, that you might have been killed. So we got off on the wrong foot." She smiled shyly. "Even so I had my own fantasy about you."

"Really?" I felt my heart skip a beat. "What was it?"

Her smile broadened. "That you and I would be here in Katmai with the brown bears, holding hands."

Her words made me melt inside. I saw her hand moving toward mine. It reminded me of that dragonfly stitching together color and light into another reality.

Our fingertips touched and I felt a tingling running up my arm. In that moment, the she-bear rose like a leviathan out of the tall grass. She was very close to us, so close we could smell her rich animal musk. Sunlight rippled off her coat like honey spilled across a table.

Joanne and I were stunned into silence. Paralyzed, I felt my heart beating heavy in my chest. Joanne's fingers twined in mine and we held on to each other. For a long moment, the she-bear peered at us, and some sixth sense told me that this was the same bear I had startled weeks ago. Her forepaw came up, just as it had before. The long, curved claws unsheathed. But she didn't bare her teeth. There was nothing menacing in her movements, no tension at all. It was as if she knew me, had been waiting in the tall grass, watching, until the right moment.

I opened my mouth as if to speak to her, and her claws sheathed themselves. The massive forepaw remained raised, and at last I was able to say Sunny's name.

The she-bear snorted, growling low in her throat as if in response. Then she backed down into the tall grass. She moved off to where I saw the tip of a small muzzle sticking up. Her cub. Then mother and child vanished, leaving me shaking and sweating.

"Dear God," I whispered. "Tell me I didn't see what I just saw." Of course, she could tell me no such thing.

Six months later, I finally got up enough nerve to bring Joanne back to the Keys. It wasn't that I wanted to go home, not really. I had a home of my own now. But I needed to complete the circle. I wanted her to meet my daddy. Later, after he died, I would come to understand that I wanted more than that, and I'd be real grateful that I got everything I wanted.

Daddy looked pale and drawn, but that's what you look like, I guess, when your liver's been pickled in bourbon for so long. Daddy's long face was as lined as a topographical map. He had that cloying sweet smell about him that a lot of old, sick people have.

I sat down by his bedside while Joanne stood just behind me. She'd asked me what he'd say when I told him and I said I didn't know. I said he wasn't much on words. When I introduced her, Daddy moved his watery blue eyes toward her and said, "Howdy."

I took his hand in mine. It was dry and leathery, like an iguana's back. Almost the same gray-green color, too, if you discounted the dark liver spots. I brushed back his hair. His forehead was damp and clammy, and there was a dark halo of sweat on the pillowcase.

I thought of him tanned and wiry-strong, stunning those gators with great swings of his Louisville Slugger. How safe I felt with him, even standing so close to danger. I guess until the moment of their deaths we all have a need to see our fathers as bigger than life, as gods, even, making everything come right, no matter how bad the situation. I know that was how it was with me and my daddy, even then.

"How are you, Daddy?"

"Ask my liver," he said. "It's been fixing to ambush me now for some time."

I tried to laugh.

"You been gone a long time, Ace," he said. "You make the most of it?"

"I believe I did."

"You're gonna stay in Alaska, aren't you?"

"I think so, yes."

He licked his lips again, and I gave him some water. His prominent Adam's apple bobbed as he swallowed. Drinking the water seemed to tire him some and I could tell he'd rather I'd given him some bourbon. He didn't ask, though. I wasn't going to do that and he knew it.

"You know," he said at length, "when I was younger I had my chances going to work for Shell Oil and Amarada Hess, just like a lot of my buddies. Didn't though. Went into business for myself. It was tough, always a struggle. Not like if I'd had a steady salary coming in from an oil company. Plus health benefits and a proper pension. Couldn't though." His eyes on me seemed to regain much of the color they'd had when he was younger. "Truth was I wasn't like my buddies, leastways not inside. And that's what really counts in life, Ace, doesn't it? Had to do what I had to do, no matter the cost, 'cause otherwise what's life all about?" His eyes, still with that old light in them, shifted to Joanne, then back to me. "She the one?"

I felt my throat close, and tears welled up in my eyes, even though I'd promised myself I wouldn't cry in front of him.

"Yes, Daddy, she is."

"Good for you, Ace," he said. "Good for you." And, keeping a tight grip on my hand, he closed his eyes. Outside the window, the power lines hummed. Three brown pelicans swooped by in formation. We both stayed with him until the afternoon grew dark and he drifted off to sleep.

TWO DOGS AT ROWENA

by Barry Lopez

The way Badgerheart eased the pie plate away, you could tell he
was thinking about the cholesterol, that he shouldn't have had it.
He pushed the dish back across the counter so the waitress could
take it away, so he could go on nursing just the mug of coffee and
pretend he hadn't had the pie.

When the woman removed the plate, he wanted to believe some
of his disturbing afternoon went with it. After a second cup of
coffee, he left a large tip and walked out to the car, a battered
yellow Ford Pinto he'd borrowed from his sister in Portland a few
hours earlier. Badgerheart's own car was in for repairs in Eugene,
as usual. He'd told Elizabeth he just wanted to go for a drive up
the Gorge, get his thoughts together.

Elizabeth, at fifty-three four years younger than Badgerheart, was
single but well thought of by her people at Warm Springs. They
admired her sharpening ability to negotiate for them. They'd requested she work out an arrangement between people on both sides
of the Columbia, Warm Springs and Yakima, to determine the fate
of a warehouse full of rock art the Army Corps of Engineers had
removed from the dark basalt cliffs of the Gorge when they began
impounding water behind the Dalles Dam in the 1950s.

The Warm Springs elders told him, in their laconic, understated
way, that Elizabeth was doing a good job—a patient, firm, courteous
woman. They liked her. The Yakima elders, he'd heard, were also

impressed with the way she conducted things, her skill for consensus.

Elizabeth herself thought things weren't going too well, that both sets of elders were doubting her. So she'd called her brother and asked him to come up to Portland. She wanted to talk it through with him. John Badgerheart had to smile to himself when he heard her on the phone. He knew she was doing all right. The elders just like to make you squirm a little.

What made him ask for the car was an old wound that had opened during their conversation. He'd been a drunk when he was young, a fighter, and the elders had lost confidence in him. They were right at the time, he couldn't criticize their position, but it hurt all the same now that he was sober not to have the faith of the men and women he most respected, the eight or ten people on the reservation to whom he went now with nearly any problem. He'd drive across the Cascades, all the way over to the east side from Eugene, just to get their guidance. At fifty-seven he felt like a teenager in their presence. They meant him to feel that way.

Badgerheart got into the yellow Pinto with its complaining door, pulled out of the dirt parking lot onto Interstate 84 and continued up the Gorge toward Mosier. A part of the old Columbia River Highway had been restored east of that town. He planned to drive those few miles up to the overview on Rowena Plateau, above the river. From there he'd descend the Rowena loops, down the wall of the Gorge, and head back to Portland, return Elizabeth's car and take the bus to Eugene.

East of Mosier the highway passed between cherry and apple orchards and climbed a basalt rise that formed a steep bluff at the eastern end of the Columbia River Gorge. He liked the view from up there. You could see a great stretch of the river disappearing into wheat country, and the high hills and bluffs of Washington State across the water. On the Oregon side you could see two oases pocketed on benches in cliffs above the interstate. He'd first become aware of these primal places when he was a boy, picking fruit with his family around Hood River. They'd represented ever since something rich and inviolate in his memory. Only a few dozen acres each, just a couple of ponderosa pine and a scatter of white oaks around permanent ponds, these natural parks had probably not been disturbed since Lewis and Clark passed through.

A single car was parked at the overview when Badgerheart pulled in. The second thing he noticed was that an array of native grasses and flowers had recently been planted in a restored plot in the middle of the parking area. To the west, over his shoulder, he saw a couple hiking away over the plateau. Off in that direction, he knew, especially this time of year, early April, the wildflowers would be spectacular—grass widow, larkspur, yellow bells, maybe early phlox and blue-eyed Mary.

He closed the car door and went over to the chain-link perimeter fence, where he stood gazing east up the Columbia for a while with his hands in his pockets, thinking about Elizabeth's negotiations, and wondering whether it was too late for him to have children.

When he turned away he descried two animals trotting in tandem across a grassland in bloom. Dogs. He guessed by the cadence of their strides that they weren't lost, and by their carriages that they were feral. They didn't belong to anybody. He watched them come on, losing them occasionally in the swales. The direction they were headed, he estimated, they would encounter a ravine too steep to cross. What then?

They were too far away to identify clearly, but the dogs looked like the medium-sized, short-haired piebald mongrels he'd known as a boy. Camp dogs. Small-game hunters. Two hundred yards off, one of the dogs halted abruptly. He peered at Badgerheart and then sat down. The other dog stopped to look back at the first dog. Their alertness and wildness spooked Badgerheart, but he started angling along the fence toward them. In a couple of minutes he was only a hundred yards away.

They were calling him, he knew that, but he wasn't sure whether to respond. One thing, he thought, if it was a bear or a wolf calling, quite another if it was a feral dog. The first dog stood up suddenly and trotted away, fetching up the other one, both of them continuing on toward the ravine. Badgerheart followed them to the ravine's edge, where he hesitated—the fear of the prey, he reflected—

before making the steep descent of forty or fifty feet. At the bottom he headed north, in the direction of the river. Strewn with boulders and glowing with robust patches of fescue and wheatgrass, the ravine ended a few minutes later in a sharp drop hundreds of feet high, like a dry waterfall. The dogs must have climbed out along the west wall. He'd missed them. He turned back, chagrined, feeling the weight of other dead ends in his life. He was trying to find a route of ascent to the east rim when part of a dog print caught his eye. He walked up and squatted over it. He scrutinized the ground for a long moment before, just beyond the partial print, an incongruity struck him. The stalks in a clump of desert parsley were swaying rhythmically in a breeze that stirred nothing else. Badgerheart stepped over to the place and put his hands close to the stems. He felt cool air running over his skin. It took only a few moments to find a niche in the wall from which the air issued.

The opening, low to the ground in a cleft of rock hard to see, was easily big enough for a dog. Badgerheart got down on his hands and knees and crawled past pale twilight into darkness. With his cigarette lighter lit, he could see the tunnel led farther down to the left, narrowed, then veered to the right. Badgerheart estimated it would be tight, but felt compelled to go on, if only the eighteen or twenty feet to where the tunnel turned.

He closed the lighter and began to pull himself ahead on his belly. Where the tunnel opened to the right he lit the lighter again. He saw it widened there, then narrowed again before twisting upward. He crawled in as far as the vertical shaft, where he could feel the cool air coming down steady in his face while he thought. It was too late in the year to encounter hibernating bears. If he went on from here he'd have to remove his boots and his jacket. He feared getting stuck. He might return to the car for a few moments, see if Elizabeth kept a flashlight. He imagined his sister, sitting back in her apartment looking over her negotiations with the Yakima people, all of her slips of paper. He took off his jacket and his boots and pushed them aside. Once more he checked his path with the lighter, then, with his arms over his head, he began to force himself up through the opening. He was barely sliding through when his

chest swelled suddenly and he was caught. He exhaled deeply, trying to make himself smaller. Stuck. He thought about the pie. He
thought about the times he'd been so drunk he couldn't make it to
the bathroom door on his knees. He thought about the lupine and
glacier lilies growing outside, the whitlow grass and fringepod, each
perfectly fitted to the landscape. He concentrated on details of
color, the shapes of leaves, the number of petals in a bloom. His
chest eased. He rose like a cork. He pulled himself free of the
embouchure.

The glow from his lighter barely brought in the walls of a wide
cave. Pitching a few stones and listening to their clatter, he determined he was near one end of it. If he hadn't gotten turned around
the corridor led north, toward the river. He started that way, light-
ing the Zippo every so often. A couple of hundred feet and he was
stopped by the first drawing, a red ocher outline of a mountain lion.
The long tail and small head were unmistakable. Above it, curving
up into the ceiling, was a herd of six mule deer.

Badgerheart leaned in closer. He saw the image of the mountain
lion outlined with a thin, scribed line, a technique that served to
separate the animal strikingly from the wall. A few feet farther on
he found a black bear underneath another array of mule deer, five
of them serried one behind the other in dark black and red ocher.
A line of mountain goats. Farther along, on the opposite wall, he
came upon a sinuous row of salmon, nine chinook lined out head
to tail. In the dim, wavering light he couldn't take the whole frieze
in at one time.

Badgerheart continued down the wall, finding more drawings as
he went. He thought the cave might be bearing gradually east. For
a stretch of two or three hundred feet he found no drawings, and
then he saw a patch of light. He stared at it for a while before his
pupils contracted and he was able to recognize the light-colored
hills of biscuit scabland on the far side of the water and in them
the cleave of the Klickitat River.

The cave opened above a place he knew, one of the parks he'd
seen so often from the Rowena overview. He recognized the arrangement of pine and oak trees, and the pattern of serviceberry

bush and poison oak around the pond. He sensed underneath its freshness, beyond its stillness, that the site had not been frequented by humans for a long time. Less than twenty acres, surrounded on three sides by tall cliffs, the fourth side falling away steeply to the Columbia, it was a place that attracted no visitors. Probably no animal larger than a brush rabbit lived here.

Badgerheart sat in the entrance to the cave for half an hour, watching fair-weather cumulus pass to the east and listening to Steller's jays in the ponderosas. It didn't seem right to him to make any tracks here, to go any farther. He remembered his father's anguish, years ago, when the whites were building all these dams, how it would have lifted his heart if he'd been able to come here. He was floating in his father's time when one of the dogs stood up, a calico animal. It had been sleeping on a ledge only fifty feet away. When it stood, Badgerheart saw the tan flank of the other dog, lying just past the first one. The dog watched him intently, but without suspicion or alarm, as if reserving a judgment.

Badgerheart directed some prayers he remembered from his childhood to what lay before him, phrases with no particular order, a litany. He spoke the words aloud in Wasco. Once or twice he stopped so he would not lose control of his voice.

A last glance at the trees, the blooming prairie stars and broomrape, the pond, the dogs, and he left.

On his way back through the cave Badgerheart stood again before the pictographs, peering at the fine lines, knowing they were more alive in the flicker of his lighter flame than they would ever be under the beam of a flashlight. He tried to recall if anyone had ever told him a story about where the Wasco people had come from, if there was an underground origin. He tried hard to remember the word for black bear but he couldn't get it.

Going back down through the hole at the end of the cave proved easier than coming up. He scuttled along to the place where he'd left his boots and jacket and crawled out. The light had changed. For a moment he wondered whether the park and the ravine into which he had emerged were close, or whether they lay apart from each other, whether the park was isolated in another afternoon.

He climbed up from the ravine and returned to his sister's car. But for it, the lot was empty. He brushed some of the dry stems and dirt off his clothing. Far up the Columbia he could see the last of the afternoon light emblazoned on the window glass of a tug guiding a line of grain barges downriver. When he turned to go, he saw the calico dog standing just past the car, poised on three feet, one paw raised tentatively, its body quivering slightly.

THE HALF-SKINNED STEER

by Annie Proulx

In the long unfurling of his life, from tight-wound kid hustler in a wool suit riding the train out of Cheyenne to geriatric limper in this spooled-out year, Mero had kicked down thoughts of the place where he began, a so-called ranch on strange ground at the south hinge of the Big Horns. He'd got himself out of there in 1936, had gone to a war and come back, married and married again (and again), made money in boilers and air-duct cleaning and smart investments, retired, got into local politics and out again without scandal, never circled back to see the old man and Rollo, bankrupt and ruined, because he knew they were.

They called it a ranch and it had been, but one day the old man said cows couldn't be run in such tough country, where they fell off cliffs, disappeared into sinkholes, gave up large numbers of calves to marauding lions; where hay couldn't grow but leafy spurge and Canada thistle throve, and the wind packed enough sand to scour windshields opaque. The old man wangled a job delivering mail, but looked guilty fumbling bills into his neighbors' mailboxes.

Mero and Rollo saw the mail route as a defection from the work of the ranch, work that consequently fell on them. The breeding herd was down to eighty-two, and a cow wasn't worth more than fifteen dollars, but they kept mending fence, whittling ears and scorching hides, hauling cows out of mudholes, and hunting lions in the hope that sooner or later the old man would move to Ten Sleep with his woman and his bottle and they could, as had their grandmother Olive when Jacob Corn disappointed her, pull the place taut. That bird didn't fly, and Mero wound up sixty years later as an octogenarian vegetarian widower pumping an Exercycle in the living room of a colonial house in Woolfoot, Massachusetts.

One of those damp mornings the nail-driving telephone voice of a woman said she was Louise, Tick's wife, and summoned him back to Wyoming. He didn't know who she was, who Tick was, until she said, Tick Corn, your brother Rollo's son, and that Rollo had passed on, killed by a waspy emu, though prostate cancer was waiting its chance. Yes, she said, you bet Rollo still owned the ranch. Half of it anyway. Me and Tick, she said, we been pretty much running it the past ten years.

An emu? Did he hear right?

Yes, she said. Well, of course you didn't know. You heard of Wyoming Down Under?

He had not. And thought, What kind of name is Tick? He recalled the bloated gray insects pulled off the dogs. This tick probably thought he was going to get the whole damn ranch and bloat up on it. He said, What the hell is this about an emu? Were they all crazy out there?

That's what the ranch is called now, she said. Wyoming Down Under. Rollo'd sold the place way back when to the Girl Scouts, but one of the girls was dragged off by a lion, and the GSA sold out to the Banner ranch, next door, which ran cattle on it for a few years and then unloaded it on a rich Australian businessman, who started Wyoming Down Under, but it was too much long-distance work and he'd had bad luck with his manager, a feller from Idaho with a pawnshop rodeo buckle, so he'd looked up Rollo and offered to swap him a half interest if he'd run the place. That was back in 1978. The place had done real well. Course we're not open now, she said. It's winter and there's no tourists. Poor Rollo was helping Tick move the emus to another building when one of them turned on a dime and come right for him with its big razor claws. Emus is bad for claws.

I know, he said. He watched the nature programs on television.

She shouted, as though the telephone lines were down all across the country, Tick got your number off the computer. Rollo always said he was going to get in touch. He wanted you to see how things turned out. He tried to fight it off with his cane, but it laid him open from belly to breakfast.

Maybe, he thought, things hadn't finished turning out. Impatient with this game, he said he would be at the funeral. No point talking about flights and meeting him at the airport, he told her; he didn't fly, a bad experience years ago with hail, the plane had looked like a waffle iron when it landed. He intended to drive. Of course he knew how far it was. Had a damn fine car, Cadillac, always drove Cadillacs, Gislaved tires, interstate highways, excellent driver, never had an accident in his life, knock on wood. Four days; he would be there by Saturday afternoon. He heard the amazement in her voice, knew she was plotting his age, figuring he had to be eighty-three, a year or so older than Rollo, figuring he must be dotting around on a cane, too, drooling the tiny days away—she was probably touching her own faded hair. He flexed his muscular arms, bent his knees, thought he could dodge an emu. He would see his brother dropped in a red Wyoming hole. That event could jerk him back; the dazzled rope of lightning against the cloud is not the downward bolt but the compelled upstroke through the heated ether.

He had pulled away at the sudden point when the old man's girl-friend—now he couldn't remember her name—seemed to have jumped the track, Rollo goggling at her bloody bitten fingers, nails chewed to the quick, neck veins like wires, the outer forearms shaded with hairs, and the cigarette glowing, smoke curling up, making her wink her bulging mustang eyes, a teller of tales of hard deeds and mayhem. The old man's hair was falling out, Mero was twenty-three and Rollo twenty, and she played them all like a deck of cards. If you admired horses, you'd go for her with her arched neck and horsy buttocks, so high and haunchy you'd want to clap her on the rear. The wind bellowed around the house, driving crys-tals of snow through the cracks of the warped log door, and all of them in the kitchen seemed charged with some intensity of purpose. She'd balanced that broad butt on the edge of the dog-food chest, looking at the old man and Rollo, now and then rolling her glossy eyes over at Mero, square teeth nipping a rim of nail, sucking the welling blood, drawing on her cigarette.

The old man drank his Everclear stirred with a peeled willow stick for the bitter taste. The image of him came sharp in Mero's mind as he stood at the hall closet contemplating his hats. Should he take one for the funeral? The old man had had the damnedest curl to his hat brim, a tight roll on the right where his doffing or donning hand gripped it, and a wavering downslope on the left like a shed roof. You could recognize him two miles away. He wore it at the table listening to the woman's stories about Tin Head, steadily emptying his glass until he was nine times nine drunk, his gangstery face loosening, the crushed rodeo nose and scar-crossed eyebrows, the stub ear, dissolving as he drank. Now he must be dead fifty years or more, buried in the mailman sweater.

The girlfriend started a story, Yeah, there was this guy named Tin Head down around Dubois when my dad was a kid. Had a little ranch, some horses, cows, kids, a wife. But there was something funny about him. He had a metal plate in his head from falling down some cement steps.

Plenty of guys has them, Rollo said in a challenging way.

She shook her head. Not like his. His was made out of galvy, and it eat at his brain.

The old man held up the bottle of Everclear, raised his eyebrows at her: Well, darlin'?

She nodded, took the glass from him, and knocked it back in one swallow. Oh, that's not gonna slow *me* down, she said.

Mero expected her to neigh.

So what then, Rollo said, picking at the horse manure under his boot heel. What about Tin Head and his galvanized skull plate?

I heard it this way, she said. She held out the glass for another shot of Everclear, and the old man poured it, and she went on.

.   .   .

Mero had thrashed all that ancient night, dreamed of horse breeding or horse breathing, whether the act of sex or bloody, cutthroat
gasps he didn't know. The next morning he woke up drenched in
stinking sweat, looked at the ceiling, and said aloud, It could go
on like this for some time. He meant cows and weather as much
as anything, and what might be his chances two or three states over
in any direction. In Woolfoot, riding the Exercycle, he thought the
truth was somewhat different: he'd wanted a woman of his own,
not the old man's leftovers.

What he wanted to know now, tires spanking the tar-filled road
cracks and potholes, funeral homburg sliding on the backseat, was
if Rollo had got the girlfriend away from the old man, thrown a
saddle on her, and ridden off into the sunset.

The interstate, crippled by orange cones, forced traffic into single
lanes, broke his expectation of making good time. His Cadillac,
boxed between semis with hissing air brakes, showed snuffling huge
rear tires in the windshield, framed a looming Peterbilt in the back
window. His thoughts clogged as if a comb working through his
mind had stuck against a snarl. When the traffic eased and he tried
to cover some ground, the highway patrol pulled him over. The
cop, a pimpled, moustached specimen with mismatched eyes, asked
his name, where he was going. For a minute he couldn't think what
he was doing there. The cop's tongue dapped at the scraggy moustache while he scribbled.

Funeral, he said suddenly. Going to my brother's funeral.

Well, you take it easy, gramps, or they'll be doing one for you.

You're a little polecat, aren't you? he said, staring at the ticket,
at the pathetic handwriting, but the moustache was a mile gone,
peeling through the traffic as Mero had peeled out of the ranch
road that long time ago, squinting through the abraded windshield.
He might have made a more graceful exit, but urgency had struck
him as a blow on the humerus sends a ringing jolt up the arm. He

believed it was the horse-haunched woman leaning against the
chest and Rollo fixed on her, the old man swilling Everclear and
not noticing or, if noticing, not caring, that had worked in him
like a key in an ignition. She had long, gray-streaked braids; Rollo
could use them for reins.

Yeah, she said, in her low and convincing liar's voice. I'll tell you,
on Tin Head's ranch things went wrong. Chickens changed color
overnight, calves was born with three legs, his kids was piebald and
his wife always crying for blue dishes. Tin Head never finished
nothing he started, quit halfway through a job every time. Even his
pants was half buttoned, so his wienie hung out. He was a mess
with the galvy plate eating at his brain, and his ranch and his family
was a mess. But, she said, they had to eat, didn't they, just like
anybody else?

I hope they eat pies better than the ones you make, said Rollo,
who didn't like the mouthful of pits that came with the choke-
cherries.

His interest in women had begun a few days after the old man had
said, Take this guy up and show him them Ind'an drawrings, jerking
his head at the stranger. Mero had been eleven or twelve at the
time, no older. They rode along the creek and put up a pair of
mallards who flew downstream and then suddenly reappeared, pur-
sued by a goshawk who struck the drake with a sound like a hand-
clap. The duck tumbled through the trees and into deadfall trash,
and the hawk shot away as swiftly as it had come.

They climbed through the stony landscape, limestone beds
eroded by wind into fantastic furniture, stale gnawed bread crusts,
tumbled bones, stacks of dirty folded blankets, bleached crab claws
and dog teeth. He tethered the horses in the shade of a stand of
limber pine and led the anthropologist up through the stiff-
branched mountain mahogany to the overhang. Above them reared

corroded cliffs brilliant with orange lichen, pitted with holes, ridged with ledges darkened by millennia of raptor feces.

The anthropologist moved back and forth scrutinizing the stone gallery of red and black drawings: bison skulls, a line of mountain sheep, warriors carrying lances, a turkey stepping into a snare, a stick man upside-down dead and falling, red-ocher hands, violent figures with rakes on their heads that he said were feather head-dresses, a great red bear dancing forward on its hind legs, concentric circles and crosses and latticework. He copied the drawings in his notebook, saying Rubba-dubba a few times.

That's the sun, said the anthropologist, who resembled an unfin-ished drawing himself, pointing at an archery target, ramming his pencil into the air as though tapping gnats. That's an atlatl, and that's a dragonfly. There we go. You know what this is, and he touched a cloven oval, rubbing the cleft with his dusty fingers. He got down on his hands and knees and pointed out more, a few dozen.

A horseshoe?

A horseshoe! The anthropologist laughed. No, boy, it's a vulva. That's what all of these are. You don't know what this is, do you? You go to school on Monday and look it up in the dictionary.

It's a symbol, he said. You know what a symbol is?

Yes, said Mero, who had seen them clapped together in the high school marching band. The anthropologist laughed and told him he had a great future, gave him a dollar for showing him the place. Listen, kid, the Indians did it just like anybody else, he said.

He had looked the word up in the school dictionary, slammed the book closed in embarrassment, but the image was fixed for him (with the brassy background sound of a military march), blunt ocher tracing on stone, and no fleshly examples ever conquered his belief in the subterranean stony structure of female genitalia, the pubic bone a proof, except for the old man's girlfriend, whom he imagined down on all fours, entered from behind and whinnying like a mare, a thing not of geology but of flesh.

·   ·   ·

Thursday night, balked by detours and construction, he was on the outskirts of Des Moines. In the cinder-block motel room he set the alarm, but his own stertorous breathing woke him before it rang. He was up at five-fifteen, eyes aflame, peering through the vinyl drapes at his snow-hazed car flashing blue under the motel sign, SLEEP SLEEP. In the bathroom he mixed the packet of instant motel coffee and drank it black, without ersatz sugar or chemical cream. He wanted the caffeine. The roots of his mind felt withered and punky.

A cold morning, light snow slanting down: he unlocked the Cadillac, started it, and curved into the vein of traffic, all semis, double and triple trailers. In the headlights' glare he missed the westbound ramp and got into torn-up muddy streets, swung right and right again, using the motel's SLEEP sign as a landmark, but he was on the wrong side of the interstate, and the sign belonged to a different motel.

Another mudholed lane took him into a traffic circle of commuters sucking coffee from insulated cups, pastries sliding on dashboards. Half around the hoop he spied the interstate entrance ramp, veered for it, collided with a panel truck emblazoned STOP SMOKING! HYPNOSIS THAT WORKS!, was rammed from behind by a stretch limo, the limo in its turn rear-ended by a yawning hydroblast operator in a company pickup.

He saw little of this, pressed into his seat by the air bag, his mouth full of a rubbery, dusty taste, eyeglasses cutting into his nose. His first thought was to blame Iowa and those who lived in it. There were a few round spots of blood on his shirt cuff.

A star-spangled Band-Aid over his nose, he watched his crumpled car, pouring dark fluids onto the highway, towed away behind a wrecker. When the police were through with him, a taxi took him, his suitcase, the homburg funeral hat, in the other direction, to Posse Motors, where lax salesmen drifted like disorbited satellites and where he bought a secondhand Cadillac, black like the wreck but three years older and the upholstery not cream leather but sunfaded velour. He had the good tires from the wreck brought over and mounted. He could do that if he liked, buy cars like packs of cigarettes and smoke them up. He didn't care for the way the Caddy handled out on the highway, throwing itself abruptly aside when he twitched the wheel, and he guessed it might have a bent frame. Damn. He'd buy another for the return trip. He could do what he wanted.

He was half an hour past Kearney, Nebraska, when the full moon rose, an absurd visage balanced in his rearview mirror, above it a curled wig of a cloud, filamented edges like platinum hairs. He felt his swollen nose, palped his chin, tender from the stun of the air bag. Before he slept that night, he swallowed a glass of hot tap water enlivened with whiskey, crawled into the damp bed. He had eaten nothing all day, but his stomach coiled at the thought of road food.

He dreamed that he was in the ranch house but all the furniture had been removed from the rooms and in the yard troops in dirty white uniforms fought. The concussive reports of huge guns were breaking the window glass and forcing the floorboards apart, so that he had to walk on the joists. Below the disintegrating floors he saw galvanized tubs filled with dark, coagulated fluid.

On Saturday morning, with four hundred miles in front of him, he swallowed a few bites of scorched eggs, potatoes painted with canned salsa verde, a cup of yellow coffee, left no tip, got on the road. The food was not what he wanted. His breakfast habit was two glasses of mineral water, six cloves of garlic, a pear. The sky to the west hulked sullen; behind him were smears of tinselly orange shot through with blinding streaks. The thick rim of sun bulged against the horizon.

He crossed the state line, hit Cheyenne for the second time in sixty years. He saw neon, traffic, and concrete, but he knew the place, a railroad town that had been up and down. That other time he had been painfully hungry, had gone into the restaurant in the Union Pacific station although he was not used to restaurants, and had ordered a steak. When the woman brought it and he cut into the meat, the blood spread across the white plate and he couldn't help it, he saw the beast, mouth agape in mute bawling, saw the comic aspects of his revulsion as well, a cattleman gone wrong.

Now he parked in front of a phone booth, locked the car although he stood only seven feet away, and telephoned the number Tick's wife had given him. The ruined car had had a phone. Her voice roared out of the earpiece.

We didn't hear so we wondered if you changed your mind.

No, he said, I'll be there late this afternoon. I'm in Cheyenne now.

The wind's blowing pretty hard. They're saying it could maybe snow. In the mountains. Her voice sounded doubtful.

I'll keep an eye on it, he said.

He was out of town and running north in a few minutes.

The country poured open on each side, reduced the Cadillac to a finger snap. Nothing had changed, not a goddamn thing, the empty pale place and its roaring wind, the distant antelope as tiny as mice, landforms shaped true to the past. He felt himself slip back; the calm of eighty-three years sheeted off him like water, replaced by a young man's scalding anger at a fool world and the fools in it. What a damn hard time it had been to hit the road. You don't know what it was like, he had told his wives, until they said they did know, he'd pounded it into their ears two hundred times, the poor youth on the street holding up a sign asking for work, the job with the furnace man, yatata yatata ya. Thirty miles out of Cheyenne he saw the first billboard: WYOMING DOWN UNDER, Western Fun the Other Way, over a blown-up photograph of kangaroos hopping through the sagebrush and a blond child grinning in a manic imitation of pleasure. A diagonal banner warned, OPEN MAY 31.

So what, Rollo had said to the old man's girlfriend, what about that Mr. Tin Head? Looking at her, not just her face but up and down, eyes moving over her like an iron over a shirt and the old man in his mailman's sweater and lopsided hat tasting his Everclear and not noticing or not caring, getting up every now and then to lurch onto the porch and water the weeds. When he left the room, the tension ebbed and they were only ordinary people to whom nothing happened. Rollo looked away from the woman, leaned down to scratch the dog's ears, saying Snarleyow Snapper, and the woman took a dish to the sink and ran water on it, yawning. When the old man came back to his chair, the Everclear like sweet oil in his glass, glances resharpened and inflections of voice again carried complex messages.

Well, well, she said, tossing her braids back, every year Tin Head butchers one of his steers, and that's what they'd eat all winter long, boiled, fried, smoked, fricasseed, burned, and raw. So one time he's out there by the barn, and he hits the steer a good one with the ax, and it drops stun down. He ties up the back legs, hoists it up and sticks it, shoves the tub under to catch the blood. When it's bled out pretty good, he lets it down and starts skinning it, starts with the head, cuts back of the poll down past the eye to the nose, peels the hide back. He don't cut the head off but keeps on skinning, dew-claws to hock, up the inside of the thigh and then to the cod and down the middle of the belly to brisket. Now he's ready to start siding, working that tough old skin off. But siding is hard work (the old man nodded) and he gets the hide off about halfway and starts thinking about dinner. So he leaves the steer half-skinned there on the ground and he goes into the kitchen, but first he cuts out the tongue, which is his favorite dish all cooked up and eat cold with Mrs. Tin Head's mustard in a forget-me-not teacup. Sets it on the ground and goes in to dinner. Dinner is chicken and dumplins, one of them changed-color chickens started out white and ended up blue, yessir, blue as your old daddy's eyes.

She was a total liar. The old man's eyes were murk brown.

Onto the high plains sifted the fine snow, delicately clouding the air, a rare dust, beautiful, he thought, silk gauze, but there was muscle in the wind rocking the heavy car, a great pulsing artery of the jet stream swooping down from the sky to touch the earth. Plumes of smoke rose hundreds of feet into the air, elegant fountains and twisting snow devils, shapes of veiled Arab women and ghost riders dissolving in white fume. The snow snakes writhing

across the asphalt straightened into rods. He was driving in a rushing river of cold whiteout foam. He could see nothing; he trod on
the brake, the wind buffeting the car, a bitter, hard-flung dust hissing over metal and glass. The car shuddered. And as suddenly as it
had risen, the wind dropped and the road was clear; he could see
a long, empty mile.

How do you know when there's enough of anything? What trips
the lever that snaps up the STOP sign? What electrical currents fizz
and crackle in the brain to shape the decision to quit a place? He
had listened to her damn story and the dice had rolled. For years
he believed he had left without hard reason and suffered for it. But
he'd learned from television nature programs that it had been time
for him to find his own territory and his own woman. How many
women were out there! He had married three of them and sampled
plenty.

With the lapping subtlety of an incoming tide the shape of the
ranch began to gather in his mind; he could recall sharply the
fences he'd made, taut wire and perfect corners, the draws and rock
outcrops, the watercourse valley steepening, cliffs like bones with
shreds of meat on them rising and rising, and the stream plunging
suddenly underground, disappearing into a subterranean darkness of
blind fish, shooting out of the mountain ten miles west on a neighbor's place but leaving their ranch some badland red country as dry
as a cracker, steep canyons with high caves suited to lions. He and
Rollo had shot two early in that winter, close to the overhang with
the painted vulvas. There were good caves up there from a lion's
point of view.

He traveled against curdled sky. In the last sixty miles the snow
began again. He climbed out of Buffalo. Pallid flakes as distant from
one another as galaxies flew past, then more, and in ten minutes
he was crawling at twenty miles an hour, the windshield wipers
thumping like a stick dragged down the stairs.

The light was falling out of the day when he reached the pass, the blunt mountains lost in snow, the greasy hairpin turns ahead. He drove slowly and steadily in a low gear; he had not forgotten how to drive a winter mountain. But the wind was up again, rocking and slapping the car, blotting out all but whipping snow, and he was sweating with the anxiety of keeping to the road, dizzy with the altitude. Twelve more miles, sliding and buffeted, before he reached Ten Sleep, where streetlights glowed in revolving circles like van Gogh's sun. There had not been electricity when he left the place. In those days there were seventeen black, lightless miles between the town and the ranch, and now the long arch of years compressed into that distance. His headlights picked up a sign: 20 MILES TO WYOMING DOWN UNDER. Emus and bison leered above the letters.

He turned onto the snowy road, marked with a single set of tracks, faint but still discernible, the heater fan whirring, the radio silent, all beyond the headlights blurred. Yet everything was as it had been, the shape of the road achingly familiar, sentinel rocks looming as they had in his youth. There was an eerie dream quality in seeing the deserted Farrier place leaning east as it had leaned sixty years ago, and the Banner ranch gate, where the companion-able tracks he had been following turned off, the gate ghostly in the snow but still flying its wrought-iron flag, unmarked by the injuries of weather, and the taut five-strand fences and dim shifting forms of cattle. Next would come the road to their ranch, a left-hand turn just over the crest of a rise. He was running now on the unmarked road through great darkness.

Winking at Rollo, the girlfriend had said, Yes, she had said, Yes, sir, Tin Head eats half his dinner and then he has to take a little nap. After a while he wakes up again and goes outside, stretching his arms and yawning, says, Guess I'll finish skinning out that steer. But the steer ain't there. It's gone. Only the tongue, lying on the ground all covered with dirt and straw, and the tub of blood and the dog licking at it.

It was her voice that drew you in, that low, twangy voice, wouldn't matter if she was saying the alphabet, what you heard was the rustle of hay. She could make you smell the smoke from an imagined fire.

How could he not recognize the turnoff to the ranch? It was so clear and sharp in his mind: the dusty crimp of the corner, the low section where the snow drifted, the run where willows slapped the side of the truck. He went a mile, watching for it, but the turn didn't come up; then he watched for the Bob Kitchen place, two miles beyond, but the distance unrolled and there was nothing. He made a three-point turn and backtracked. Rollo must have given up the old entrance road, for it wasn't there. The Kitchen place was gone to fire or wind. If he didn't find the turn, it was no great loss; back to Ten Sleep and scout a motel. But he hated to quit when he was close enough to spit, hated to retrace black miles on a bad night when he was maybe twenty minutes away from the ranch.

He drove very slowly, following his tracks, and the ranch entrance appeared on the right, although the gate was gone and the sign down. That was why he'd missed it, that and a clump of sagebrush that obscured the gap.

He turned in, feeling a little triumph. But the road under the snow was rough and got rougher, until he was bucking along over boulders and slanted rock and knew wherever he was, it was not right.

He couldn't turn around on the narrow track and began backing gingerly, the window down, craning his stiff neck, staring into the redness cast by the taillights. The car's right rear tire rolled up over a boulder, slid, and sank into a quaggy hole. The tires spun in the snow, but he got no purchase.

I'll sit here, he said aloud. I'll sit here until it's light and then walk down to the Banner place and ask for a cup of coffee. I'll be cold but I won't freeze to death. It played like a joke the way he imagined it, with Bob Banner opening the door and saying, Why, it's Mero, come on in and have some java and a hot biscuit, before he remembered that Bob Banner would have to be 120 years old to fill that role. He was maybe three miles from Banner's gate, and the Banner ranch house was another seven miles beyond the gate. Say a ten-mile hike at altitude in a snowstorm. On the other hand, he had half a tank of gas. He could run the car for a while, turn it off, start it again, all through the night. It was bad luck, but that's all. The trick was patience.

He dozed half an hour in the wind-rocked car, woke shivering and cramped. He wanted to lie down. He thought perhaps he could put a flat rock under the goddamn tire. Never say die, he said, feeling around the passenger-side floor for the flashlight in his emergency bag, and then remembering the wrecked car towed away, the flares and car phone and AAA card and flashlight and matches and candle and power bars and bottle of water still in it, and probably now in the damn tow driver's damn wife's car. He might get a good enough look anyway in the snow-reflected light. He put on his gloves and buttoned his coat, got out and locked the car, sidled around to the rear, bent down. The taillights lit the snow beneath the rear of the car like a fresh bloodstain. There was a cradle-sized depression eaten out by the spinning tire. Two or three flat ones might get him out, or small round ones—he was not going to insist on the perfect stone. The wind tore at him; the snow was certainly drifting up. He began to shuffle on the road, feeling with his feet for rocks he could move, the car's even throbbing promising motion and escape. The wind was sharp and his ears ached. His wool cap was in the damn emergency bag.

My Lord, she continued, Tin Head is just startled to pieces when he don't see that steer. He thinks somebody, some neighbor, don't like him, plenty of them, come and stole it. He looks around for tire marks or footprints but he don't see nothing except old cow tracks. He puts his hand up to his eyes and stares away. Nothing in the north, the south, the east, but way over there in the west, on the side of the mountain, he sees something moving stiff and slow, stumbling along. It looks raw and it's got something bunchy and wet hanging down over its hindquarters. Yeah, it was the steer, never making no sound. And just then it stops and it looks back. And all that distance Tin Head can see the raw meat of the head and the shoulder muscles and the empty mouth without no tongue open wide and its red eyes glaring at him, pure teetotal hate like arrows coming at him, and he knows he is done for and all of his kids and their kids is done for, and that his wife is done for and that every one of her blue dishes has got to break, and the dog that licked the blood is done for, and the house where they lived has to blow away or burn up and every fly or mouse in it.

There was a silence and she added, That's it. And it all went against him too.

That's it? Rollo said in a greedy, hot way.

Yet he knew he was on the ranch, he felt it, and he knew this road, too. It was not the main ranch road but some lower entrance he could not quite recollect that cut in below the river. Now he remembered that the main entrance gate was on a side road that branched off well before the Banner place. He found another good stone, another, wondering which track this could be; the map of the ranch in his memory was not as bright now, but scuffed and obliterated as though trodden. The remembered gates collapsed, fences wavered, while the badland features swelled into massive prominence. The cliffs bulged into the sky, lions snarled, the river corkscrewed through a stone hole at a tremendous rate, and boulders cascaded from the heights. Beyond the barbwire something moved.

He grasped the car-door handle. It was locked. Inside, by the dashboard glow, he could see the gleam of the keys in the ignition where he'd left them to keep the car running. The situation was almost comic. He picked up a big two-hand rock, smashed it on the driver's-side window, and slipped his arm in through the hole, into the delicious warmth of the car, a contortionist's reach, twisting behind the steering wheel and down, and had he not kept limber with exercise and nut cutlets and green leafy vegetables he could never have reached the keys. His fingers grazed and then grasped, and he had them. This is how they sort out the men from the boys, he said aloud. As his fingers closed on the keys, he glanced at the passenger door. The lock button stood high. And even had it been locked as well, why had he strained to reach the keys when he had only to lift the lock button on the driver's side? Cursing, he pulled out the rubber floor mats and arranged them over the stones, stumbled around the car once more. He was dizzy, tremendously thirsty and hungry, opened his mouth to snowflakes. He had eaten nothing for two days but the burned eggs that morning. He could eat a dozen burned eggs now.

The snow roared through the broken window. He put the car in reverse and slowly trod the gas. The car lurched and steadied in the track, and once more he was twisting his neck, backing in the red glare, twenty feet, thirty, but slipping and spinning; the snow was too deep. He was backing up an incline that had seemed level on the way in but now showed itself as a remorselessly long hill, studded with rocks and deep in snow. His incoming tracks twisted like rope. He forced out another twenty feet, spinning the tires until they smoked, and then the rear wheels slewed sideways off the track and into a two-foot ditch, the engine died, and that was it. He was almost relieved to have reached this point where the celestial fingernails were poised to nip his thread. He dismissed the ten-mile distance to the Banner place: it might not be that far, or maybe they had pulled the ranch closer to the main road. A truck might come by. Shoes slipping, coat buttoned awry, he might find the mythical Grand Hotel in the sagebrush.

On the main road his tire tracks showed as a faint pattern in the pearly apricot light from the risen moon, winking behind roiling clouds of snow. His blurred shadow strengthened whenever the wind eased. Then the violent country showed itself, the cliffs rearing at the moon, the snow rising off the prairie like steam, the white flank of the ranch slashed with fence cuts, the sagebrush glittering, and along the creek black tangles of willow, bunched like dead hair. Cattle were in the field beside the road, their plumed breath catching the moony glow like comic-strip dialogue balloons.

His shoes filled with snow, he walked against the wind, feeling as easy to tear as a man cut from paper. As he walked, he noticed that one from the herd inside the fence was keeping pace with him. He walked more slowly, and the animal lagged. He stopped and turned. It stopped as well, huffing vapor, regarding him, a strip of snow on its back like a linen runner. It tossed its head, and in the howling, wintry light he saw he'd been wrong again, that the half-skinned steer's red eye had been watching for him all this time.

FIBER

by Rick Bass

I

When we came into this country, runaways, renegades, we were like birds that had to sing. It was only ten years ago but it feels like a hundred, or maybe a thousand. No person can know what a thousand years feels like, though in the first part of my life, I was a geologist, and was comfortable holding a foot-long core of earth and examining such time—a thousand years per inch.

In the section of my life after that one, I was an artist, a writer of brief stories, comfortable holding a sheaf of ten or twelve papers in which a lifetime, even several lifetimes, passed. A few thousand people would read my slim books. They would write letters to me then and talk about the characters in those stories as if they were real people, which strangely saddened me.

Then came the third life. I became an activist. It was as if some wall or dam burst within me, so that everything I wrote had to be asking for something—petition signatures, letters to Congress, etc.—instead of giving something.

But any landscape of significance, of power—whether dramatic or understated—will alter us, if we let it. And I am being bent yet again, though not without some fracturing; now I am into my fourth life, one that is built around things more immediate than the fairy-wing days of art. Even this narrative, this story, is fiction, but each story I tell feels like the last one I'll do—as if I've become like some insect or reptile trying to shed the husk of its old skin—and even now as I struggle toward the perceived freedom of the next phase of my life—the light ahead—neither you nor I can really be sure of how much of any story is fiction, or art, and how much of it is activism.

I am trying hard to move forward cleanly into the next territory. But still, things slip and fall back; the old, even when it is buried beneath the new, sometimes rises and surges, pierces through, and reappears.

Sometimes it feels as if I am running toward the future, with a hunger for it, but other times, as if I am simply fleeing the past, and those old skins. It's so hard not to look back.

I cut sawlogs to sell to the mill. Prices are high on the back end of an election year (low interest rates, new housing starts), as the economies of man heat to incandescence, fueled by China's child labor, Mexico's slave labor—fueled by the five-dollar-an-hour slave labor even in our own country—and in sawing those logs, the first thing I notice is whether the log I cut is an old tree or a young tree. I don't mean whether it's a big one or not; all the logs I cut are of roughly the same size—big enough so that I can almost get my arms around them. They are each a hundred inches long, a figure I can measure off in my sleep, or can pace blindfolded. I've cut so many hundred-inch logs that I tend to see the world now in hundred-inch increments. That's the size log the L-P mill over in Idaho needs for its laser mill, which makes short (eight-foot) two-by-fours. There's not a lot of waste. Those fucking lasers don't leave much curf.

So the logs I cut are all about the same size, but each one is a different weight and density, based mostly on age, and based also on whether the tree got to be that big by growing quickly, or slowly.

The first cut you make into the log will show you this—will tell you just about all you'd ever want to know about that tree's history. I can handle larger individual logs, and sometimes I'll hump some big-ass honker, tight, green old-growth spruce or fir—four hundred fucking pounds packed into that hundred-inch length—but mostly

I try to carry out only the medium-sized ones, which fill up the back of the truck quickly enough. Some of them will be eighty or ninety years old, if they grew slowly, in a shadowy light-starved place (the kind of woods where I best like to work in summer); and others, the same size, will be only twenty or thirty years old, with their growth rings spaced a quarter inch apart or wider—trees that are seemingly made up of liquid sunlight, trees like pipe straws sucking up water and sucking down sunlight, trees of no real integrity or use, weakened from having grown too fast, and without ever having been tested.

But I get paid for volume, not quality, and I load them into the truck too, a hundred inches at a time, though they feel light as balsa wood, after having just handled an eighty- or ninety-year-old log, and I feel guilty thinking of some carpenter three thousand miles away—Florida, perhaps—building some flimsy-shit house with those studs, the wood splitting like parchment at the first tap of a nail, and the carpenter cursing some unknowable thing, groping with his curse to reach all the way back to the point of origin, which is, what? The mill? Me? The sunlight? The brutality of supply and demand, and the omnipresent hypercapitalism here at post-consumer century's end? Finish the house, stucco over the mistakes, paint it bright red and blue, sell the sonofabitch, and move on. What're they going to do, dissect the house to cross-examine each strut, each stud? Who knows what's inside anything? More and more I'm trying not to look back at who I was, or even who I am, but at the land itself. I am trying to let the land tell me who and what I am—trying to let it pace and direct me, until it is as if I have become part of it.

This country—the Yaak Valley, way up in the northwest tip of Montana—burns and rots, both. The shape of the land beneath the forests is like the sluggish waves in an ancient, nearly petrified ocean—the waves of the northern Rockies sliding into the waves of the Pacific Northwest—so that it is like being lost, or like having found the rich dense place you were always looking for. You can walk around any given corner, and in less than a hundred paces go from fire-dependent ponderosa pine and grassland into the shadowy, dripping, mossy cedar-and-hemlock forests, rich with the almost sexual smell of rot. Tree frogs, electric-red salamanders, wood thrushes, ferns; climb a little farther, past the trickling waterfall, past the mossy-green skull of a woodland caribou, and you come to a small glacier, across which are sculpted the transient, sun-melting tracks where a wolverine passed by the day before. The tracks and scourings of the glacier across the stone mountain, beneath all that ice, are only slighty less transient.

Down the sunny back side of the mountain, you can pass through one of the old 1910 burns, where there are still giant larch snags from that fire, each one a hollowed-out home to woodpeckers and martens, bear cubs and flying squirrels. This old burned-out forest still has its own peculiar vital force and energy and seems to almost *seethe*, drunk or intoxicated on the health of so much available sunlight, and drunk on the health of the rich fire-blackened soil— the nutritiousness of ashes.

Then, farther down the mountain, you'll be back into damp creek-side silent old growth: more moss, and that dark Northwest forest—spruce and fir.

Back home, in your cabin, your dreams swirl, as if you are still traveling, still walking, even in your sleep, across this blessed landscape, with all its incredible diversity, and the strength that brings.

In the first life, back in Louisiana, I took things. Just the oil, at first, from so deep beneath the ground, and from such a distant past that at the start it did not seem like a taking; but then, gradually and increasingly, from the surface.

I took boats, big boats, from their moorings at the marina at night: sailed them all night long—sometimes alone, other times with my wife, Hope. Before dawn we would sail back toward shore, then open the boat's drain plug to try to sink it, or sometimes would even torch the boat, and swim back in that last distance to shore, and then watch, for a while, in the darkness, the beautiful flaming spectacle of waste.

I would take everything, anything. The manhole covers to flood sewers in the street. License plates. Once, a sewing machine. From a back yard in suburban Lafayette, a picnic table. It was as if I was trying to eat the world, or that part of it. The newspapers began reporting the strange disappearances. They couldn't make rhyme or reason of it—there seemed no logic to it.

I went in through windows and from dresser tops took jewelry and other riches. I didn't ever sell anything: I just took it. It pleased me. I would place the objects elsewhere. There are diamond necklaces hung in the boughs of cypress trees in Louisiana, pearl earrings in bird nests in the Atchafalaya.

I took cars: got in them and drove a short distance, then hid them, or sank them. It filled a need in me. I would look at my two hands and think, What are these made for, if not to take?

II

I believe in power. What I mean to say is I ascribe great value to it, and like to observe power in action. I like the way continents are always straining to break apart or ride up on and over one another, and I like the way the seedlings in the forest fight and scramble for light.

I like all that goes on in the hundred years of a tree's life, or the two hundred or five hundred years of its span—all the ice and snow, the windstorms, the fires that creep around the edges of some forests and sweep through and across others, starting the process all over, and leaving behind a holy kind of pause, a momentary break in power, before things begin to stretch and grow again, as vigorously as ever.

It feels good after sitting hunch-shouldered at a desk these last ten or twelve years to be hauling real and physical things out of the woods: to get the green sweet gummy sap of fir stuck to my gloves and arms; to have the chunks of sawdust tumble from the cuffs of my overalls; to have the scent of the forest in my hair. The scent of leather gloves. The weight of the logs as real as my brief life, and the scent of blue saw smoke dense in my leather boots. The sight of bright-cut, new yellow pinewood—a color that soon fades as it oxidizes, just as the skin of a gleaming fish fades quickly, immediately after it dies, or the hue of a river rock is lost forever after it is taken from the waters of its particular stream . . .

They can never find me. They have been up here looking for me—with warrants—and may come again, but I have only to slip into the woods and disappear for a while. And perhaps this is where the activism came from, after the storytelling—the desire to defend a land that defended me. The desire to give, for once, after a life-time of taking. Perhaps one reason none of us knows what's inside the heart or core of anything is that it's always changing: that things are always moving in a wave, or along an arc, and that the presence of one thing or one way of being indicates only that soon another will be summoned to replace it, as the night carves out the next day.

I thought I was made all along for writing short stories, and maybe one day again I will be—as forests recycle through succes-sion—but this landscape has carved and fit me—it is not I who have been doing the carving—and I can feel, am aware of, my change, so that now what I best fit doing is hauling logs, one at a time.

I'm short—a low center of gravity—with short legs, but long arms, and a heart and lungs that don't get tired easily. The red meat, the core of me, is stronger than ever. Certain accessories or trappings, such as ligaments, cartilage, disks, etc., are fraying and snapping—I get them mended, stitched back together, stapled and spliced or removed—but the rest of me is getting stronger, if slower, and I keep hauling the logs out one at a time, stepping gently over and around the fairy slippers and orchids, and choosing for my harvest only the wind-tossed or leaning trees, or the trees that are crowded too close together, or diseased. I try and select individual trees like notes of music. As one falls or is removed, others will rise, and with each cut I'm aware of this.

Art is selectivity—that which you choose to put in a story—and it's what you choose to leave out, too. This new life is still a kind of music, a kind of art, but it is so much more real and physical and immediate. It feels right to be doing this—hauling the logs out, carrying them over my shoulder one at a time like a railroad tie, some as dense and old as if soaked with creosote, or green life: and the more I carry, the stronger and more compact I get—the better I fit this job. As I choose and select, I listen to that silent music all around me, faint but real, of what I am doing—not imagining, but *doing*.

Sometimes I work in the rotting areas, other times in the burns. I become smeared with charcoal, blackened myself as if altered, and that night heading home I will stop and bathe in a stream and become pale again under the fierce stars and will sometimes think about the days when I wrote stories, and then further back, about the days when I practiced geology, and then even further, to child-hood and joy and wonder: but without question, these days I am a black beast moving slowly through magical woods, growing shorter each year under those logs, as each year a disk is removed—as if I am sinking deeper and deeper into the old rot of the forest, until soon I'll be waist-deep in the soil—and it is neither delicious nor frightening. It is only a fit.

A thing I do sometimes, when I have a log I'm really proud of, is to haul it out and carry it on my back and place it in the road next to some other logger's truck, or sometimes even in his truck, like a gift.

It is nothing more complex than trying to work myself out from under some imbalance of the past. It will take a long time. I haul the heaviest, densest logs I can handle.

People are curious about who's doing it—the log fairy, they call him—and here, too, I take precautions not to get caught.

I know I'll get back to hauling the balsa-wood logs from the fields of light. I know it's not going to make a difference, but I try only to select the densest, heaviest blowdown logs from the old forests of darkness, and I try to envision them, after their passage to Idaho, or Texas, or wherever they go, as standing staunch and strong within their individual houses' frameworks. I picture houses and homes getting stronger, one at a time—one board at a time—as they feed on my magical forest, and then I imagine those strong homes raising strong families, and that they will act like cells or cores scattered across the country—like little stars or satellites— that will help shore up the awful sagging national erosions here at century's end. It's a fantasy, to be sure, but you tell me which is more real: an idea, such as a stated passion or desire of one human's emotions—susceptible to the vagaries of the world, and fading through time—or a hundred-inch, 250-pound green juicy fir on one's mortal shoulder. You tell me which is fantasy and which is real.

I am so hungry for something real.

As I said, when we came up here to escape the law, we were artists: that second life. I breathed art, inhaled it—as the timber companies are inhaling this forest's timber—and I exhaled it, too. It was easy to write stories, even poems. I don't know what I'm doing, telling this one—only that for a moment, and one more time, it is as if I have stepped in a hole, or have put back on one of the old, dry coats shed from an earlier time.

It was like a pulse, back then. There was an electricity between me and the land, and there was one between Hope and the land, too, and one between Hope and myself.

I'd work in my notebooks, sitting out at the picnic table, the sunlight bright on that paper, my pen curlicuing words and shapes across that parchment like lichens spreading across the page in time-lapse warp speed—and Hope would paint landscapes with oils, as she had done down in the South.

Back then she had worked in greens and yellows and had always walked around with dried smears of it on her hands and face, so that she seemed of the land, and of the seasons, down there, as I tried to be—the incredibly fertile, almost eternal spring of greens and yellows, in the South. But then once we got up to this valley, the colors changed to blue fir, and blue rock, and to white glaciers, and white clouds; and those became the colors affixed to her body, the residue of her work. There are four distinct seasons up here, as if in some child's fairy-tale book, except that after the South's slow motion, the seasons in Yaak seem almost to gallop—the quick burning flash of dry brown heat, *August*, then an explosion of yellow and red, *October*, then more blue and white, blue and white, then winter's black-and-whiteness, seeming to last forever, but snatched away finally by the incandescence of true spring—and even now after a decade (the trees in the forest around us another inch larger in diameter, since that time), Hope is still searching to settle into the rhythms of this place—the fast rhythms on the surface, as well as the slower ones frozen in the rock below.

Between her chores of running the household and helping raise the children, I do not see much blue paint smeared on her, or any other color. And we just don't talk about art anymore. An overwhelming majority of the art we see discourages us, depresses us— no longer inspires us—and whether this is a failure within us, or within the artists of this age, we're not sure.

It seems like a hundred years, not ten, since we first came up here. Back then I would stumble through the forest, pretending to hunt—sometimes taking a deer or elk or grouse—but mostly just thinking about stories: about what had to be at stake, in any given story, and about the orthodox but time-tested critical progressions, or cyclings, of beginning, middle, and end, and about resolutions within a story, and epiphanies—all the old things. They were new to me then and seemed as fresh as if none of it had ever been done before.

I did not know the names of the things past which I was walking, or the cycles of the forests, or the comings and goings, lives and deaths, the migrations, of the animals. At night, hiking home after I'd traveled too far or been gone too long, I did not know the names of things by their scent alone, as I passed by them in the darkness.

Those kinds of things came to me, though, and are still coming, slowly, season after season, and year after year; and it is as if I am sinking deeper into the earth, ankle-deep in mulch now. I keep trying to move laterally—am drawn laterally—but recently it has begun to feel as if perhaps the beginnings of some of my old desires are returning, my burrowing or diving tendencies: the pattern of my entering the ground vertically again, as I did when I was drilling for oil; desiring to dive again, as if believing that for every emotion, every object, every landscape on the surface, there is a hidden or corresponding one at depth. We tend to think there are clean breaks between sections of anything, but it is so rarely that way, in either nature or our own lives: things are always tied together, as the future is linked, like an anchor, to the past.

Hope and I don't talk about art anymore. We talk about getting our firewood in for winter, or about the deer we saw that day. We talk about the wildflowers, or the colors of leaves—that's the closest we come to discussing the shadow or memory of her work, and we do not come close to discussing mine, either, or the memory or buried shadow of it. We talk about *things*, instead, and hand things to each other, for us to touch: a stone found on the mountain that day, or an irregular piece of driftwood. A butterfly, wind-plastered and dried, pinned to the grill of the truck, looking remarkably like the silk scarves and blouses she would often paint. We step carefully, desiring to travel further into this fourth life: being pulled into it by unknown or rather unseen rhythms. Walking quietly, carefully, as if believing perhaps we can sneak away from those old lives, and be completely free of them, and in pace—once more—with the land.

The logs that get you are almost always late in the day. You overextend, in your love, your passion for the work—the delicious physicality of it: the freedom of being able to work without acknowledging either a past or a future.

You spy a perfect fallen tree just a little bit out of your reach, and at the bottom of a steep slope. You have to cross a tangle of blowdown to get to it. It's a little larger than you should be carrying and a little too far from the truck—you've already hauled a day's worth—but all of these things conspire within you, as you stare at the log, to create a strange transformation or alteration: they reassemble into the reasons, the precise reasons, that you *should* go get that log.

And always, you do, so that you will not have to go to bed that night thinking about that log, and how you turned away from it.

III

There are seventy-six species of rare and endangered plants in this forest—Mingan Island moonwort, kidney-leaved violet, fringed onion, maidenhair spleenwort—and I know them all, each in both its flowering and dormant state. Most of them prefer the damp, dark depths of the last corners of old growth up here, though others prefer the ashes of a new fire, and appear only every two hundred years or so.

Still others seek the highest, windiest, most precarious existences possible, curled up in tiny clefts at the spartan tops of mountains, seeking brief moisture from the slow sun-glistening trickle of glaciers. I know all of them, and I watch carefully as I walk with the log across my back, across both shoulders like a yoke. Again it is like a slow and deliberate, plodding music—the music of humans— choosing and selecting which step to place where, to avoid those seventy-six species, whenever I am fortunate enough to find any of them in the woods where I am working. They say the list is growing by a dozen or so each year. They say before it's all over, there won't be anything but fire ants and dandelions. They say . . .

That is my old life. This is my new one. My newest one. This one feels different—more permanent.

Still, the old one, or old ones, try to return. My right side's stronger than my left, so I use it more. By the end of the day it's more fatigued than the left, and it feels sometimes as if I'm being turned into a corkscrew; and because of this slight imbalance, accumulated and manifested over time, my steps take on a torque that threatens to screw me down deeper and deeper into the ground, like the diamond drill bits I'd fasten to the end of the pipe string when I worked in the oil fields. And late in the day I find myself once again daydreaming about those buried landscapes, and other hidden and invisible things.

A midnight run to town with four gleaming, sweet-smelling larch logs—hundred-inch lengths, of course, and each one weighing several hundred pounds. A cold night: occasional star showers, pulsings of northern lights, sky electricity. Coyote yappings, on the outskirts of town. A tarp thrown over the back of my truck, to hide the logs. One in one logger's truck, another in his neighbor's truck. So silent. They will think it is a strange dream when they look out in the morning and see the gift trees, the massive logs, but when they go out to touch them, they will be unable to deny the reality.

The third log into the back of yet another sleeping logger's truck, and the fourth one in the front yard of the mill itself, standing on end, as if it grew there overnight.

Home, then, to my wife and children and the pursuit of peace, and balance. In the winter, Hope and I sleep beneath the skins, the hides, of deer and elk from this valley.

There is an older lady in town who works on plow horses—gives them rubdowns, massages, hoists their hips and shoulders back into place when they pop out. She says they're easy to work with, that a horse won't tense up and resist you when you press or lean in against its muscles—and when my back gets way out of line, I go visit her, and she works on it. I lie there on her table by the woodstove while she grinds her elbow and knee into certain pressure points, and she pulls and twists, trying to smooth it all back into place, and she uses a machine she calls "Sparky," too, which I have never seen, because she uses it only on my back. It sends jolts of electricity deep into my muscles—which, she says, are but electrical fibers, like cables, conduits for electricity—and the sound that Sparky makes as she fires round after round of electricity into me (my legs and arms twitching like some laboratory frog's) is like that of a staple gun.

And sometimes I imagine that it is: that she is piecing me back together; that she is pausing, choosing and selecting which treatments to use on me that day, so that I can go back into the woods to choose and select which wood to take out and send to the far-away mills, who will then send the logs to . . .

We are all still connected, up here. Some of the connections are in threads and tatters, tenuous, but there is still a net of connectivity, through which magic passes.

Whenever a new car or truck enters the valley, I run and hide. I scramble to the top of a hill and watch through the trees as it passes. They can never get me. They would have to get the land itself.

The scent of sweat, of fern, of hot saw blade, boot leather, damp bark: I suck these things in like some starving creature. All the books in my house now sit motionless and unexamined on their shelves, like the photos of dead relatives, dearly loved and deeply missed. Sometimes I pull them down, touch the spines, even say their names aloud, as one would the name of one's mother, "Mom," or one's grandmother, "Grandma."

But then I go back out into the woods.

Once, carrying a log across a frozen pond, I punched through the ice and fell in up to my chest—the cold water such a shock to my lungs that I could barely breathe—and I had to drop the log and skitter out, then build a quick fire to warm up. (The heater in my old truck doesn't work.) Some days, many days, it feels like two steps forward, two steps back, as the land continues to carve and scribe us at its own pace.

And now when I take my pickup truck to the mill, and off-load my logs next to the millions of board feet that are streaming through it like diarrhea through a bloated pig's butt in the feedlot— what difference do I think it will make? How does my fantasy stand up then, under the broad examination of reality?

In protest, I haul the logs more slowly than ever. In protest, I take more time with them. I touch them, smell them. I tithe the best ones to strangers. Sometimes I sit down and read the cross section of each log, counting the growth rings. Here is where one seedling grew fast, seeking light, struggling for co-dominance. Here is where it reached the canopy and was then able to put more of its energy into girth and width rather than height—*stability*. Here—this growth ring—is the drought year; then the succession of warm, wet growing years. Here—the next band of rings—is where the low-intensity fire crept through and around the forest, scorching the edges of but not consuming the tree.

I read each of the logs in this manner, as if reading the pages of some book. Maybe someday I will go back to books. Maybe someday I will submerge back into the vanished or invisible world, and will live and breathe theory, and maybe Hope will start painting again.

But right now I am hauling logs, and she is gardening, raking the loose earth with tools, though other times with her bare hands, and it feels like we are falling, and as if we are starving, and as if I must keep protesting, must keep hauling logs.

We try not to buy *anything* anymore—especially anything made of wood. It's all such utter, flimsy shit. One touch, one stress on it, and it all splinters to hell—a hammer or ax handle, a stepladder, a chest of drawers . . . It is all such hollow shit, and we are starving.

Before I burned out in that third life, I was asizzle. I remember awakening each morning to some burning smell within me—scorched metal against metal. Manatees, ivory-billed woodpeckers, whales, wolves, bears, bison—I burned for it all, and did so gladly. The forest loves its fires.

The reason I think I left the second life—left art, left storytelling—was because it had become so safe, so submerged. It wasn't radical enough. They say most people start out being radical and then gravitate toward moderation, and then beyond moderation to the excesses of the right, but for me it has been the opposite—as if the land itself up here is inverted, mysterious, even magical, turning humans, and all else, inside out, in constant turmoil, constant revolution.

We—all painters and writers—don't want to be political. We want to be pure, and *artistic*. But we all know, too, I think, that we're not up to the task. What story, what painting, does one offer up to refute Bosnia, Somalia, the Holocaust, Chechnya, China, Afghanistan, or Washington, D.C.? What story or painting does one offer up or create to counterbalance the ever-increasing sum of our destructions? How does one keep up with the pace? Not even the best among us are up to this task, though each tries; like weak and mortal wood under stress, we splinter, and try to act, create, heal. Some of us fall out and write letters to Congress, not novels; others write songs, but they are frayed by stress and the imbalance of the fight. Some of us raise children, others raise gardens. Some of us hide deep in the woods and learn the names of the vanishing things, in silent, stubborn protest.

I want to shock and offend. Hauling *logs*? My moderation seems obscene in the face of what is going on on this landscape, and in this country—the things, the misery, for which this country is so much the source, rather than a source of healing or compassion.

Paint me a picture or tell me a story as beautiful as other things in the world today are terrible. If such stories and paintings are out there, I'm not seeing them.

I do not fault our artists for failing to keep up with, or hold in check, the world's terrors. These terrors are only a phase, like a fire sweeping across the land. Rampant beauty will return.

In the meantime, activists blink on and off like fireflies made drowsy over pesticide meadows. Activism is becoming the shell, the husk, of where art once was. You may see one of them chained to a gate, protesting yet another Senate-spawned clear-cut, and think the activist is against something, but the activist is for something, as artists used to be. The activist is for a real and physical thing, as the artist was once for the metaphorical; the activist, or brittle husk-of-artist, is for life, for sensations, for senses deeply touched: not in the imagination, but in reality.

The activist is the emergency-room doctor trying to perform critical surgery on the artist. The activist is the artist's ashes.

And what awaits the activist's ashes: peace?

IV

There is, of course, no story: no broken law back in Louisiana, no warrant, no fairy logs. I am no fugitive, other than from myself. Here, the story falls away.

It—storytelling—has gotten so damn weak and safe. I say this not to attack from within, only to call a spade a spade: a leftover lesson from art. I read such shit, and see such shit paintings, that I want to gag; one could spray one's vomit across the canvas and more deeply affect or touch the senses—what remains of them— than the things that are spewing out into the culture now.

The left has vanished, has been consumed by the right. On one day, the Sierra Club announces it is against all logging on national forests—"zero cut"—and the next day it turns around and endorses the re-election of President Clinton, who has just endorsed the industrial liquidation of five billion board feet of timber in one year alone. Hell, yes, employment is up, this year; what about after the election, when the five billion drops back to zero because it's all been cut or washed away by erosion? Clinton tosses in the Tongass National Forest in Alaska—old-growth coastal rain forest—gives the timber company a hundred-year lease on it. And the Sierra Club, bastion of radicalism, endorses him.

Trying to shore up his base among the environmentalists—a long, nasty word for which we should start substituting "human fucking beings"—Clinton designates a couple million acres of Utah desert as a national monument; the year before, he signed a Senate bill protecting California desert. He's made moves in the direction of protecting some Pacific Northwest old growth, too, but nothing permanent for the Yaak; whether planned or not, he is making a political trade of rock for timber—trading the currency of the Yaak's wildness for votes and red rock—and this is an alteration, a transformation, that will not bear scrutiny; it is not grounded in reality, it cannot be done, it is superficial, flimsy, it is theft. He is not the environmental President. He is trading rock for timber. Each has its inherent values, but each is different.

The Yaak, perched up on the Canadian line like some hunch-shouldered griffin high in a snag looking down on the rest of the American West, can act as a genetic pipeline to funnel its wild creatures and their strange, magical blood down into Yellowstone and the Bitterroot country, and back out toward the prairies, too. It can still resurrect wildness. There is still a different thrumming in the blood of the Yaak's inhabitants.

The Nature Conservancy won't even get involved up here. The timber companies owned the land along the river bottoms in the Yaak, and they clear-cut those lands and left town rather than wait for the trees to grow back as they're always bragging they'll do: but before leaving town (shutting down the mill behind them, so that now we have to export our wood, and jobs, to Idaho), the timber companies subdivided the hell out of those clear-cut lands, turned them into ranchettes, like cow turds all up and down the river, and still I couldn't get the Conservancy to become active up here.

When I wrote to them, they wrote back and told me the valley wasn't important enough. They hadn't ever even seen the damn place. Now the vice president of the timber company—Plum Creek—that's selling off these lands in such tiny fragments sits on the board of directors of The Nature Conservancy's Montana chapter.

I don't mean to speak ill of anyone, and certainly not of a man I've never met, but Plum Creek's got tens of thousands of acres in the south end of the Yaak, in the Fisher River country, which is the only route by which a wandering grizzly can pass down out of the Yaak and into the rest of the West.

Plum Creek owns the plug, the cork, to the bottleneck—these lands were given to it by Congress more than a hundred years ago—and so now the situation is that one man—one human, more heroic than any artist or group of artists ever dreamed of being—will do either the right thing, and protect that land, or the wrong thing, and strangle the last wildness.

If you think I'm going to say *please* after what they've already done to this landscape, you can think again. It is not about being nice or courteous. It is not even about being radical. It is simply about right versus wrong, and about history: that which has already passed, and that which is now being written and recorded.

I can hear my echo. I recognize the tinny sound of my voice. I know when an edge is crossed, in art: when a story floats or drifts backward or forward, beyond its natural confines. And I understand I am a snarling wolverine, snapping illogically at everything in my pain, snapping at everyone—at fellow artists, and at fellow environmentalists.

I am going to ask for help, after all. I have to ask for help. This valley gives and gives and gives. It has been giving more timber to the country, for the last fifty years, than any other valley in the Lower 48, and still not one acre of it is protected as wilderness.

I load the logs slowly into the back of my ragged truck and drive them slowly to the mill in protest. The valley cannot ask for anything—can only give—and so like a shell or husk of the valley I am doing the asking, and I am saying please, at the same time that I am saying, in my human way, fuck you.

Somebody help. Please help the Yaak. Put this story in the President's, or Vice President's, hands. Or read it aloud to one of them by firelight on a snowy evening with a cup of cider within reach, resting on an old wooden table.

The firelight on the spines of books on the shelf flickering as if across the bones or skeletons of things; and outside, on that snowy night, the valley holding tight to the eloquence of a silence I can no longer hear over the roar of my own saw.

Somebody please do this. Somebody please help.

EARLY LESSONS

by Rita Mae Brown

Every county in America has a Dead Man's Curve named for the first speeder to fly off the road and crash below.

Our Dead Man's Curve was at the southeastern corner of the county, a mile from the Mason-Dixon Line. But the name should be changed to Fat Ass Curve, for reasons that will soon be apparent.

Julia Buckingham, "Juts," and her sister, Louise, "Wheezie," pulled together in times of crisis and fought the rest of the time. There was peace in our family only when someone was dying or some outsider had the temerity to criticize one sister to the other.

Mother told me their wrangling started in 1911 when sister Louise was sent to McSherrystown Academy in Littlestown. That's where the impressionable Louise embraced the Catholic Church. Actually, it was more like a death grip.

The rest of the family, staunch Lutherans, feigned horror at backsliding into the Church of Rome. I use the word "feigned" deliberately, because there never was a Buckingham who gave a damn about theological matters. But it was something to talk about.

Mother was six in 1911. Louise was twelve or eleven or possibly ten, depending on when she told the story. The older she got, the younger she became when she trooped off to McSherrystown Academy.

"If you can't pick on somebody, what's the use of living?" Mother would say by way of explanation for the latest tiff. Then she'd grab the phone, dialing her sister, "Beat your beads." She'd hang up before the outrage became intelligible.

Louise's explanation for this endless competitiveness between herself and Juts was simply that Julia was terminally immature.

"Wheezie, does that mean Momma's gonna die?"

"Not soon enough."

One particular summer morning back in 1950 the two sisters begged a car from my father. In those days only terribly rich families owned more than one car. Uncle Mearl, Louise's husband, refused to let her borrow his Nash, the Big Black Cockroach. I was too young to appreciate the wiles Mom must have inflicted on Daddy to get the car.

Waking me up at three in the morning, Mom put me in the backseat with a blanket, a pillow, a deck of cards, and a fishing pole. She hurtled up the steep hill that was RD #1, Queen Street Hill, and picked up Aunt Louise waiting impatiently on the front porch.

I couldn't sleep so I stared out the window as the soft rolling countryside, corn already at two feet, gave way to flat sandy soils.

Louise applied light makeup along with hot-pink lipstick. "I need my sunglasses." Mother winced.

Wheezie tied a hankie around her wrist, a habit. "I keep up with the fashions, and I'm telling you, pink is in this summer."

"Mother?"

"If you have to go to the bathroom already you can just hold it. I am not stopping every five minutes to accommodate the smallest bladder in the world."

"I don't have to go to the bathroom."

"Oh."

"I want to know how far it is to the Chesapeake Bay?"

"Two hours give or take."

"Why don't you go to sleep?" Aunt Louise suggested.

"Can't." I stood up and leaned against the front seat. "What's the Chesapeake Bay look like?"

"It's big," came Mother's informative reply.

At age almost-six I wanted to know more. "What color is it?"

"Blue. Well, sometimes green and sometimes brown. It's special."
Mother, skinny, was eating a pickled egg handed her by Louise,
who wiped her hands on a dish towel. Pickled eggs were always
packed for road trips.

"Keep your eyes on the road, Juts."

"I am. Just give me another one."

"Didn't you eat breakfast?"

"No. It was bad enough I had to get up at two-thirty."

"How come we got up so early?"

"To see the sunrise over the bay—best time to fish."

"Do I have to kill the fish if I catch it?"

"You can throw it back," Mother said.

Louise commandeered the conversation so Juts could concentrate
on driving. "The Chesapeake Bay is special because it's not saltwa-
ter but it's not freshwater. That means fish and birds live there that
don't live anywhere else."

"Will I see them?"

"If you keep your trap shut. Birds don't like noisy little girls."
Mother rolled along.

We reached Gunpowder Neck as the orange rim of the sun
nudged over the Chesapeake Bay. Birds with little feet scurried
along the water's edge. Birds with long legs stood still in rushes and
birds flew overhead only to dive into the water. I had never seen
such creatures.

Mom and Wheezie limbered their lines after the sun cleared the
horizon. Mom handed me my little red-and-yellow fishing pole.

She unfolded chairs. Mine was a canvas sling-back chair, which
meant when I sat down I couldn't get up without rolling out of the
chair and knocking it over.

Much discussion ensued as to appropriate bait. Aunt Wheezie
liked flies. She waxed eloquent on the properties of flies, which she
tied herself. Mother stuck to little red worms. I didn't want any
bait because I didn't want to catch any fish. I wanted to stare at
this sparkling expanse of water.

"Momma, what's on the other side?"

"More Maryland."

"Where's Virginia?"

"Farther down. Where the Potomac runs into the bay."

"Delaware's above us and there's a Delaware Bay—not as big as the Chesapeake though. This is the granddaddy." Louise settled down.

The cooler was between them. Each had a bucket filled with water for their catch. I had a small bucket.

Mom and Aunt Wheezie were silent for fifteen minutes, intent on their fishing. A lifetime to them.

"I don't know why you bother with those red worms."

"They wiggle. A fly doesn't wiggle."

"You catch a better grade of fish with flies. Salmon like flies."

"There aren't salmon in the bay."

"I know that. I was discussing a better grade of fish. You'll just pull up stuff that feeds on the bottom." She wrinkled her nose.

"Yeah. Yeah." Mother shaded her eyes, stuck her pole in the sand, and fetched a straw hat out of the car for Louise, baseball caps for me and her, black caps with an orange H in the middle for Hanover High.

"Julia, I wish you wouldn't wear those things. You look like a farmhand."

"And you, of course, look like the queen of England."

Mary was queen at that time. King George was still alive.

"Ha ha."

"I'm sure the queen goes fishing every day. Probably ties her own flies, too."

"Did you bring a crab cage?" Louise changed the subject.

"No, but I bet Queen Mary would have thought to bring one, and those chicken necks you throw in smell so lovely, too."

"Daddy will kill you, Momma, if you stink up his car."

"You know why the fish aren't biting? Because they hear us." Louise pinched her pink lips together.

We shut up. A small white wooden boat glided down the center of the water. No one else was around Gunpowder Neck.

The fish disdained Louise's fly. She reeled in her line, tied on another one, casting it out with a flick of her wrist. Mother observed. The red worms weren't appealing that morning either.

After a while they both fell asleep. The ragged shoreline enticed me. I couldn't fall asleep. I listened to the different bird cries, the loud squawking of the seagulls. Every now and then a fish would break water, but I was too young to know what kind it was, and I didn't want to awaken the sleeping Gorgons to find out.

I lived on a farm. I could identify red-tailed hawks, blue jays, gray fox, red fox, muskrats, but everything was different here. Even the smell was different, no rich earth smell but a brackish odor, not unpleasant. The sand underfoot seemed to have no smell at all.

The rising heat finally roused Mom.

"Catch anything?"

"No, ma'am."

"I don't know why the fish aren't biting." Louise, on hearing us, roused herself.

"It's that dreadful shade of lipstick you're wearing." Mother lit up a Chesterfield.

"Aunt Louise."

"Huh?"

"We aren't having any luck, are we?"

"Not a nibble. I'm hungry for soft-shell crabs," Mother announced.

"Well—" Louise drawled out the word.

"We aren't going to catch a minnow." Mother reeled in her line.

Within minutes Mom and Wheezie were packed up, rumbling down the sandy shell road, turning out onto the paved highway. Soon we saw a white sign with a red crab on it swaying in the light breeze.

No matter how Mother prodded, I wasn't going to eat a soft-shell crab. Anything with eight legs is too much for me.

"It's a great delicacy." Wheezie tied a bib around her neck.

"Can't get this anywhere else in the world." Mother did likewise.

"I hate crabs."

"How do you know? You never ate one."

"Yes, I did. At the Flag Day picnic."

"That was crab cake not a crab." Mother informed me as the waitress took her order. "Well?" She stared at me.

"A hamburger and fries."

"Coward," Mom muttered.

"More for us." Aunt Wheezie also ordered soft-shell crabs. "Juts, better put on a blouse—your shoulders are getting red."

As Mother hopped up to fetch her blouse, I asked my aunt, checking herself in a small handheld mirror, "Think a crab could grow big enough to eat us?"

"They do. I mean they eat us when we're dead. Crabs feed on the bottom of the bay."

Mother sat down as the crabs and my hamburger were delivered. I could hardly look at the smallish cooked creatures. I had visions of them crawling over a dead man's face pulling off his nose, kind of like me eating the cherry on the sundae first.

"Mmm." Mother attacked the first crab.

"Mom, Aunt Wheezie says crabs eat dead people."

As she sucked a tiny claw, she nodded. "Yep. Dead anything. I think that's why the meat is so sweet."

As I turned green, they laughed at me.

"Someone's got to clean up. They're Nature's garbagemen," Aunt Wheezie helpfully added.

"I thought that's why we buried our dead. So things wouldn't eat them."

"Yes, but we can't get everybody. Some people drop in the woods or fall off boats. When your number's up, it's up." She was grabbing her second crab as it reposed on the newspaper. "Seven or seventy. Makes no matter. When your number's up, adios."

"Julia, the Lord calls. Don't tell her stuff like that."

"Calls what, Louise? You use that phrase at every funeral we attend. I want to know exactly what the Lord says when He calls. I mean, is He talking into a giant telephone in the sky? Does He ever make a mistake dialing and say 'Excuse me, wrong number'?"

Eyebrows knit together, Louise sipped her Coke then placed the cold bottle on the table exactly where its wet ring was. "I'm not lowering myself to this discussion."

"Does God care if a soft-shell crab dies?" I asked.

"He knows if a sparrow dies. Of course, He cares if the crab dies," Aunt Wheezie answered with conviction.

"Does He care that you're eating the crab?"

"No." Mother reached for her third, little peppercorns sticking to its underbody. "Everybody eats everybody. It's the law of nature."

"It's not like that. Kid, don't listen to her." Louise ate more slowly than Mother, which was a mistake because Mom would grab a crab off her newspaper if she wasn't careful.

"It most certainly is." Mother leaned over in my direction so I guarded my french fries. "Out there in the bay and the ocean tiny things float around. A slightly bigger bug eats them, a snail eats the bug, and a fish eats the snail. A crab eats the fish, but a squid eats the crab—"

"You don't know what a squid eats." Louise laughed.

"I know it would squirt ink in your face. Anything to blot out that lipstick, Louise. You've got to get away from the pinks."

"I'm not wearing red. Looks loose." She cast a sideways glance at me.

"Oh, balls." Mother merrily returned to her subject. "So each animal is slightly bigger than the animal it eats until finally there's a shark or a whale."

"Julia Ellen, whales don't eat sharks. They swim around the ocean and filter plankton between their teeth."

"Since when are you a marine biologist?"

"I read National Geographic. The only magazine you've ever read in your life is Silver Screen."

"Only for the hairdos!"

"Ha!"

"She reads them for the clothes, too." I defended Mother.

"Yes, well," Aunt Louise sniffed, "someone once told her she resembled Mary Pickford. She doesn't remotely resemble Mary Pickford but it went to her head."

"You know, I could be real mean right now." Mother shook a claw at her sister.

"Now?"

They both glanced at me as I left my seat. No one wanted to be in the middle of a fight between the Buckingham sisters.

"Sit down." Mother ordered as people were looking at us. Then she whispered, "I'm not going to throw it at her."

"As I was saying." Aunt Wheezie smiled sweetly at me and spoke a touch too loudly. "There's a food chain. Everything makes sense."

"Louise, I was the one saying it."

"Yes, well, we agree."

Mother laughed.

"Anything else, ladies?" The waitress returned, fishing in her apron for the bill.

"Nothing, thank you." Aunt Louise was overly polite.

They argued about who eats whom most of the way home, with Aunt Louise finally conceding that a disaster might rupture the food chain.

Mother said people could mess it up. We could kill off all the animals like we killed off the dodo bird. They argued some more.

In those days gas stations were few and far between.

Aunt Louise, needing to answer nature's call, asked Mother to pull over. We happened to be at Dead Man's Curve, about three miles from home.

"Louise, go in front of the car. By the time a car passes us they won't look back."

For whatever reason, perhaps because her bladder was pressing, Aunt Louise didn't ask what would happen if a car came from the opposite direction. Mother helpfully turned off the lights.

As luck would have it, a car did come around in the opposite direction and slowly, too, since the curve was feared. At the exact right moment Mom cut on the lights and Louise emitted a blood-curdling scream as the other car driver honked.

"I'll kill you!" Louise screamed as his taillights receded.

Mother was laughing so hard she was crying. Louise yanked open the car door, picked up her purse, and bopped Mother over the head with it. Mom was so weak with laughter she couldn't fight back.

"I hate you," Louise yelled, but within seconds she was laughing, too. "You are the worst sister in the world."

Mother, practically in convulsions, squeaked, "I know."

After that moment Mother always referred to the spot as Fat Ass Curve.

I became interested in the survival of animals and plants after that, and I also learned never to ask Mom to stop so I could go to the bathroom by the side of the road.

MINK RIVER

by Larry Watson

From time to time Barden looked in his wife's closet to see if the box was still there. Once he found it, as he always did, back behind the shoes and the wrapping paper, he would pick the box up, hefting it to check if it still held its contents. Its weight never changed.

On one occasion, Barden's wife came into the room just as he began his search.

"Can I help you?" Helen asked.

Her voice startled him, but Barden was neither apologetic nor defensive about his activity. "You know what I'm doing," Barden said.

"It's still there, if that's what you're wondering."

In spite of her confession, Barden pushed aside one of Helen's coats and looked for himself. Yes, the box was there, just as she said. Just as Barden knew it would be.

Not much smaller than a shoe box and made of brown plastic, the box held the remains of James Robert Candell, Helen's son from her first marriage, killed in an automobile accident on April 19, 1993. Barden was convinced that until Helen opened that box and scattered her son's ashes neither she nor their marriage would return to normalcy.

And what would normalcy mean? To Barden something quite modest and ordinary. For Helen to laugh and not have her laughter suddenly brought up short on guilt's choke chain. For her to be able to risk tears without worrying they would never stop. For her to partake of life's simplest pleasures—food, wine, conversation, sex—without sorrow's sudden intrusion. For Helen to spend less time on her work—she was a computer systems analyst—and more time on those activities that she once enjoyed: Walking. Working in her garden. Reading her beloved British mysteries. Visiting her friends. And Barden was willing to admit it—he wanted Helen to scatter those ashes for his sake as well. He wanted pleasure and ease back in his own life, and neither could be his as long as Helen was married to the memory of her dead son.

Was this jealousy? Barden supposed it was. He was jealous of James. But only in death. When James was alive, Barden seldom felt anything for him but pity and annoyance.

James had been a quiet young man, uncomfortable in the presence of others, but more than a few people mistook his shyness for arrogance or even insolence. His physical appearance contributed to the impression. He seldom smiled. He was tall and stiff in his movements, long-necked and narrow-eyed, and as he looked down at the world from his somber height, he seemed to be judging it and finding it inadequate.

In truth, it was James who was, by most of the world's standards, deficient. He had few friends, male or female, of duration or intimacy. He seemed to be without personal or professional ambition or direction. He was a restless, indifferent student, who, at the time of his death, was enrolled at his third college. Recently, his academic performance was somewhat improved, perhaps because the Wisconsin college he attended had a course of study that allowed James to pursue his special interest. The college was noted for its natural-resources programs—many of them pertaining to ecology and wildlife—and James was a birder of exceptional skill. With his binoculars and field guide in hand, he was everything he could not be in the classroom—focused, attentive, patient.

In fact, on the day of his death, James was returning from a preserve in northeast Wisconsin that served as a habitat for more than two hundred species of bird. James was driving back to the university when a drunk driver swerved across the center line, instantly killing them both.

Helen took some comfort from the fact that her son had spent his final day in a place he loved. Barden said nothing, but his judgment of the circumstances of James's death was less generous. It happened on a Monday, a spring day when classes were in session, and, according to one of the other students with whom James rented a house, James had left town early in the morning. Barden knew, as Helen did, that James's time outdoors escalated in proportion to the troubles he was having with the world of clocks, schedules, and responsibilities.

This habit of escaping to the woods was so contrary to Barden's own nature that neither he nor James could ever understand, much less appreciate, the other. Barden's life was oriented toward accomplishment. Academic scholarships. Honor rolls and deans' lists. Law school. Partnership in a firm of standing and repute. And Barden always felt that whatever success he had enjoyed had not been achieved by gifts of intellect or personality but by hard work, self-discipline, perseverance. Once he began observing James and his difficulties, Barden wished that he could offer his own life in example or at least give the boy some simple advice. But Barden arrived late on the scene—he and Helen met when James was in high school—and Barden knew his rights were limited. Besides, he doubted James would listen. Neither demonstrated obvious contempt for the other, but neither were there any signs of affection. Because they both loved and respected Helen, they tolerated and treated each other politely, but there was little beyond that. As different as they were, Barden always knew Helen could not draw love for each of them from the same well.

At one time Helen had declared her intention to scatter James's ashes. On the way home from the memorial service, the box resting on the floor behind the front seat, Barden asked her what she planned to do with the cremains. (He had not known, until James's death, that there was a special term for the remains of cremated bodies. Barden wasn't sure if it was the word itself he hated, or the unctuous way the funeral director said it. Nevertheless, because Helen used the word, Barden did, too.)

"I'm not sure," she said. "I was going to ask Bill . . ." Bill was her first husband and James's father. He had remarried, and he and his wife (his third) lived in Portland, Oregon. When Helen called him with the news, he told her that he wouldn't attend the funeral. If he did, he said, it would "upset the equilibrium" of his new family.

And you were going to consult him, Barden wanted to say. A man you've spoken to on fewer than ten occasions since your divorce more than fifteen years ago? Instead, Barden said, "It should be your decision."

"I thought . . . ," Helen's voice trailed away, and she turned toward her window. Over the succeeding months, Barden grew accustomed to her unfinished sentences and her unfocused looks. "I thought maybe someplace James loved. Someplace . . . I could scatter them someplace."

"Any ideas?" Barden asked.

It took a long time for her to answer. "Not so far."

"You'll let me know?"

"I will."

But no ideas were forthcoming, and when they returned to their home in Minneapolis, the box went into Helen's closet, where it had rested now for more than a year, a period of time long enough for Barden to wonder if that would be its permanent residence.

For the first few months, Barden continued to bring up the matter. At first, he simply asked Helen whether she had yet thought of a place for James's ashes. She usually just shook her head, and because Barden could tell how much even that minimal response cost her, he did not push.

The box remained in its place and Helen in hers—trapped under grief's bell jar—and Barden went further and began to make suggestions for disposition of the ashes.

"How about the back yard of the house in Anoka?" he suggested. Helen and James lived there from James's birth until her marriage to Barden, when they moved into his condominium. "That's a huge lot. I bet the people there would let you bury the ashes back by those cottonwoods."

"I'd feel funny about it," Helen said. "I mean, it's their house now."

Barden was careful not to simply throw out a list of places—he didn't want to imply that any urgency was involved—so he always waited a respectful period of time, at least a week and usually longer, before he suggested another location.

"How about that lake where you and James used to rent a cottage every summer?"

"Your uncle's farm?"

"Yellowstone? You said he loved it when the two of you drove out to Yellowstone."

"The hill behind your parents' house? Where he found the hawk's nest?"

"The river that James used to canoe?"

Barden knew that grief had a course to run and that, contrary to what self-help or pop-psychology books might say, its course could not be predictably charted. But Barden was not a patient man. Furthermore, he did not believe that predicaments—whether they were emotional or legal—were resolved by waiting and doing nothing.

Accordingly, on a morning in September, he confronted Helen in their kitchen.

"Could I talk to you for a moment?" Barden asked. The small unit of time he requested was only barely an exaggeration. They both had to leave for work in less than an hour; Barden didn't intend this to be a matter for discussion or debate.

When she heard his request, Helen put her hands behind her and backed up against the dishwasher. At the sight of her, Barden almost relented and abandoned his plan. His wife was a small woman, yet she had always given off an impression of both self-assurance and vitality. Furthermore, she had full breasts, a narrow waist, wide hips, great legs, and her body's voluptuousness came through even when it was fully covered, as it was now in her work attire, a silk blouse and wool skirt. But at that moment, viewed across the kitchen, she merely looked small, and wished to be smaller still, as if she wanted to leave her physical being completely.

"What is it?" Helen said. She had no reason to be frightened or worried, yet both emotions were in her voice, her posture.

"I've made reservations," Barden said, "at a hotel in Door County for the last weekend in October."

"Door County? Wisconsin?"

Barden nodded. "Where the Pages have their cottage." Their friends had often encouraged them to join them for a weekend, calling the vacation area, the tiny peninsula where Wisconsin stuck its thumb out into Lake Michigan, "Cape Cod in the Midwest."

"And where . . ."

Barden nodded again. "I've sent away for information about the preserve that James was visiting. It's called the Mink River Estuary. I've got a brochure with directions."

"Are you sure that's—"

"—I'm sure. I think we should go there. And I think we should take the cremains and scatter them there." Barden could have said more, but he stopped himself. He did not want Helen to acquiesce simply to please him. Either the idea alone was enough to convince her or it was not.

"The last weekend in October, you said?"

"Fall's a busy season there. I had trouble finding a room."

She turned and looked at the clock on the microwave, though Barden was certain she knew the time. "I should get going," Helen said.

"We'd want to leave on Friday. It's a long drive. Seven hours maybe. Then we can get up Saturday morning and look for the preserve. Come home on Sunday. How does that sound?"

"The last weekend in October . . ." She continued to stare at the clock, as if its green numbers were not counting off minutes and hours but days and weeks.

"Six weeks," Barden said.

"Six weeks. Report cards used to come out every six weeks. God, that seemed so long . . ."

"If we're not going, I'll have to know soon. If reservations aren't canceled within a certain period of time, you still pay for the room. One night anyway."

"All right."

"All right—what?"

"All right we'll go."

"And take the ashes?"

"And take the ashes." Helen's voice had been getting softer and softer, and when she said this Barden wondered if he actually heard her or only read her lips. He did not ask her to repeat herself.

No one thing caused Barden's foul mood. All across Wisconsin the fall colors were past their peak, and all those brilliant reds, greens, and golds that he had hoped to see had faded to duller tones of rust, tan, or wine and looked as though they wore a dulling layer of dust. Traffic was heavier than he expected. They arrived in Door County too late to find a place to eat—restaurants had either closed for the year or had such long lines that it was impossible to get in without a reservation. At the hotel, Helen did not leave the brown plastic box in the trunk but brought it into the room and placed it under the folding rack their suitcase rested on.

No matter what brought on his ill temper, Barden should not have made it worse by drinking, and on an empty stomach at that. He had brought along a bottle of Merlot, with a very specific idea for its use. They would eat a decent dinner, return to their room, and build a fire. Barden would uncork the wine, and they would make love on the floor in front of the flames.

The fireplace was gas, and its odor was not woodsmoke but a sulfurous combination of burned matches and rotting eggs. Helen worried that gas might be leaking, and Barden turned off the fire.

Certainly, he should have let sex wait, at least one more night, at least until Helen had let go the weight she had carried with her on this trip. But Barden had difficulty deviating from a plan. What's more, he thought that making love might reverse the day's disappointments.

It did not. The act was, as it had so often been in months past, hurried and, for all their years of practice, even a bit clumsy—too much muscle and bone and too little languor and tenderness. Their noses bumped and their teeth clashed. Barden's fingers caught in Helen's hair, and he pulled too hard to get free. Their hip and pubic bones banged against each other as if they were coupling with furniture. The bed frame was fastened to the wall and clattered against its bolts. Their sweaty chests stuck to each other and made a vulgar sucking sound when they popped free.

After, Helen jumped quickly from the bed and went to the bathroom. When she returned, she did not lie down beside Barden but sat on the edge of the bed. She switched on the lamp and began doing something with her watch that did not need to be done. Barden put his finger in the middle of Helen's bare back and ran it lightly down the shadowed curve of her spine. She arched away from his touch.

"I'm trying to fix this," Helen said.

"Just get a new band."

"I can fix this one."

Barden had drunk most of the bottle of wine, and it had left behind an ache high in his chest and in his shoulders. He wondered if he was allergic to something in red wine because he never felt this after drinking a Chablis or a Chardonnay. In an effort to ease the throbbing, he got out of bed and walked to the window. He was naked, and he held the curtains closed while he peered out through the small gap.

"We're parked between a Lexus and a Mercedes," he announced. "Both of them with Illinois plates."

"Judy Page said that the people in the cottages on each side of them are from Chicago."

"I couldn't believe how crowded the streets were. Jesus, do they come here just to shop?"

"And eat, apparently."

Barden looked further down the line of cars. A Land Rover. Two Jeep Grand Cherokees. "I can't see James here."

When Helen said nothing in response, Barden turned to look at her. She had dropped her watch, and pulled the sheet up to her chest. She wore the fearful, bewildered expression he had come to know so well—*what do you mean? no, don't tell me, I don't want to know.*

"I just meant," Barden quickly said, "out there. Here. Door County. With all the BMWs and the Cadillacs. James in his rusty old Toyota."

"He . . . he was here in a different season."

"Spring. Still, it's got to be busy here in spring." Barden returned to the bed. As soon as he lay down, the ache returned to his shoulders.

"Did he ever talk to you about coming here?" Barden asked. Helen had gathered the sheet so tightly to her body that he couldn't use it to cover himself without pulling it from her.

She shook her head, a gesture that deepened his irritation. What if I weren't looking at you, he thought; I wouldn't know if you had answered me or not.

"Did you buy James that truck?"

"You know I did."

"New or used?"

"New."

"Do you remember what you paid for it?"

Barden didn't know why he persisted with this line of questioning. None of the information about James and the financing of his truck was of any interest to him. What Barden wanted was something quite different. He wanted an admission from Helen, a statement that her son was not perfect, that James, James and not the world—and certainly not his mother—was responsible for James's unhappiness.

Helen's hair had gone almost completely gray, but she still wore it long and loose. Now, when she shook her head again, hair moved back and forth across her back like a waving curtain. He didn't need to see her face to know she was crying. How could Barden have forgotten—James was driving his truck when he was killed. It must have seemed to Helen as though, like an attorney building a case, Barden was trying to prove that she was partly to blame for her son's death because she bought him the vehicle he died in.

Barden used to think, naively, that the ashes of human remains were like the weightless scraps that floated in the smoky air when paper was burned. Scattering ashes like that, he imagined, would have been like creating a snowfall, although with black and gray flakes rather than white.

But he had long ago looked into that box, and what he saw set him right. Inside a plastic bag—sealed with a wire twist-tie of the sort you used at the grocery store to close your bags of produce— was a fine pale powder, as heavy and dense as unmixed concrete and laced through with tiny bits of teeth or bone.

He thought of crossing the room again, of opening the box and the bag and dumping its contents over his naked body, turning himself chalk white with the powdered remains of Helen's son. This is how sorry I am, he could say. This is the penance I'm willing to do. I'll wear this ash until you tell me I'm forgiven.

But Barden remained in bed, and instead tried to back up the conversation, to ease the situation by giving himself an innocent motive. "I'm sorry," he said, "but I was just wondering what the truck cost. Compared to the cars out there. That Mercedes . . . I don't think I paid that much for the condo." Barden remembered something that old Lyle Hennigan, the attorney who gave him his first job in law, used to say: *When they say, I'm sorry* but *they're not really sorry.*

Helen got out of bed, pulling the sheet with her. Then she made her own apology.

"I'm the one who should be sorry," she said. "Sometimes I can't talk about anything without . . . It's like I'm still raw. After all this time."

Barden could see his marks all over Helen. Her lips were still reddened and smeared from his kisses. Her hair was tangled on one side, where Barden had knotted his fingers during their lovemaking. She wrapped the sheet tightly around herself, hugging and flattening her breasts and causing their swell to show above the fabric. There, where his beard had rubbed against her, the skin was chafed and pink.

He could see too how tired she was, yet her fatigue had not

dimmed her sensuality but caused it to burn even brighter. Her reserves had dwindled until you could see her core, and it was carnal. Barden felt himself filling again with desire.

"Come back to bed," he said, and patted the mattress beside him.

Helen spun in a tight circle, and as she did, she unwound herself from the sheet. In what seemed the same motion she threw it overhead, and somehow it opened and billowed out as though caught by a breeze. Under the sheet's cover, she scurried into the bathroom, where she closed and locked the door behind her.

They had trouble finding the preserve, although the directions were specific and clear.

First, they missed their turn off the main highway. Traffic was heavy again, the county roads were not well marked, and the glittering bay waters kept pulling their eyes in the wrong direction, away from the land and out to where tilting sailboats seemed to be suspended among the waves. They ended up driving all the way to the rocky tip of the peninsula and then had to backtrack.

Then, once they turned into the county's interior, the landscape changed so drastically, from beaches, towering pines, roadside shops and galleries to rolling countryside, tilled and treeless, that they doubted they could possibly be drawing closer to an estuary. They finally found the parking lot after driving by it twice, so modest was the sign announcing the preserve. It was close to noon when they parked the car, having driven more than an hour to get to a destination less than twenty miles from their hotel.

Helen had put the box in a backpack, and as soon as she got out of the car, she shouldered the pack and set off down a trail. Barden stayed behind a moment and studied the maps at the information kiosk. There was also a list of rules and regulations, covering, among other matters, hunting, fishing, and using motorized vehicles. One item caught his attention: visitors were forbidden to take anything out of or leave anything in the preserve.

Ashes? Barden doubted the prohibition could extend to a few handfuls of ash. That would be like forbidding people to leave the dust they kicked from their shoes, the carbon dioxide they expelled from their lungs.

Barden set off in pursuit of his wife, but he made no attempt to hurry. The trail was undermined by a network of roots from the surrounding trees, and some of the roots had pushed to the surface and made walking the trail like stepping over a web of thick ropes and cables. Barden worried that a misstep could easily result in a twisted ankle or a sprained arch. Besides, he wasn't sure what he would say to Helen if he caught up to her. From the time they got up that morning, their exchanges had been awkwardly brief and formal. The day's solemn purpose could certainly have been the reason, yet Barden felt there was something more. It seemed to him as though their relationship had changed during the night, and in the day's new light they behaved not like a long-married couple but like a man and woman new to intimacy, as if they had sex before they knew anything about each other and now had little to talk about but the act itself, a topic they were too embarrassed to discuss.

Barden followed Helen down the Fern Trail. He could see how it had been named. The path was bordered by ferns, growing in every spot that was not already occupied by a live or fallen tree. The plants started at ankle height and went up, a few of them almost waist-high. Like the leaves of the trees, the ferns had changed their color but without variation. Every fern had dried to a deep gold, and where the sun managed to find an opening in the heavy foliage overhead, these plants shone with gold's brilliance.

Why not here, Barden thought? Why not dump those ashes here and be done with it? But Helen was nowhere nearby.

The ferns thinned and soon gave out completely. Barden was amazed at how quickly the spirit of the place changed. Trees before and trees now, but these seemed older by centuries, and all of them competing for light, water, air. They leaned at improbable angles. They exposed their roots so it looked as though they clung to the earth with claws. Many trees had split, cracked, or toppled, and they decayed where they fell. The air was dim and smelled of rot. Why not here? The earth looked welcoming, ready to turn anything fallen—as small as a leaf, as large as a dead bird, as insubstantial as ash—to the humus the years had been building.

The trail widened, turned, descended slightly, and brought another change.

Here was a stand of aspen, their skinny white trunks as straight as soldiers at attention. The canopy thinned, and in the middle of the sunlit path, Helen stood, staring overhead. Barden approached her cautiously, and when he came close, she whispered one word: "Birds."

He looked up, too. Among the highest branches, hundreds of sparrows—or so they seemed to Barden—leaped and tumbled from tree to tree. He intended to make an observation about how sparrows reminded him of junior businessmen, always in motion, always scurrying around in order to impress someone with their busyness, yet never really doing anything, but Helen set out again down the path before he could frame the thought in words.

They did not stop again until the Mink River came into sight. They stepped out of the trees into marshland. Barden was six feet tall, and many of the rushes and waving grasses were a foot or two taller than he. The earth was boggy and wet, and they had to stride from one tiny hillock to another, the only secure footing available.

At the kiosk, Barden had read that the Mink River surged regularly with tidal movement from the Great Lake. "Do you think the tide is in?" he asked.

At the sound of his voice, two ducks splashed into flight from where they had paddled unseen along the bank.

"I don't think I can get any closer to the river," Helen said.

The river! Of course! That had been Helen's destination all along. She planned to pour James's remains into the river, to let his ashes swirl and dissolve in the dark water.

"Don't try," Barden said. "If you slipped in that muck, you'd have a hell of a time getting your foot out."

She gazed out across the river, its near bank as inaccessible as its far side.

"Let's go back," Barden suggested. "You can find a spot back up the trail."

"You go ahead."

"I don't want you trying to make it down to the river."

"I'll be all right. I'm not going to do something I shouldn't. Go. I'll be along."

Barden felt he had no choice but to give her the privacy she requested. He looked at his watch. It had taken them half an hour to hike from the car. He'd wait farther up the trail, and if Helen didn't appear in forty-five minutes, he'd come back for her.

When he reached the aspen grove, he stepped fifteen or twenty feet off the path and sat down on the trunk of a fallen tree, an oak and the only tree in the area not covered in white bark.

Overhead, the dun-feathered sparrows were still flying from branch to branch for no purpose that Barden could discern. Ducks aside, these common birds were the only ones he'd seen, far from the many species the visitors guide promised.

But then, Barden knew he did not have a birder's eye or ear. Perhaps mingled with all that sparrow chat was the song of a bird so rare its call was almost never heard. And perhaps what he saw as the most commonplace of birds was a kind of sparrow never before seen or catalogued. But Barden did not have the patience to wait hours for a glimpse of a feather he had never seen before. Nor did he have the temperament to walk away and not feel disappointment or frustration when he saw nothing new or exotic. He did not have the disposition to say, sparrows . . . what's wrong with sparrows?

What was he thinking? That he did not have James's ability to take the world on its own terms? Birds, after all, do not wait for us; we must wait for them.

No, Barden knew he had an eye tuned for other plumage—there, for instance, the bright blue of Helen's jacket as she came up the trail.

While he watched, she stepped off the path and, picking her way among the rocks, branches, and undergrowth, moved farther from him.

He thought to call out to her, to announce his position, but he did not. And once he did not, he felt he had to remain silent. If he shouted to her now, he might frighten her. Or intrude.

As Helen moved farther back among the trees, the white trunks obscured his view of her, but he saw that she had unslung the pack and was carrying it by its strap. That had to mean she had decided, since she was unable to get to the river, that this sunlit grove was the next-best place for James's ashes.

Helen suddenly dropped down, and for an instant Barden thought she had stumbled and pitched forward, but then he could tell: she was kneeling to prepare a place for the remains, falling to her knees in the dirt . . .

Barden remembered when they got the news of James's death. The spring day had been rainy and warm, and the clouds finally cleared around sunset. Helen took advantage of the remaining light to do some work in her flower beds. Barden answered the telephone, and when the caller asked for Helen, he took the portable phone out to her. Barden assumed the call was business-related; Helen was frequently phoned at home by people who had questions about their new computer systems.

Her hands were muddy, and, smiling, she indicated that Barden should hold the phone to her ear. After Helen listened for a moment, her smile eroded and she said, "What? What?" Barden mistakenly believed she was having trouble hearing, and he pressed the phone harder to her ear.

Helen in turn tried to back away, whether from the phone's pressure or the caller's message Barden couldn't know, but he kept walking with her. Finally, she escaped the only way she could—by falling back down into the soft wet dirt.

What should Barden have done at that moment? Was his job, as husband to Helen but not father to her child, to remain on his feet and to do exactly as he did—to say into the receiver, "Please stay on the line; she'll be right with you," and then to get behind Helen and try to lift her up out of the mud grief had dropped her into? Or was his place down in the dirt with his wife?

For that matter, where did he belong now? Here, a hundred yards away, while Helen performed in private her life's most difficult duty? Or there, kneeling at her side, their knees sinking into the decaying yellow leaves while together they watched James's ashes fall and powder the earth?

As difficult as it had been to get Helen to come to this place, how much harder would it be for her now to leave it?

While he pondered these questions, Helen rose, turned, and, to Barden's astonishment, called out to him.

"Can you come here a minute?" she shouted.

Where once Barden stepped cautiously through the undergrowth, now he ran, heedless of his footfall, toward Helen. As he bounded past the aspens, the black streaks and spots on their white trunks looked like marks of punctuation, the dashes, commas, periods, and parentheses of faint, unreadable texts.

Just before he reached her, Helen shouted another question: "Can you remember where we are? I mean, this exact spot?"

"How did you know I was here?"

"Didn't you say you were going to wait? I just assumed . . . And when I was coming up the trail, I saw you sitting over there—"

"The aspen grove," Barden said quickly. "That's what I call it. In my mind, I mean. I think of this as the aspen grove."

Helen smiled. "The aspens. I just call it 'the aspens.' " She looked around. "It doesn't matter. As long as I can find my way back here." She touched Barden's arm reassuringly. "Not that I'm ever going to. I just need to know I can."

With her hand still on his arm, Barden led her back toward the path.

"Oh, God," Helen said with a laugh. "This is awful. Are they aspens? Maybe they're birch . . ."

"The skinny white trees," Barden suggested. "How's that? We can come back to the place where all the skinny white trees grow."

"I just wish I knew. It's embarrassing. To be my age and still not know the difference between an oak tree and an elm."

As they walked up the trail, it was Barden who looked back.

Even at this short distance, in the middle of the afternoon, those trees already looked like the ghosts of trees. He wasn't sure if he should keep his next thought or say it out loud. Before he could decide, his tongue let it go.

"James would have known."

VÍCTOR

by Julia Alvarez

Whenever Don Bernardo comes to the national park, he asks for Víctor's father as his guide. "And tell him to bring Víctor along," he invariably adds.

Today, Don Bernardo has a strange guest with him. Víctor can tell that Don Bernardo is not quite at ease with this lady, as if she were here to report on his work as director of parks. But she seems harmless enough. A skinny lady who is not americana but looks americana in her blue pants and T-shirt with letters written across it. She is carrying a notebook, and from a ribbon around her neck dangles a pen where the Virgencita's medallion should go.

Don Bernardo looks down and notices Víctor. "Ho, there, Víctor! How is the little man?"

As he always does when he doesn't know what to say or where to look, Víctor lifts his unbuttoned shirt over his head. He hides underneath it like the lizard under the frond of the elephant fern.

"Mira, muchacho," his father scolds in a voice that threatens to cuff his ear. After all, Don Bernardo made a point of introducing this lady as an honored visitor who writes books and teaches in an American school. "You can say hello like a person."

"Hello," Víctor says loud and clear, like a person.

Don Bernardo laughs. "Víctor is as smart as a pencil," he tells the lady, who smiles at him and says, "Is that so?" Just as she is not americana but looks americana, she is dominicana but speaks Spanish as if she were worried there might be a little stone in among the words that will crack her mouthful of white teeth. Each word is carefully spoken and cleanly finished before the next one starts. "So tell me, Víctor," she says, "what grade are you in?"

Víctor glances at his father. "In the third grade," he offers.

"Did you complete it or are you about to start it this September?"

Looking over her shoulder, Víctor spots the red-eyed bobo flying through the trees as if stitching together the forest with the rise and fall of its wings. If the lady is here to see the park, she should not miss the flight of the bobo. "Look!" he points. "A bobo!"

She turns around, craning her neck to see what he sees.

Víctor keeps pointing, but the lady is not quick enough and the bobo disappears into the dark-green curtain of the rain forest.

"Bo-bo," the lady says the name slowly, writing it down in her little book. "Where were we?" she asks when she looks back up.

"Lead on, Víctor!" Don Bernardo commands.

Víctor darts ahead, his shirt flapping behind him like the tail of the bobo when it sits on the branch of the cedar, calling bo-bo, bo-bo, bo-bo, as if it were trying to talk like a person, expecting an answer.

The lady walks behind him on the trail. "Wow," she says over every little thing.

"Wow-oh." Víctor tries out the words under his breath. "Wow-oh, wow-oh." The words sound like the call of the big-eyed lechuza at night.

"Wow! Look at that flower!" The lady points.

"That's a campana," Víctor explains. "Careful when you touch it. Wasps love to build in its leaves."

"It's so so beautiful," the lady says, writing down the name of the flower in her notebook. "Cam-pa-na." She breaks it down into little pieces as if she were about to feed the word to a baby who cannot chew solid food. Her voice is clear and measured like a schoolteacher's. "What is *that*?" She looks up. Behind her, Don Bernardo stops to listen.

"That little bird singing is a barrancolí," Víctor explains. "And over there is a tinaja," he adds. "You want me to cut one down for you?"

"Cut it down?" A scolding look spreads across the lady's face.

"I can cut you an orchid if you prefer." Víctor hesitates. His father has taught him to figure out what will please a turista so the tip will be a good one. The ladies, when they come, always like a delicate orchid or tufted bromeliad to take home to the capital in their jeeps or scouts. The chauffeur, usually along carting the ice chest, carries it back in his free hand.

Don Bernardo catches up and wags his finger. "You know better than to disturb things in the rain forest, Víctor."

"You know better," his father agrees. Víctor recognizes the look that says, You have put your foot down beside a wasp nest. Watch out.

"I know better." Víctor nods.

"Víctor is as smart as a pencil," Don Bernardo repeats. "How old did you say you were, Víctor?" He winks at the lady as if preparing her for a merriment.

Víctor looks at his father. "Ten," he says solemnly.

"But, Víctor," Don Bernardo says, eyeing him kindly, "you have been ten years old for the last three years I have been coming to the park."

"You mean to say he doesn't know how old he is?" the lady asks Don Bernardo. The director of parks glances at his feet. Every time he comes to the park, he teases Víctor and his guests smile along with him.

"Don't you know how old you are, Víctor?" the lady persists.

Víctor lifts his shirt over his head and looks up at the trail. It winds through the trees and then up the incline toward the collection of white rocks the turistas like to photograph. "Nine," he tries, and then, "fourteen," but none of the numbers seem to please the lady, who shakes her head at Don Bernardo.

"Something should be done about this," she says, making a note in her book. Don Bernardo nods gravely, his hands in his pockets. Víctor glances at his father, who narrows his eyes at his son as if to say, Stand very still, boy. If you don't make a move, maybe the wasps will go away.

. . .

They continue down the trail, but the exploration is no fun anymore.

"One-two-three-four," the lady makes him slowly count out loud.

"What is the first month of the year, Víctor?"

"October?"

"Víctor! The *first* month? I already told you."

He tries a few more before he gets it right. They stop by a bush of bejuco de gato so the lady can write the name down.

"Those leaves are good for pain," Víctor explains to her.

"How do you spell bejuco anyhow?" she asks Don Bernardo, who spells the word for her. That gets her started on something else. "Can you spell *your* name, Víctor?"

Víctor feels silence tingling the inside of his mouth—as if he had taken a bite of bejuco de gato and his tongue had gone numb. He looks down at the lady's pants covered with melao and amor seco, nettles that are hard to take out. "You want me to pick those off?" he offers her.

"V-I-C-T-O-R," she instructs him.

He repeats the letters after her.

"Well done!" Don Bernardo nods, but he does not add his usual phrase, "Víctor is as smart as a pencil." Perhaps he will no longer ask for Víctor every time he visits the park.

"Onetwothreefourfive!" Víctor pipes up, wanting to impress them both. Sure enough, Don Bernardo is laughing again!

At the fork in the trail, Don Bernardo explains to the lady that one path leads to the river, the other climbs up to the white rocks. The lady decides she wants to see the river, but then she confuses things by saying, "So take a right, Víctor."

"To the river?" he asks her just to make sure.

That look comes on her face again. "Which is your left, Víctor, and which is your right?"

"It depends," he says, outsmarting her for once. "Which way do you want to go?"

This time even she laughs, little hiccup laughs that sound like the calcalí calling to the sun as it rises up in the morning.

At the river, Don Bernardo and the lady sit on the rocks and talk in low, earnest voices about matters that sound important. "Thirty percent officially," Don Bernardo is explaining, "but it depends what you mean by illiteracy."

Víctor looks over at his father, perched on a fallen log, a papagallo stem in his mouth. He wishes he had picked one, too, for the sweet sap tastes so good on a hot day. Víctor can tell his father is calculating how much Don Bernardo will tip them for this tour. The farther the turistas go, the more they tip. But Don Bernardo and his guest had barely gone two kilometers before the lady discovered that Víctor did not know his numbers. The walk slowed as the lady stopped often to draw figures with a stick on the forest floor.

Beyond them, the trail cuts through to the heart of the green preserve. So many things are disappearing that will never be seen again on this earth! Or so Víctor has overheard at the lodge when his father attends the mandatory workshops the forestry service gives for the guides. But Víctor sees no sign of danger: the cocaría, whose flower stains blue and whose seeds if chewed cure toothache, is bursting with blossoms. Beside it, the leaves of cola de caballo bob in the slight breeze of late afternoon. The day is waning and there is still so much to show. The bamboo knock against one another like knuckles rapping on a desk asking for attention.

Bo-bo, bo-bo, calls the bobo.

"Bo-bo, bo-bo," Víctor answers back.

"Ho, Víctor!" Don Bernardo wakes Víctor from his daydreaming. "Time to head back."

A soft light is falling through the canopy of thick branches. The air is cool. The forest is always so much more pleasant than the village schoolhouse with the sun beating down on its zinc roof.

As they climb back up the stone steps, the lady notices a narrow footpath that cuts away from the river in the same general direction as the trail. "Where does this go?" she wants to know.

"That's an old mule track up to the white rocks," Víctor's father explains. "But it's too overgrown to walk."

"It looks fine," the lady says. "It'll give us some new things to look at. Don't you think so, Don Bernardo?" she addresses the director of parks. But it is clear from her face that her mind is already made up.

"There's a lot of campanas," Víctor begins, seconding his father's hesitation.

But the lady has already sprung forward, thrashing through the undergrowth so that all Víctor sees through the bobbing of the fern fronds is the blue of her pants and the flash of white paper in her little book. The men exchange a look. Finally, Don Bernardo shrugs and says, "Let's go."

Víctor has almost caught up to her when he hears the cry that comes as no surprise. She has pressed through a narrow avenue of campanas and the wasps are after her.

Quick, Víctor looks around and snaps off a branch from a nearby guayuyo tree. Beating a way toward her through the buzzing in the air, he yanks her by the hand back out to the river. Her notebook falls to the ground as she races beside him, Don Bernardo and his father giving them a wide berth as they jump into the water.

When she comes to the surface, Víctor can see that one eye is already swollen shut. He searches the bank for the leaves of bejuco de gato to ease the pain and oreja de burro to keep down the swelling. Meanwhile his father and Don Bernardo are rubbing guayuyo leaves on their arms and face to keep away the few wasps who have followed the intruders to the river. The forest has gone absolutely still. Not even the bold bobo calls to find out what is going on.

As soon as the lady is soothed with the leaves he has brought her, Víctor rubs guayuyo on his own face and arms, and runs off to retrieve the little book filled with things he has tried to teach her about the rain forest.

ACKNOWLEDGMENTS

Once again, we are in debt to members of the literary community. Our contributors have been generous in donating their stories to The Nature Conservancy and good spirited in their willingness to participate in this unusual anthology. We are deeply grateful.

We are fortunate to have the encouragement of members, staff, and volunteers at the Conservancy, who recognize the importance of giving voice to nature; to have the support of John C. Sawhill, Mike Coda, Stephanie Meeks, and others at the organization's headquarters; and to have the wise literary counsel of Anne Dubuisson and Elizabeth Kaplan.

Ethan Nosowsky of Farrar, Straus & Giroux has been enthusiastic, committed, responsive—all we could ask of an editor.

Thanks to Vee Vee Coleman for helping move things along.

Thanks to Dusty and Mike for being in our landscapes.

Thanks, everyone, for letting us bring these voices together.

THE NATURE CONSERVANCY

Founded in 1951, The Nature Conservancy is a private organization widely recognized as one of the most successful in the field of conservation. Its mission is to preserve plants, animals, and natural communities that represent the diversity of life on Earth by protecting the lands and waters they need to survive. Thus far, it has protected more than ten million acres in the United States and Canada and has helped like-minded partner organizations protect millions more in Latin America and the Pacific.

The Conservancy's staff of twenty-two hundred, a national volunteer force of more than twenty thousand, and a membership of more than nine hundred thousand have together created and maintain more than sixteen hundred preserves—the largest private system of nature sanctuaries in the world.

The Conservancy is now engaged in a pioneering regional approach to conservation whose goal is to conserve a collection of places that together sustain the full range of biological diversity. The work is being done in ecological regions—geographic areas that reflect natural boundaries, not political ones. The regions capture the heart of our natural heritage. From the Adirondacks to California's Great Central Valley, from the Great Lakes to the Southern Blue Ridge, and from Brazil to Micronesia, each reflects nature's own borders, with distinct geology, climate, and species.

Each site in this effort is a "Last Great Place," the Conservancy's designation for large areas of land and water of great biological significance. At each, the organization works closely with public and private partners to show that economic, recreational, and other development can occur while preserving nature.

For information about the Conservancy and its work, contact:

THE NATURE CONSERVANCY
International Headquarters
1815 North Lynn Street
Arlington, Virginia 22209
(800) 628-6860
www.tnc.org

ABOUT THE AUTHORS

Julia Alvarez

Julia Alvarez is originally from the Dominican Republic and returns often to her native land. She is the author of three novels, *How the García Girls Lost Their Accents, In the Time of the Butterflies*, and *¡Yo!*, and two books of poems, *Homecoming* and *The Other Side: El Otro Lado*. She teaches at Middlebury College.

" 'Víctor' was inspired by my visit to Armando Bermúdez National Park in the Dominican Republic. As a native of the island, I grew up hearing about one of our national treasures, Pico Duarte, the highest peak in the Caribbean, located in a vast forest since turned into a national park with the help of The Nature Conservancy. I always longed to go there. It took an invitation four decades later from The Nature Conservancy to write a story based on a visit to the park to finally get me there, fulfilling a childhood dream. At the park, I met another national treasure, a young tour guide named Víctor, who knew everything there was to know about the rain forest. Soon after we were introduced, I found out he didn't know how to read. My first reaction was, Oh my God, what a tragedy! He must be taught his alphabet! Instead I kept quiet and listened to this boy with his encyclopedic knowledge of the forest around us. That first impulse, though, to take him in hand and 'teach him what he didn't know' inspired the character of the lady in my little story. Thank God I didn't get the comeuppance the lady in my story got. Instead, I paid attention to Víctor, and from our hike came the inspiration for this story as well as a lesson on different kinds of knowing.

But the story, I hope, also acknowledges the limitations of knowledge without vision. Despite all he knows, my Víctor character does not realize the danger the rain forests are in, just as my educated lady has no vision beyond what can be written down."

RICK BASS

Rick Bass is the author of five books of fiction—most recently, a novel, *Where the Sea Used to Be*—as well as seven books of natural history, including *The Book of Yaak*. He lives in northwest Montana, where he is a member of the Yaak Valley Forest Council and is a board member of Round River Conservation Studies as well as the Cabinet Resources Group and the Montana Wilderness Association. The University of Georgia Press will publish a special edition of "Fiber" in the fall of 1998.

"I'm grateful to The Nature Conservancy and North Point/Farrar, Straus and Giroux for publishing this story, which was written out of a deep frustration and an inability to convince the various national conservation organizations that this biologically unique, extraordinarily rich and magical little green valley—the Yaak Valley of northwest Montana— has a value beyond the current one, which is clear-cutting the national forests and subdividing for development the privately held river-bottom lands: lands that were given to the railroads by Congress and then sold to the timber companies . . . I am asking The Nature Conservancy, again, and Congress, and readers, to please get involved in helping out the wild Yaak."

RICHARD BAUSCH

Richard Bausch's short stories have appeared in *The New Yorker, Esquire, The Atlantic Monthly, Harper's, Playboy*, and other magazines. His 1984 novel *The Last Good Time* was made into a movie, written and directed by Bob Balaban and released by Samuel Goldwyn. In 1996, the Modern Library published his volume *Selected Stories*. His eighth novel, *In the Night Season*, appeared in early summer of 1998.

"The central event of 'Glass Meadow' was told to me as a childhood memory by a wonderful storyteller named William Kimble, a prominent attorney from Tucson, Arizona. His son, Cary Kimble, is my very dear friend. William was the older brother in the story. I moved the time forward and added the batty parents, and imagined a man in the present asking the reader to envision this family as they were back in the 1950s. I think the story is about the curious effect a certain kind of goofy exclusive happiness has on those who come in contact with it."

RITA MAE BROWN

Rita Mae Brown is the author of more than twenty novels as well as screenplays and teleplays.

"I have long loved the Chesapeake Bay, and this story recounts my first visit."

DAVID JAMES DUNCAN

David James Duncan is the grandson of a Butte, Montana, miner, the father of three children who love the Blackfoot River, a lifelong fly fisherman, and the author of *River Teeth*, *The Brothers K*, and *The River Why*.

"Montana's Big Blackfoot River is the breathtakingly beautiful home of a food chain ranging from endangered bull trout, grizzly bears, elk, and eagles to conscientious fly-fishing cattle ranchers. It is enjoyed by tens of thousands of people annually, helps create thousands of sustainable jobs, and gives life to millions of creatures. It is the inspiration of Norman Maclean's legendary novella and Robert Redford's eponymous movie A River Runs Through It. *It is the property of every American. It is also the proposed site of a gigantic corporate-run cyanide heap-leach gold mine.*

"Cyanide gold-mining technology is devastating watersheds, aquifers, sustainable human economies, wildlife, and avian flyways worldwide. Yet 84 percent of gold goes to jewelry alone. The proposed Blackfoot River gold project is an unnecessary risk made possible by mining laws signed into effect by President Ulysses S. Grant in the same year that

Emperor Napoléon Bonaparte was limping home from his failed invasion of Prussia. The original purpose of Grant's 1872 mining law was to people the American West. The corporate miners who now benefit from this legal anachronism do not people a place at all: they rape it and abandon it, bequeathing busted "boom towns," gargantuan toxic waste heaps, ruined aquifers, dead rivers, dead wildlife, and terribly expensive Superfund sites to the American people.

"The Blackfoot River Valley is a mad hornet's nest. The gold mine's primary developer—the Phelps Dodge Corporation of Arizona—has sensibly withdrawn from the fray. But the cyanide mine remains on line. When Montana governor Marc Racicot, an outspoken Blackfoot goldmine supporter, presided over a 1996 Nature Conservancy–brokered Blackfoot River land acquisition, I thought I might be ill. Instead, I wrote "A Blackfoot River Fable"—a satire that tries to describe how thousands of us feel. Long live the Blackfoot."

GRETEL EHRLICH

Gretel Ehrlich was born in Santa Barbara, California, and educated at Bennington College and UCLA Film School. She moved to Wyoming in 1976, where she lived and worked on sheep and cattle ranches for seventeen years. Her books include Geode, Rock, Body (poems), To Touch the Water (poems), The Solace of Open Spaces (essays), Drinking Dry Clouds (short stories), Heart Mountain (novel), Islands, the Universe, Home (essays), Arctic Heart (poems), A Match to the Heart (memoir), Yellowstone: Land of Fire and Ice, and Questions of Heaven (travel memoirs). Forthcoming in 1998 is a nonfiction volume, Any Clear Thing That Blinds Us with Surprise, about Greenland, to be followed by a volume of fiction. Her books have been translated into Italian, Japanese, French, and German.

Her work has appeared in Harper's, The Atlantic Monthly, The New York Times, Time magazine, Life magazine, Architectural Digest, Antaeus, and Outside, among many others. She received a National Endowment for the Arts Creative Writing Fellowship in 1981, a Whiting Foundation Award in 1987, and a Guggenheim Fellowship in 1988. The American Academy of Arts and Letters honored her with the Harold B. Vurcell Award for distinguished prose in 1986. She now divides her time between the central coast of California and Wyoming.

"I flew to Anchorage, Alaska, then on to Iliamna and Tularik Creek, where I stayed at Gram's B and B, itself worthy of a story. That was in September 1996. All the birds had gone and most of the animals, except eagles, bears, and caribou. The weather turned bad. It was blustery: rain mixed with snow. On the one good day, Mac Minard, a Fish and Game biologist, was kind enough to fly me around the Tularik Creek drainage from source to mouth. We didn't crash. He is a fine pilot. But I almost wished we had. I loved that barren country so much, I didn't want to leave."

BARBARA KINGSOLVER

Barbara Kingsolver's books include the novels *Animal Dreams*, *The Bean Trees*, and *Pigs in Heaven*, as well as collections of short stories, poetry, and the best-selling essay collection *High Tide in Tucson*. She has also contributed to numerous literary anthologies and writes articles on environmental issues. She grew up in rural Kentucky and has two daughters, whom she raises with her husband, Steven Hopp, a musician and biologist. Her forthcoming novel, *The Poisonwood Bible*, is set in Africa.

BARRY LOPEZ

Barry Lopez is the author of four story collections, among them *Field Notes* and *Winter Count*. His stories appear regularly in *The Paris Review*, *American Short Fiction*, *Esquire*, *Manoa*, *The Georgia Review*, and elsewhere. He is also the author of several works of nonfiction, including *Arctic Dreams* and *Crossing Open Ground*, and is the recipient of a National Book Award and other honors.

"In the spring of 1996, I spent a day in the Columbia River Gorge with John Fowles, the English writer, searching for a wild orchid, Calypso bulbosa, variously called Pacific calypso orchid, deer's-head orchid, and fairy slipper. John, a knowledgeable and keen observer of wild flow-

ers, had wanted for many years to find this orchid in its natural setting. We located several patches in groves of old-growth Douglas fir. Later, we drove up on the Rowena Plateau and wandered about in silence, our shoulders hunched against a cold wind. In some way, 'Two Dogs at Rowena' was planted in my mind that afternoon. Weeks later, after I'd drafted the story, I realized The Nature Conservancy's Tom McCall Preserve, which includes the isolated park imagined in the story and is adjacent to the area where John and I walked, made the story a candidate for this collection. Our guides that day were Jerry Igo and Barbara Robinson. Ms. Robinson was later kind enough to verify my memory of flowers in bloom on the plateau that day.''

ERIC LUSTBADER

Eric Lustbader (he dropped his middle name, Van, several years ago) was born and raised in Greenwich Village. He is the author of more than twenty best-selling novels, including *The Ninja*, *Black Heart*, *Second Skin*, and *Dark Homecoming*. His novels have been translated into eighteen languages; his books are best-sellers worldwide. He is a graduate of Columbia College, with a degree in sociology. Before turning to writing full time, he enjoyed successful careers in the New York City public school system, where he holds licenses in both elementary and early-childhood education, and in the music business, where he worked for Elektra Records and CBS Records, among other companies.

"Sometimes, though not often, fiction and reality come together to create an astonishing whole. On my flight back from Alaska, I was wondering how in the world to frame a story that would convey the profound effect the Kenai and Katmai had had on me. I didn't want to write about what I had seen; that was surface stuff. I wanted to go beneath, to describe what Alaska evoked in its people. It took quite some time for me to find the key—not until Labor Day weekend, in fact, nearly three months later, when my wife and I were having lunch with a friend who told us an eerie incident from her past that connected with my feelings for Alaska in such an essential way I asked her permission

to draw from it to create my own story. She readily agreed; the result is 'Hush.'"

JILL MCCORKLE

A native of North Carolina, Jill McCorkle graduated from University of North Carolina-Chapel Hill and obtained a master's in writing at Hollins College, Virginia. She has taught at UNC-Chapel Hill, Tufts University, Harvard University, and in the Bennington College M.F.A. program. She lives near Boston with her husband and children.

"*I grew up in southeastern North Carolina in a town that during my childhood had a population of about ten thousand and then doubled in size as I-95 came through. The construction of the interstate seemed ongoing during my childhood, and I spent a lot of time in the strip of woods that separated my neighborhood from the service road. There the land was flat and filled with pines. At one time there was a wild chicken running around in the woods and we would stalk it only to find that we were more afraid of it than it was of us. I never actually went on a snipe hunt, but I had friends who did; by the time someone invited me to go, I knew better. My friend Emma Beckham is the one whose family used tape recorders, and though the circumstances of this story are not in any way Emma's story, I had the great pleasure of once hearing Emma and her brother's whispering childhood voices forever preserved on an aging, much treasured cassette. I knew then that this was a story I wanted to pursue, bringing to it a story of trust and betrayal, as well as the sights and sounds of that wonderful patch of woods that no longer exists.*"

HOWARD NORMAN

Both of Howard Norman's novels, *The Northern Lights* and *The Bird Artist*, were short-listed for the National Book Award. He has written a collection of short stories, articles on ethnography and natural history, and film scripts. He is the recipient of a Lannan Award in fiction, a Guggenheim Fellowship, and the New England Booksellers Association Award for Excellence. His forthcoming books are *The Museum Guard* and *The 100 Year Overdue Library Book*. He lives in Vermont and Washington, D.C., with his wife, the poet Jane Shore, and their daughter, Emma.

"My friend Brad Northrup, an excellent naturalist, and I traveled around Northern California for about a week. The abundance of late-autumn birds was inspiring. We went from sandhill cranes to acorn woodpeckers to ducks in the lowland estuaries of Point Reyes—where, on Sunset Beach, we saw a gathering of white pelicans. In the almost-constant rain, we had very good luck. Country music stations on in the car. A lot of walking. The magnificent Dye Creek Reserve was a new place for both of us. 'Ghost,' 'ghosting,' 'ghostly,' words engendered by the sight of those white pelicans, I think was finally the organizing principle—the central image—when working on 'The Chauffeur.' That, and the desire to experience vicariously a profession other than writing: that of a chauffeur. That vicariousness always seems absolutely essential to writing, in my experience."

ANNIE PROULX

Annie Proulx is the author of a short-story collection, *Heart Songs and Other Stories*, and the novels *Postcards*, *The Shipping News*, and *Accordion Crimes*. She lives in Wyoming.

"The starting point for 'The Half-Skinned Steer' was The Nature Conservancy's ten-thousand-acre Ten Sleep Preserve on the southwest slope of Wyoming's Bighorns. For twenty years, the property was a Girl Scout national summer camp. It was purchased by the Conservancy in 1991. I spent three wonderful days hiking in the preserve and learning something of the place from the husband-and-wife manager team Phil Shephard and Anne Humphrey.

"The most obvious feature of the preserve is a spectacular canyon, but the diverse terrain is habitat for many animals and plants, including three extremely rare species that grow only in the Bighorns. Good country too for mountain lions, hawks, and eagles. Perhaps the most interesting

places in the preserve are the archaeological sites, sheltered overhangs protecting brilliant Native American pictographs on the walls. The meanings and functions of Wyoming and Montana pictographs are not yet well understood, and there is little information available on these sites.

"The story of the half-skinned steer is based on an old Icelandic folktale, 'Porgeir's Bull,' which I have heard in several versions in Canada. In these tales, the bull haunts Porgeir's descendants for nine generations. Even today in Manitoba the spectral bull is believed to appear on the night prairies in the guise of a barking dog.

"The story I have told does not claim to present the preserve, the pictographs, local people, or events in a realistic way; it is fiction loosely attached to a certain place."

LEE SMITH

Lee Smith's most recent book, *News of the Spirit*, a collection of stories and novellas, was published in 1997. She is the author of many other works of fiction, including the novels *Fair and Tender Ladies, Oral History*, and *Saving Grace*. She lives in North Carolina.

"Instead of traveling someplace far away for this story, I seized the opportunity to look in my own back yard and satisfy my curiosity about the fabled Bluff Mountain Nature Conservancy Preserve, only a mile or so (as the crow flies) from our beloved cabin up in Ashe County, North Carolina. I hiked the mountain with Nature Conservancy guide Jane Thompson and the knowledgeable Judy and Bill Watson; then I spent a wonderful day talking to Earlene Barker, who grew up near Bluff Mountain and was kind enough to share with me some of the stories I use here, stories that have been passed down in her family for generations."

LARRY WATSON

Larry Watson is the author of the novels *Montana 1948, Justice*, and *White Crosses*. He has also published stories and poems in *The Gettysburg Review, New England Review, High Plains Literary Review*, and elsewhere. He teaches writing and literature at the University of Wisconsin-Stevens Point.

"*My wife, Susan, and I have a place in Door County, Wisconsin, not far from the Mink River Estuary, a Nature Conservancy preserve. We were walking there on a fall day when the idea for the story came to me.*"

ABOUT THE EDITORS

JOSEPH BARBATO and LISA WEINERMAN HORAK have written extensively for The Nature Conservancy and co-edited the popular Conservancy anthology *Heart of the Land: Essays on Last Great Places*. Barbato is a contributing editor to *Publishers Weekly*.